Paul Fortunatus Mundé

Mt. Sinai Hospital Reports

Vol. I - For 1898

Paul Fortunatus Mundé

Mt. Sinai Hospital Reports
Vol. I - For 1898

ISBN/EAN: 9783337173562

Printed in Europe, USA, Canada, Australia, Japan

Cover: Foto ©ninafisch / pixelio.de

More available books at **www.hansebooks.com**

MT. SINAI HOSPITAL REPORTS

VOLUME I

FOR 1898

EDITED FOR THE MEDICAL BOARD

BY

PAUL F. MUNDÉ, M.D., LL.D.

1899

CONTENTS.

PREFACE.

The Mount Sinai Hospital has existed since 1856. During its first decade it was called the "Jews' Hospital." The growth of the Institution is best characterized by the fact that while its annual admissions numbered two hundred in 1856, there are now three thousand. The original subdivision of the service was a simple one, viz., into a medical and a surgical department. At present a medical, a surgical, a gynecological, an ophthalmological and otological, and a children's department are in working order, having been established twenty or more years ago. During the last two years two new places were created in the Medical Staff for a consultant neurologist and a consultant dermatologist. The new and enlarged Hospital, the erection of which is in preparation, will furnish the opportunity for special services. The work of the pathologist was greatly facilitated during the same period.

The vast material of the Institution was never sufficiently utilized in the interest of medical science and art; indeed, very few publications based upon the experience gathered in the Mount Sinai Hospital have seen the light. At last the means for publishing this first annual volume have been granted by the Directors, and it is with intense gratification and pride that the undersigned launches the new enterprise.

A. JACOBI, M.D., LL.D.,
President of the Medical Board.

MEDICAL AND SURGICAL STAFF FOR 1898.

CONSULTING PHYSICIANS.

A. JACOBI, M.D. E. G. JANEWAY, M.D.

CONSULTING SURGEONS.

THOMAS M. MARKOE, M.D. DANIEL M. STIMSON, M.D.

CONSULTING DERMATOLOGIST.

S. LUSTGARTEN, M.D.

CONSULTING NEUROLOGIST.

B. SACHS, M.D.

ATTENDING PHYSICIANS.

JULIUS RUDISCH, M.D. MORRIS MANGES, M.D.
ALFRED MEYER, M.D. N. E. BRILL, M.D.
B. SCHARLAU, M.D.
(Diseases of Children.)

ATTENDING SURGEONS.

A. G. GERSTER, M.D. WILLIAM F. FLUHRER, M.D.
(Genito-urinary Service.)

GYNECOLOGIST.

PAUL F. MUNDÉ, M.D.

OPHTHALMIC AND AURAL SURGEON.

EMIL GRUENING, M.D.

ADJUNCT ATTENDING PHYSICIANS.

D. H. DAVISON, M.D. HENRY W. BERG, M.D.
HENRY KOPLIK, M.D.
(Diseases of Children.)

ADJUNCT ATTENDING SURGEONS.

HOWARD LILIENTHAL, M.D. WM. W. VAN ARSDALE, M.D

ADJUNCT OPHTHALMIC AND AURAL SURGEONS.

CHARLES H. MAY, M.D. CARL KOLLER, M.D.

ADJUNCT GYNECOLOGIST.

JOSEPH BRETTAUER, M.D.

PATHOLOGIST.

F. S. MANDLEBAUM, M.D.

ASSISTANT PATHOLOGIST.

E. LIBMAN, M.D.

ADMITTING PHYSICIAN.

MAX ROSENBERG, M.D.

HOUSE STAFF.

From January 1st, 1898, to July 1st, 1898.

House Physician,	*House Surgeon,*
LOUIS HAUSWIRTH, M.D.	HARRY RODMAN, M.D.
Senior Assistant Physician,	*Senior Assistant Surgeon,*
W. G. ECKSTEIN, M.D.	WALTER M. BRICKNER, M.D.
Junior Assistant Physician,	*Junior Assistant Surgeon,*
L. W. ALLEN, M.D.	SIDNEY ULFELDER, M.D.
First Provisional Assistant Physician,	*First Provisional Assistant Surgeon,*
L. A. S. BODINE, M.D.	A. G. FOORD, M.D.
Second Provisional Ass't Physician,	*Second Provisional Assistant Surgeon,*
E. M. LAZARD, M.D.	F. L. ADAMS, M.D.

From July 1st, 1898, to January 1st, 1899.

House Physician,	*House Surgeon,*
LOUIS HAUSWIRTH, M.D.	WALTER M. BRICKNER, M.D.
Senior Assistant Physician,	*Senior Assistant Surgeon,*
W. G. ECKSTEIN, M.D.	SIDNEY ULFELDER, M.D.
Junior Assistant Physician,	*Junior Assistant Surgeon,*
A. G. FOORD, M.D.	L. W. ALLEN, M.D.
First Externe,	*First Externe,*
L. B. MEYER, M.D.	L. A. S. BODINE, M.D.
Second Externe,	*Second Externe,*
I. STRAUSS, M.D.	E. H. EISING, M.D.
Provisionals,	*Provisionals,*
M. THORNER, M.D.	ED. A. ROSENBERG, M.D.
H. SCHWARZ, M.D.	E. D. LEDERMAN, M.D.

I.

DEPARTMENT OF INTERNAL MEDICINE.

STATISTICS OF MEDICAL SERVICE DURING THE YEAR 1898.

GRAND TOTAL OF ALL DISEASES.

Treated	1020
Cured	494
Improved	351
Unimproved	54
Died	121

	Total.		Cured.		Improved.		Unimproved.		Died.	
General Diseases.	M	F	M	F	M	F	M	F	M	F
A. Diphtheria		4		4						
Erysipelas	1	2	1	2						
Febricula	1		1							
Influenza	1		1							
Malaria	12		12							
" tertian	15	5	15	5						
" double tertian	3	1	3	1						
Malarial cachexia	1	1	1	1						
Measles		1		1						
Typhoid fever	53	26	47	25					6	1
Typho-malarial fever	3		3							
B. Arthritis deformans		2				2				
" gonorrhœal	12	8	8	4	4	4				
Carcinomatosis, general		3								3
Debility	1		1							
Diabetes mellitus	5	3			4	2			1	1
Goitre, exophthalmic	1	6			1	4		2		
Insolation	1	1		1					1	
Morbus Addisonii	1	3				2		1	1	
Multiple sarcoma	1	2					1			2
Rheumatism, acute articular	28	35	26	32	2	2				1
" chronic "	2	5			2	3				
" muscular	3	1	2	1	1					
Senility	3	2					3	2		
Septicæmia	1								1	
" puerperal		1		1						
Syphilis	8	2			8	1		1		
Total males, 157; females, 114; grand total, 271.										
Total	157	114	121	78	22	20	4	6	10	8
Diseases of the Circulatory System.										
Angina pectoris	1				1					
Aortic, double		1								1

	Total.		Cured.		Improved.		Unimproved.		Died.	
Diseases of the Circulatory System— *Continued.*	M	F	M	F	M	F	M	F	M	F
Aortic obstruction	1	..	..	..	1	..	..	..	..	..
" regurgitation	..	1	..	..	..	1	..	..	..	..
Chronic myocarditis	7	1	..	..	6	..	..	..	1	1
Endarteritis	..	1	..	..	..	1	..	..	..	..
Epistaxis	..	1	..	1	..	..	..	..	..	..
Mitral, double	2	1	..	..	1	1	..	..	1	..
" obstructive	1	8	..	..	1	8	..	..	..	..
" regurgitation	6	5	..	..	4	3	..	1	2	1
Mitral and aortic	2	5	..	..	2	3	..	..	..	2
Phlebitis	..	1	..	1	..	..	..	..	..	..
Tachycardia	1	..	1	..	..	..	..	..	..	..
Thrombosis	1	..	..	..	..	..	..	..	1	..
Ulcerative endocarditis	4	..	..	..	..	..	..	..	4	..
" " gonorrhœal	1	..	:	..	..	..	..	..	1	..
Total males, 27; females, 25; grand total, 52.										
Total	27	25	1	2	18	17	..	1	10	5
Diseases of the Blood.										
Anæmia, primary	5	20	..	11	5	9	..		..	..
" secondary	1	3	..	1	1	2	..	..	..	..
" pernicious	1	1	1	..	..	..	..	..	..	1
Chlorosis	..	5	..	1	..	4	..	..	..	..
Leukæmia, myelo-splenic	2	1	..	..	1	..	..	1	1	..
" pseudo	1	2	..	..	1	1	..	..	..	1
Total males, 10; females, 32; grand total, 42.										
Total	10	32	1	13	8	16	..	1	1	2
Diseases of the Respiratory System.										
Abscess of lung	1	..	..	..	..	..	..	..	1	..
Asthma	6	3	4	2	2	1	..	..	..	..
Bronchitis, acute	6	1	6	1	..	..	..	..	..	..
" chronic	7	2	2	..	5	2	..	..	..	..
Emphysema	13	3	..	..	13	3	.	..	..	..
Gangrene of lung	1	..	..	..	..	..	..	..	1	..
Malignant disease of pleura	1	..	..	..	1	..	..	..	..	..
Phthisis, pulmonary, acute	1	..	..	..	.	..	..	..	1	..
" " chronic	31	17	2	..	21	13	2	1	6	3
Pleurisy with effusion	12	8	10	7	2	1	..	..	..	..
" dry	6	4	5	4	..	..	1	..	..	..
Pneumonia, catarrhal	2	1	2	1	..	..	..	..	..	..
" croupous	25	18	23	18	..	..	1	..	1	..
Pyopneumothorax	1	..	..	..	..	..	..	..	1	..
Tracheal diverticulum	..	1	..	..	..	1	..	..	..	..
Tuberculosis, acute miliary	2	2	..	..	..	..	.	1	2	1
Bronchiectasis	2	..	..	..	2	..	..	..	..	..

	Total.		Cured.		Improved.		Unimproved.		Died.	
Diseases of the Respiratory System—*Continued.*	M	F	M	F	M	F	M	F	M	F
Empyema	1						1			
Total males, 118; females, 62; grand total, 180.										
Total	118	62	54	31	46	21	5	2	13	4
Diseases of the Cutaneous System.										
Eczema	4	1	3	1			1			
Epithelioma of leg	1						1			
Furunculosis	1				1					
Purpura hæmorrhagica	1		1							
Sarcoides pigmentosum (typus Kaposi)	2		1		1					
Scabies	1		1							
Total males, 10; females, 1; grand total, 11										
Total	10	1	6	1	2		2			
Surgical Diseases.										
Mastitis		1		1						
Mastoiditis		1		1						
Pes planus	1	4				3	1	1		
Pott's disease		1				1				
Tuberculosis of ankle	1				1					
Total males, 2; females, 7; grand total, 9.										
Total	2	7		2	1	4	1	1		
Diseases of the Digestive Tract.										
Abdominal tumor	3	3			1	1	1	2	1	
Appendicitis, acute	6		6							
" subacute	6				6					
" chronic	2		1		1					
Cholecystitis	3	1	3	1						
Cholelithiasis	4	3	1		3	3				
Colitis, acute	4	2	3	2						
" chronic	4		3		1					
" mucous		1		1						
" ulcerative		2		1						1
Colon, carcinoma of			1							1
Constipation	7	9	6	4	1	5				
Dilatation of stomach, acute	1	1			1					
Duodenum, carcinoma of	1								1	
" stricture of	2				2					
Dysentery, acute	20	1	20	1						
" chronic	1	1			1	1				
Enteroptosis		1				1				
Fecal impaction	3	4	3	4						

Diseases of the Digestive Tract—*Continued.*	Total.		Cured.		Improved.		Unimproved.		Died.	
	M	F	M	F	M	F	M	F	M	F
Gastralgia	1	1	1	1						
Gastritis, acute.	1	3	1	3						
" chronic.	11	5	2	3	9	2				
Gastric carcinoma	6	4			2	1	1	1	3	2
" ulcer	1	6	1	5						
Gastro-duodenitis	6	4	5	4	1					
Gastro-enteritis	4	3	2	3	2					
Hemorrhoids	2		2							
Hypochlorhydria		1		1						
Intestinal auto-intoxication	10	6	10	6						
Intestine, adhesions of	1								1	
Lip, epithelioma of	1		1							
" tuberculosis of	1		1							
Liver, carcinoma of	2	1					1	1	1	
" cirrhosis of	5	3			2	1	2		1	2
" abscess of	2		1						1	
" syphilis of	1				1					
Movable spleen		1				1				
Œsophagus, carcinoma of	2								2	
" stricture of, spasmodic	1		1							
" " " syphilitic	1				1					
Pancreatitis, acute		1		1						
Pancreas, carcinoma of, and of suprarenal body and lung	1								1	
Peritonitis, chronic		1				1				
" tubercular	1	1			1					1
Pharyngitis	1				1					
Rectum, carcinoma of	1								1	
" prolapse of	1				1					
Stomatitis	1				1					
Tonsillitis	8	2	8	2						
Ulcers of stomach and colon (tubercular)	1								1	
Vomiting of pregnancy		3		3						
Total males, 141; females, 75; grand total, 216										
Total	141	75	83	46	39	17	5	4	14	7
Diseases of the Genito-Urinary System.										
Carcinoma uteri		1						1		
Cystitis, acute		2		1		1				
" chronic	1		1							
Epididymo-orchitis	2				2					
Gonorrhœa	1				1					
Hæmaturia	1				1					
Movable kidney		2				2				
Nephritis, acute	4	2	4	2						
" chronic	20	21			15	16	1	2	13	3

	Total.		Cured.		Improved.		Unimproved.		Died.	
Diseases of the Genito-Urinary System— *Continued.*	M	F	M	F	M	F	M	F	M	F
Pelvic exudate	..	1	..	..	..	1	..	..	..	..
Prostatic abscess	1	.	1	..	..	..	..	..	..	..
Pyelitis	4	..	3	..	1	..	..	..	..	..
Pyelo-nephritis	1	1	..	..	..	1	..	..	1	..
Pyosalpinx	..	1	..	..	..	1	..	..	..	..
Renal calculus	..	1	..	1	..	..	..	..	..	..
Retroflexio uteri	..	1	..	..	..	..	..	1	..	..
Tuberculosis of genito-urinary tract	1	..	..	..	..	..	1	..	..	..
Uræmia	11	3	..	..	2	..	..	..	9	3
Total males, 56; females, 36; grand total, 92.										
Total	56	36	9	4	22	22	2	4	23	6
Diseases of the Nervous System.										
Cranial.										
Acromegaly	1	..	..	..	1	..	..	..	..	..
Apoplexy	9	4	3	..	4	3	..	..	2	1
Cephalalgia	3	1	1	1	2	..	..	..	..	..
Cerebro-spinal syphilis	3	1	..	..	2	..	..	..	1	1
Encephalophia saturnina	1	..	..	..	..	..	..	..	1	..
Meningitis, tubercular	2	2	..	.	..	..	..	..	2	2
" purulent	1	..	..	..		..	..	..	1	..
Sarcoma of brain	1	..	..	..	..	..	..	..	1	..
Total males, 21; females, 8; grand total, 29.										
Total	21	8	4	1	9	3	..	..	8	4
Spinal.										
Ataxia paraplegia	1	..	..	..	..	..	1	..	..	..
Hemorrhage	1	..	..	..	..	..	..	..	1	..
Landry's paralysis	1	..	..	..	1	..	..	..	..	..
Myelitis	..	1	..	..	..	..	..	..	1	..
Syphilis	2	..	1	..	..	..	..	..	1	..
Syringomyelia	1	..	..	..	..	..	1	..	..	..
Locomotor ataxia	4	1	..	..	3	1	..	..	1	..
Total males, 10; females, 2; grand total, 12.										
Total	10	2	1	..	4	1	2	..	4	..
Peripheral.										
Neuralgia	3	..	1	..	1	..	1	..	..	..
Neuritis	3	4	1	1	2	3		..	..	2
Neuroma	1	..	..	..	1	..	..	..	..	..
Occupation neurosis	1	..	1	..	..	..	..	..	..	..
Optic nerve atrophy	1	..	..	..	..	..	1	..	..	.
Sciatica	18	5	10	2	8	3	..	.	..	..
Total males, 27; females, 9; grand total, 36.										
Total	27	9	13	3	12	6	2	..	..	2

Diseases of the Nervous System—*Continued.*	Total.		Cured.		Improved.		Unimproved.		Died.	
General.	M	F	M	F	M	F	M	F	M	F
Astasia abasia	2	..	2	..	..	..	..	..	..	..
Epilepsy	1	..	..	..	..	..	1	..	..	..
General paresis	5	..	..	..	1	..	4	..	..	..
Hysteria.	11	7	7	4	4	..	..	3	..	..
Incipient dementia	1	..	..	..	1	..	..	..	..	..
Insomnia	..	1	..	1	..	..	..	..	..	..
Mania, acute.	1	..	..	..	..	..	1	..	..	..
" postpartum	..	1	..	1	..	..	..	..	..	..
Neurasthenia	18	20	2	5	16	12	..	3	..	..
Total males, 39; females, 29; grand total, 68.										
Total	39	29	11	11	22	12	6	6	..	..
Poisons.										
Alcoholism	1	1	1	..	..	1	..	..	..	..
Mercurialism	1	..	1	..	..	..	..	..	..	..
Plumbism	2	..	1	..	1	..	..	..	..	..
Total males, 4; females, 1; grand total, 5.										
Total	4	1	3	..	1	1	..	..	..	..

II.

A STUDY OF THE CASES OF TYPHOID FEVER OBSERVED IN THE HOSPITAL FROM 1883–1898.

By J. RUDISCH, M.D.,
ATTENDING PHYSICIAN.

In the following contribution I have made a study of the typhoid fever cases treated in the Hospital from January 1, 1883, to January 1, 1898. Apart from the interest which is attached to the consideration of a long series of typhoid fever cases, I believe this series is of special interest, because the patients are almost entirely of one class. They comprise for the most part members of the poor Jewish working classes, who are badly nourished, overworked, of poor physique, but moderate in eating and rarely alcoholic to any degree.

Typhoid fever statistics can be compiled from almost innumerable points of view, and I have, therefore, chosen to review the cases from certain aspects only. These are the following: The number of cases treated; the mortality; the comparative frequency of occurrence in males and females; the mortality according to sex; the frequency of occurrence and mortality according to age; the influence of the duration of the disease, before admission to the Hospital, on the mortality; the frequency of occurrence of the various complications and their mortality; and, finally, what is of special interest, the influence of the Brand treatment on the mortality and the occurrence of complications.

Whenever of interest, I have inserted references to the statistics of other writers. These statistics are cited mainly from Liebermeister's work on typhoid fever in Von Ziemssen's Encyclopædia, from Curschmann's recent monograph in the Nothnagel series, and from Osler's reports.

TABLE I.

SHOWING THE NUMBER OF CASES TREATED ANNUALLY, THE NUMBER OF RECOVERIES AND DEATHS, AND THE PLAN OF TREATMENT.

Year.	No. o Recoveries.	No. of Deaths.	Total No. of Cases.	Percentage of Deaths.	Plan of Treatment.
1883.....	45	8	53	15.09	Antipyretic.
1884.....	27	2	29	6.20	"
1885.....	22	3	25	12.00	"
1886. ..	51	12	63	19.04	"
1887...	28	4	32	12.50	"
1888....	44	5	49	10.20	"
1889. .	73	8	81	9.87	"
1890.....	85	3	88	3.40	"
1891.....	58	13	71	18.31	"
1892.....	67	7	74	9.46	"
1893. .	59	10	69	14.50	"
1894. ..	67	8	75	10.66	Brand.
1895....	58	8	66	12.12	"
1896.....	97	8	105	7.61	"
1897....	85	9	94	9.57	"
Totals.	866	108	974	11.09	

Comments.—The cases dying within twenty-four hours after admission have been excluded from the series, as it would be manifestly unfair in trying to show the results of treatment in the Hospital. The antipyretics used were as follows: In 1883, quinine, carbolic acid, and salicylic acid; 1884, quinine and salicylic acid; in 1885, quinine; in 1886, 1887, and 1888, quinine and antipyrin; in 1889, antifebrin, quinine, and antipyrin; in 1890, phenacetin and quinine. After that phenacetin was almost exclusively used. A few cases in the earlier years were treated with Brand baths. In 1891 to 1893, inclusive, the baths were used on a small number of patients, but they were first used as routine treatment since 1894, being applied in two-thirds of all the cases since that time. The cases that were treated in the earlier years with antipyretics were occasionally also treated with hydrotherapeutic methods. In the same way, the cases on the Brand treatment occasionally received antipyretics, but these only when some contra-indication arose to the use of the baths. In 1897 five cases were treated at the outset on the Woodbridge plan: similarly, in 1896, three cases were treated in this way. No inferences will be drawn as to the results of this method of treatment, as the cases in which it was used were too few in number.

Conclusions from Table I.—The total number of cases was 974. Of these 866 recovered and 108 died, giving a mortality of 11.09 per cent. (The lowest mortality in any one year occurred in 1890, being 3.40 per cent. The highest mortality in any one year was in 1896, being 19.04. Both series were on the same plan of treatment. This shows plainly the fallacy of trying to draw conclusions from short series of cases.) This compares very favorably with the mortality of typhoid fever given by other writers during the same period. Thus Curschmann states that the mortality of typhoid fever nowadays ranges between 9 and 12 per cent, 14 per cent being the highest: and that lower or higher mortalities than this are due to special circumstances. His own statistics show that in 3,686 cases the mortality was 9.80 per cent, and in the second series of 3,600 cases 9.30 per cent. In New York the mortality at one of the large hospitals during the same period from which our statistics are taken was 11.93 per cent, and in another hospital 15.82 per cent.

Before the Brand treatment was introduced in the Hospital there occurred 634 cases of the series; of these 11.83 per cent died. After its introduction 340 cases occurred, with a mortality of 9.70 per cent, showing a reduction in the mortality of 2.13 per cent. To compare an approximately equal number of cases before and after 1894, I have tabulated the cases from 1889 to 1893, inclusive, which are 383 in number, with a mortality of 12.01 per cent compared with the mortality of 9.70 per cent after 1894 in 340 cases.

TABLE II.

Showing the Number of Males and Females Annually, and the Mortality according to Sex.

Year.	No. of Males.	No. of Females.	Deaths in Males.	Deaths in Females.
1883......	35	18	5	3
1884.... .	17	12	1	1
1885.......	18	7	1	2
1886......	34	29	6	6
1887....	20	12	4	..
1888	33	16	3	2
1889	37	34	6	2
1890........	41	47	1	2
1891 ...	49	22	10	3
1892	37	37	2	5
1893	37	32	4	6
1894	43	32	4	4
1895.... .	39	27	4	4
1896.......	61	44	6	2
1897	52	42	7	2
Totals......	563	411	64	44

Table II shows that the total number of males was 563, and females 411. Of the males 64 died, and of the females 44, giving a mortality rate of 11.37 per cent for the males and 10.70 per cent for the females. It is, therefore, seen that while the number of males admitted was larger, the absolute mortality among them was also larger. This corresponds to the experience of most authors, and it is generally explained that the larger number of males is due to the fact that as a rule the sum total more males are admitted to the hospitals for treatment than females, for all diseases. The statistics of Murchison and Curschmann, however, show a greater frequency and a higher mortality rate for females.

TABLE III. (*a*)

SHOWING THE OCCURRENCE AND MORTALITY ACCORDING TO AGE.

Age in years.	Number of recoveries.	Number of deaths.	Total.	Percentage of deaths.
1	2	3	5	60.00
2	6	0	6	0.00
3	5	0	5	0.00
4	9	1	10	10.00
5	9	2	11	11.72
6	14	2	16	12.50
7	19	1	20	5.00
8	11	0	11	0.00
9	21	3	24	12.50
10	15	1	16	6.25
11–15	81	9	90	10.00
16–20	226	25	251	9.96
21–25	200	26	226	11.50
26–30	123	13	137	9.49
31–35	61	10	71	14.08
36–40	42	6	48	12.50
41–45	14	1	15	6.66
46–50	4	1	5	20.00
51–55	1	1	2	50.00
56–60	2	1	3	33.00
61–65	1	1	2	50.00
66–70	0	0	0	0.00
71–75	0	1	1	100.00

TABLE III. (*b*)

THE SAME AS TABLE III. (*a*), ARRANGED ACCORDING TO DECADES.

Age in years.	Recovered.	Died.	Total.	Percentage of deaths.
1–10	111	13	124	10.40
11–20.	307	34	341	9.97
21–30	323	39	362	10.77
31–40	103	16	119	13.44
41–50	18	2	20	10.00
51–60	3	2	5	40.00
61–75	1	2	3	66 00

Between the ages of 1 and 5 years there were 37 cases, of which 31 recovered and 6 died, giving a mortality of 16.21 per cent. Between the ages of 6 and 10 years there were 87 cases, of which 80 recovered and 7 died, giving a mortality of 8.75 per cent.

These tables show that the greatest number of cases occur between the ages of 10 and 30. In this period the fourth hemi-decade shows the largest number of cases. Up to 5 years of age the cases were very infrequent, as they also were after the age of 40. The mortality seems very high above the age of 50, and lower before than after 30. The lowest mortality is between the ages of 10 and 30. Between 30 and 40 it increases almost 3 per cent. The two youngest cases were respectively 6 and 10 months old; the oldest case was of the age of 74. All three cases died.

TABLE IV. (a)

SHOWING THE NUMBER OF CASES AND THE PERCENTAGE OF DEATHS ACCORDING TO THE DURATION OF THE DISEASE BEFORE ADMISSION. 886 CASES ARE TABULATED.

Duration.	No. of cases.	No. of deaths.	Percentage of deaths.
0 days	3	0	0.00
1 day	3	0	0.00
2 days	6	0	0.00
3 "	20	1	5.00
4 "	39	2	5 13
5 "	52	3	5.77
6 "	65	3	4 61
7 "	115	8	6 95
8 "	91	7	7 69
9 "	31	1	3.22
10 "	68	10	14.70
11 "	21	4	19.05
12 "	20	0	0 00
13 "	2	1	50.00
2 weeks	212	34	16.02
2½ "	13	2	15.38
3 "	74	9	12.16
4 "	33	3	9.09
5 "	6	3	50.00
6 "	7	2	28.57
7 "	3	1	33.00
8 "	2	0	0 00

Summed up according to duration in weeks:

Up to 1 week,	303 cases,	17 deaths	= 5.61 per cent.
" 2 weeks,	445 "	57 "	= 10.56 "
" 3 "	87 "	11 "	= 12.53 "
After 3 "	51 "	9 "	= 17.64 "

This tabulation shows that the largest number of cases was admitted with an illness already lasting about two weeks. It demonstrates that the mortality increases progressively with the lateness of arrival of the patients in the Hospital. Of those sick a week or less outside, only 5.61 per cent died.

It has been claimed that the Brand treatment would be specially efficacious if the cases came in early. To get at the truth of this statement the following table has been compiled.

TABLE IV. (*b*)

CASES SINCE 1894 (WHEN THE BRAND BATHS WERE FIRST EXTENSIVELY USED) CLASSIFIED AS IN TABLE IV. (*a*). 330 CASES ARE TABULATED.

Duration.	No. of cases.	No. of deaths.	Percentage of deaths.
0 days	3	0	0.00
1 day	2	0	0.00
2 days	3	0	0 00
3 "	8	0	0.00
4 "	16	0	0.00
5 "	16	2	12.50
6 "	21	0	0.00
7 "	54	3	5.55
8 "	28	2	7.14
9 "	15	0	0.00
10 "	25	5	20.00
11 "	12	2	16.66
12 "	10	0	0.00
2 weeks	70	11	15.71
2½ "	4	0	0.00
3 "	28	3	10.71
4 "	8	1	12.50
5 "	3	0	0.00
6 "	2	2	100.00
7 "	1	1	100.00
8 "	1	0	0.00

Summed up according to duration in weeks:

Up to 1 week,	73 cases,	5 deaths	= 6.85 per cent.
" 2 weeks,	160 "	20 "	= 12.50 "
" 3 "	32 "	3 "	= 9.38 "
After 3 "	15 "	4 "	= 26.66 "

A consideration of this table shows that the cases admitted early and treated with the Brand baths did not have a better prognosis, for 6.85 per cent of the cases died, against 5.61 per cent of the whole series, or 5.02 per cent for the cases up to 1894 (230 cases, 12 deaths). The reduction in the mortality since the use of the Brand baths seems to have occurred in the cases which were sick over two weeks outside. We would lay no stress on this point, however, as the number of cases (73) is too small. A larger number of cases would probably show a much more favorable result.

TABLE V.

SHOWING THE FREQUENCY OF OCCURRENCE OF THE VARIOUS COMPLICATIONS AND THEIR MORTALITY, IN THE ENTIRE SERIES OF CASES, AND ALSO THE FREQUENCY BEFORE AND AFTER 1894.

Complications.	No. of cases	No. of deaths.	Per cent.	No. of cases before 1894.	No. of cases after 1894.
Hemorrhage	57	13	22.80	35	22
Pneumonia	35	10	28.05	20	15
Perforation	20	19	95.00	10	10
Furunculosis	14	3	20.71	12	2
Otitis media	13	1	7.69	9	4
Phlebitis	11	1	9.09	6	5
Parotitis	10	0	0.00	8	2
Hemorrhage and perforation	8	8	100.00	3	5
Pleurisy with effusion	7	1	14.18	4	3
Acute nephritis	7	2	28.57	6	1
Meningitis	6	4	66.66	5	1
Pregnancy	6	1	16.66	6	0
Hemorrhage and pneumonia	5	2	40.00	3	2
Peritonitis	5	4	80 00	4	1
Hemorrhage and peritonitis	4	1	25.00	3	1
Pyelitis	3	1	33.33	2	1
Erysipelas	3	0	0.00	3	0
Hemorrhage and phlebitis	2	1	50.00	1	1
Appendicitis	2	1	50.00	1	1
Post-typhoid dementia	3	1	33.33	3	0
Corneal ulcer	2	0	0.00	2	0
Cystitis	2	0	0.00	2	0
Multiple synovitis	2	0	0.00	2	0
Meningitis and pneumonia	1	1	100.00	0	1
Acute delirium	1	0	0.00	1	0
Erythema nodosum	1	0	0.00	1	0
Herpes zoster	1	0	0.00	1	0
Ulceration of pharynx	1	0	0.00	1	0

Died from the effects of the fever (toxæmia) alone, 35 cases.

Comments.—1. As the histories do not always state what form of pneumonia was present, all the cases are grouped together. 2. Of the 10 parotitis cases, 6 suppurated; 1 of these was bilateral. 3. The case of phlebitis that died involved the left external iliac vein. This was followed by pulmonary embolism and empyema; in the pus typhoid bacilli were found in pure culture. 4. The case of pleurisy with effusion that died was complicated with mitral stenosis. 5. One of the appendicitis cases was accompanied by peritonitis, the other was not. 6. Of the otitis media cases 3 were followed by mastoid disease; 1 of these died. 7. Pregnancy was present in 6 cases; abortion followed in 3 of these; 1 of the latter died of peritonitis secondary to the uterine condition.

Complications of Special Interest.—1. The case of phlebitis referred to above under heading 3. This occurred in a woman of 46 and resulted fatally.

2. A case which recovered after having had repeated hemorrhages, peritonitis, and lobar pneumonia.

3. A case in which profuse hemorrhage occurred in the third week from internal hemorrhoids; and a case in which the patient cut his left radial artery and then lay on his hand, the sheets and buttocks being full of blood, the case at first looked like one of typhoid hemorrhage. Both cases recovered.

4. One case of suppuration of the axillary glands.

5. Two cases of pericarditis which recovered.

6. In 1883 occurred 2 cases of suppurative thyroiditis, 1 in a patient of 21 in the fourth week, and 1 in a patient of 11 years in the eighth week. The second case also had hemorrhages from the bowels, and erysipelas. Both patients recovered.

7. One case was complicated with measles and one with scarlet fever.

8. One case of facial paralysis; this is an exceedingly rare complication, Curschmann having met with only one case in a series of 6,000 patients.

9. One case, a girl of 17, developed phlebitis of both femoral veins, osteomyelitis of the inferior maxilla, and pyelitis. During her relapse she developed signs of a lobar pneumonia, which later proved to be tubercular. She left the Hospital in a very fair condition; she still had signs in her lungs, a discharging sinus from osteomyelitis, and pus and casts in her urine.

10. One case of marasmus ending fatally. This is a very rare condition.

Conclusions from Table 5.—1. Most deaths (almost one-third) occurred from the effects of the toxæmia without any complications. The usual percentage is 30 to 50. Of next importance are the cases of perforation, of which all but one (?) died. Hemorrhage and pneumonia make up a large part of the remaining mortality. Peritonitis and meningitis each carried off four patients. The relative frequency of these complications as causes of death corresponds very closely to that shown in Curschmann's tables.

2. The mortality in cases which had hemorrhages and no other complication was 25 per cent. The mortality in pneumonia cases was about 33 per cent. Phlebitis was the cause of death in but one instance (referred to above). Otitis media seems not to have been an unfavorable complication, only 1 case having died.

3. The number of cases in pregnant women is quite large compared to that given in other statistics. For instance, Osler reports 1 case in 685 typhoids. Curschmann, however, reports 38 cases in 1,117 typhoids. In the series here reported only 1 of the cases died. This does not seem to be in accord with the general opinion regarding the prognosis in pregnancy. Thus Liebermeister reports 6 deaths in 18 cases; Curschmann, 14 cases with 5 deaths, but he himself believes that the prognosis is not as bad as previous authors would make us believe.

4. Parotitis and erysipelas did not influence the mortality. The furunculosis cases give a mortality of about

21 per cent, which seems quite high. It is probable that the complication was not reported in the histories as often as it occurred.

Frequency of Complications, with Comparisons with Other Statistics.—1. Hemorrhage occurred in about 5 per cent of the cases. Liebermeister gives the frequency as 4 to 6 per cent; Griesinger as 5.3 per cent; Homolle as 4 65 per cent, in a tabulation of 10,000 cases; and Liebermeister puts it at 7.3 per cent of the cases. 2. Pneumonia occurred in about 3 per cent of the cases. Other authors give figures varying from 7 per cent to 14.4 per cent. 3. Perforation occurred in about 2 per cent of the cases. The absolute number that usually occurs is not over 3 per cent. Griesinger's series gives a frequency of 3.2 per cent. 4. Phlebitis occurred in 1 per cent of the cases. This is rather below the average. 5. Parotitis occurred also in 1 per cent of the cases. The usual figure given is 0.3 to 0.5 per cent, but Hoffman reports 16 cases in 1,600 cases, corresponding exactly to the figures in our statistics. Of his cases 9 died. The complication is generally considered a serious one, but our figures do not bear this out. 6. The other complications noted need no special comment as to their frequency.

TABLE VI.

SHOWING FREQUENCY OF OCCURRENCE OF COMPLICATIONS BEFORE AND AFTER 1894. THERE WERE 634 CASES BEFORE 1894 AND 340 CASES AFTER 1894.

Complication.	Before 1894.	Percentage.	After 1894.	Percentage.
Hemorrhage	45	7.09	26	7.65
Perforation	13	2 05	15	4.41
Pneumonia	23	3.63	21	6.16
Phlebitis	7	1.04	6	1.76
Furunculosis	12	1.89	2	.59
Acute nephritis	6	.95	1	.29

Conclusions.—These statistics, which really do not cover a large enough number of cases to be very demonstrative, show:

1. That perforations have increased. We cannot lay any stress on this point, as comparatively few autopsies were made and there was no way of determining the correctness of the diagnosis.

2. That the number of hemorrhages has very slightly increased.

3. Pneumonia has decidedly increased, as has phlebitis.

4. Furunculosis and acute nephritis have decreased.

Some of these results are at variance with those found in other statistics; thus, while our statistics show an increase in the number of cases of pneumonia, Liebermeister's figures show a decrease of 4 per cent and a reduction in mortality of 20 per cent. His figures also show a reduction of 2 per cent in the number of hemorrhages, while our figures give an approximately equal number before and after.

RELAPSE.

1. The total number of relapses for the entire series was 82, giving a percentage of 8.42. The number in various epidemics has ranged from 1.4 per cent up to 17 per cent. Liebermeister reports 8.6 per cent; Osler, 7.88 per cent; Wagner, 8.74 per cent; Gerhardt, 6.3 per cent; Ziemssen, 13 per cent; and Murchison, 3 per cent.

2. Of the 82 relapse cases, 7 died, giving a mortality of 8.53 per cent, or a lower mortality rate than the cases without relapse show (892 cases, 101 deaths = 11 32 per cent). This comparatively low mortality in relapse cases has been frequently noted; thus, while among 10,823 cases in the Hamburg epidemics of 1886–87 8.5 per cent died, the relapse cases showed a mortality of only 4.9 per cent.

3. Of the 82 relapse cases, 48 occurred before 1894 in 634 cases, giving a percentage of 7.57 per cent; after 1894 we find 340 cases with 34 relapses, 10 per cent—showing an increase of 2.5 per cent in the number of relapses since the introduction of the Brand treatment.

If we compare the figures of 1889–94 we find 393 cases, with 27 relapses, or 6.89 per cent, compared to 10 per cent since 1894, showing again a decided increase. This is in accord with the general consensus of opinion.

4. The deaths in the 48 relapse cases before 1894 number 4, and in the 34 cases since then 3, giving almost exactly the same mortality.

5. Of the 7 deaths in the relapse cases, 4 were due to the toxæmia alone, 1 to perforation, 1 to perforation and hemorrhage, and 1 to hemorrhage and meningitis.

6. In the 77 remaining cases,

5 cases had hemorrhages only.
1 case had hemorrhages and lobar pneumonia.
3 cases had pneumonia.
2 cases had pyelitis.
2 cases had phlebitis.
2 cases had furunculosis.
1 case had appendicitis, hemorrhages, and nephritis.
1 case had double mastoid disease and broncho-pneumonia.
1 case had herpes zoster.

Summary.—1. The cases were more frequent in males, and in them the mortality was slightly higher.

2. The greatest frequency occurred between the ages of 15 and 20.

3. The mortality in cases sick less than a week outside was 5.61 per cent, and increased progressively with the duration of the disease outside.

4. The Brand treatment reduced the mortality a little over 2 per cent. This reduction occurred in the cases which had been sick two weeks or longer outside.

5. Since the introduction of the Brand treatment there has been an increase in the number of cases of pneumonia and phlebitis, and a decrease in the number of cases of furunculosis and nephritis.

6. Relapses have increased 2.5 per cent.

7. The mortality in the relapse cases is almost 3 per

cent lower than in the other cases. The death rate in the relapse cases before and since the introduction of the Brand treatment is practically the same.

8. The Brand treatment has not reduced the number of complicated cases as a whole, but has decreased the number of deaths from toxæmia, which is the greatest single factor in the production of the mortality of typhoid fever.

For the compilation of the statistics I am highly indebted to my collaborators, Drs. E. Libman and A. G. Foord.

III.

STATISTICS OF FIVE HUNDRED CASES OF LOBAR PNEUMONIA.

By ALFRED MEYER, M.D.,
ATTENDING PHYSICIAN.

The following statistics of 500 lobar pneumonias are culled from all the cases of the primary type that have occurred in the medical service of Mount Sinai Hospital during the ten years ending January 1, 1898. The medical service includes 2 adult male wards of about 44 beds, 1 adult female ward of about 24 beds, and a children's ward of about 26 beds. The children's service includes both sexes up to the age of 14 years.

TABLE I.

	Cases Treated.			Died.			
Age.	Male.	Female.	Total.	Male.	Female.	Total.	Percentage.
4-12 months....	6	7	13	4	5	9	69.34
1-5 years......	22	25	47	3	7	10	21.27
6-10 "	23	15	38	0	3	3	7.89
11-20 " ..	77	27	104	7	4	11	10.57
21-30 "	90	36	126	5	5	10	7.93
31-40 "	64	20	84	15	2	17	20.23
41-50 "	36	16	52	12	7	19	36.53
51-60 "	22	5	27	9	2	11	37.03
61-70 "	6	0	6	3	0	3	50.00
71-80 "	2	1	3	0	1	1	33.33
Total..........	348	152	500	58	36	94	18.88

Total cases, 500. Total deaths, 94.

Mortality of series, 18.88 per cent.

Youngest case in series, 4 months (died).

Oldest " " " 77 years (recovered).

Twenty-three cases died within forty hours after admission. Excluding these, the mortality for series is 14.20 per cent.

A study of this table indicates a rather favorable mortality per cent: 94 deaths out of 500 cases = 18.88 per cent. Omitting 23 cases that died within forty hours after admission, the mortality for the series is only 14.20 per cent. Pye-Smith reports a mortality of 25.5 per cent out of 434 cases. Now, as it is well known that for a number of reasons hospital statistics are apt to be unfavorable as compared to those drawn from private practice, our own results, taken exclusively from hospital records, are comparatively more favorable than the figures indicate. As the cases cover a period of ten years, there is less probability of the introduction of certain chance elements that might influence the mortality during a particular year. Aufrecht reaches the conclusion, after a careful study of mortality for sixteen years, and after excluding all variations due to locality, season, individuality, and therapeutics, that the varying mortality (his own figures, 6.6–25.3 per cent) is dependent upon the varying virulence of the pneumococcus.[1] How large a rôle in the reduction of our own mortality is played by the fact that our patients do not belong to the drinking class I shall leave undetermined.

Mortality according to Age.—A further study of this table shows (last column) a very high mortality under 12 months (9 out of 13 cases = 69.34 per cent), an almost uninterrupted fall in the mortality up to 30 years of age, and then a rise for every decade up to 70 years, which latter gives a mortality of 50 per cent. The mortality is nearly three times greater between 31 and 40 than it is between 21 and 30, and nearly twice as great between 41 and 50 as it is between 31 and 40. All authors agree as to the influence of age on mortality, though their figures vary.

Morbidity according to Sex.—Of the 500 cases, 348 were males and 152 were females—*i.e.*, 69.6 per cent and 30.4 per cent respectively. The difference is mainly due to cases occurring after 10 years of age, and is greater than

[1] I refer to this question again in Table IX.

can be accounted for by the disproportion in the size of the male and female services, which is about 2 to 1. Our result agrees with the general verdict that men are more liable to pneumonia than women. Aufrecht seems to think it still uncertain whether sex plays any rôle in the causation of pneumonia, but presents figures which seem to indicate a prevalence three and one-half times greater among men than women.

Mortality according to Sex.—There were 36 deaths out of 152 female cases=23.68 per cent; there were 58 deaths out of 348 male cases=16.66 per cent—a proportion that agrees almost exactly with that given by Juergensen in Ziemssen's "Encyclopædia," who says that "pneumonia is, *cœteris paribus*, a more dangerous affection in the female than in the male sex in the ratio of 3 to 2."

TABLE II. (*a*)

CRISES.

Day.	Male.	Female.	Total.
5th	6	5	11
6th	2	3	5
7th	42	11	53
8th	18	3	21
9th	29	5	34
10th	13	6	19
11th	11	3	14
12th	4	3	7
13th	2	2	4
2 weeks	2	4	6
2½ "	14	3	17
3 "	4	1	5
4 "	4	0	4
Total	151	49	200

TABLE II. (*b*)

LYSES.

No. of days.	No. of cases.
9 days....	1
10 "	3
12 "	3
13 "	3
2 weeks...	4
2½ " ...	19
3 " ...	12
4 " ...	11
5 " ...	1
6 " ...	3
7 " ...	2
8 " ...	1
Total......	63

Showing average duration of pyrexia.

Out of 263 cases there were 63 lyses and 200 crises.
Of 200 crises, 79 fell on even days, 121 on odd days.

In this table all cases are considered as having defervesced by crisis in which the temperature fell from 103° or over to normal within forty-eight hours. This may appear as an arbitrary classification, but I believe it has at least this to recommend it, that it is a compromise between the twenty-four-hour limit allowed by some and the seventy-two hour limit allowed by others. Out of 263 cases with complete histories, there were 200 crises—that is, a little more than 75 per cent of the cases. Aufrecht gives a smaller percentage, 57.5 per cent out of 1,501 cases.

The proportion on the even and odd days respectively was:

Even days	39.5
Odd "	60.5

Juergensen's figures are:

Even days	38.7
Odd "	61.3

The closeness of the two sets of figures is striking.

The Average Duration, estimated from the beginning of the disease to the cessation of fever, was:

For 200 crisis cases, 10 days.
" 63 lysis " 22 "
" 263 " 13 "

The most frequent duration was about a week—125 cases ended between the fifth and ninth days inclusive = 47.53 per cent.

TABLE III.

SITE.

Lobe.	Right upper.		Right lower.		Right middle.		Entire right lung.		Right bilobar.		Total right lung.		Left upper.		Left lower.		Entire left lung.		Involving both lungs.		Total left lung.		Total both lungs.	
	RIGHT LUNG.												LEFT LUNG.											
Sex.	M.	F.	M.	F.	M.	F.	M.	F.	M.	F.	M.	F.	M.	F.	M.	F.	M.	F.	M.	F.	M.	F.	Male and female.	
4–12 mos	1	1	0	0	0	0	0	2	0	0	1	3	1	0	0	0	0	1	1	0	1	1	Right upper.. ..	46
1– 5 yrs	2	2	4	4	0	0	1	2	0	0	7	8	2	4	4	2	3	5	2	4	9	11	Right lower......	76
6–10 " ..	2	0	3	1	0	0	1	0	0	0	6	1	2	2	4	4	1	1	0	1	7	7	Right middle .	3
11–20 " ..	6	1	12	5	0	0	6	2	5	1	29	9	2	0	11	4	7	0	6	0	20	4	Entire right lung.	51
21–30 " ..	8	3	14	5	0	1	13	2	4	1	39	12	6	3	18	5	9	5	11	4	33	13	Two lobes, right lung.	24
31–40 " .	7	3	5	8	2	0	6	1	6	2	26	14	5	4	19	4	9	1	9	5	33	9	Left upper.......	36
41–50 " ..	3	1	8	2	0	0	6	2	2	1	19	6	3	0	11	6	2	1	5	4	16	7	Left lower.......	102
51–60 " ..	3	1	3	1	0	0	5	0	1	0	12	2	1	1	7	1	0	0	4	1	8	2	Entire left lung..	45
61–70 " ..	0	0	1	0	0	0	1	0	1	0	3	0	0	0	1	0	0	0	1	0	1	0	Total lobes......	383
71–80 " ..	2	0	0	0	0	0	1	0	0	0	3	0	0	0	1	0	0	0	0	0	1	0	Bilateral pneumonia.	58
Total. ..	34	12	50	26	2	1	40	11	19	5	145	55	22	14	76	26	31	14	39	19	129	54	Total cases......	325

In this series of 383 sites, the frequency of occurrence and percentages (including the cases which had pneumonic processes in both lungs) of the more common sites, is as follows:

Left lower lobe, 102 cases, 26.62 per cent.		Total right lung.	52.21 per cent.
Right " " 76 " 19.84 "		" left "	47.78 "
Entire right lung, 51 " 13.31 "		Total cases involving both lungs,	15.14 "
" left " 46 " 12.01 "			

This table requires but little comment. The figures agree with those of other authors in that they show a more frequent involvement of the right lung than of the left; the difference is somewhat less than the one usually observed, perhaps because the bilateral cases are included in the calculation. The left lower lobe was the most frequent seat of disease, occurring in 26.62 per cent of the cases. This also agrees with experience gained elsewhere. Pye-Smith gives the following figures in his 434 cases: left base, 151; right base, 140.

TABLE IV.

SITE IN RELATION TO MORTALITY.

	RIGHT LUNG.												LEFT LUNG.									
Lobe.	Right upper.		Right lower.		Right middle.		Entire right lung.		Right bilobar.		Total right lung		Left upper.		Left lower.		Entire left lung.		Involving both lungs.		Total left lung.	
Sex	M.	F.	M.	F.	M.	F.	M.	F.	M.	F.	M.	F.	M.	F.	M.	F.	M.	F.	M.	F.	M.	F.
4–10 mos.	0	1	0	0	0	0	0	1	0	0	0	2	0	0	0	0	0	1	1	0	0	1
1– 5 yrs..	0	0	1	2	0	0	1	0	0	0	2	2	0	0	0	0	0	2	0	0	0	2
6–10 " ..	0	0	0	0	0	0	0	0	0	0	0	0	0	0	0	1	0	0	0	0	0	1
11–20 " ..	0	0	1	0	0	0	1	1	0	0	2	1	0	0	0	1	0	0	0	0	0	1
21–30 " ..	0	0	1	0	0	1	0	0	0	1	1	2	0	0	1	0	1	2	2	1	2	2
31–40 " ..	0	0	1	0	0	0	2	0	1	0	4	0	0	0	3	0	0	0	2	2	3	0
41–50 " ..	1	0	2	0	0	0	1	2	0	0	4	2	0	0	1	0	0	0	2	2	1	0
51–60 " ..	2	0	0	0	0	0	1	0	0	0	3	0	0	0	2	0	0	0	3	0	2	0
61–70 " ..	0	0	0	0	0	0	1	0	0	0	1	0	0	0	0	0	0	0	1	0	0	0
71–80 " ..	0	0	0	0	0	0	1	0	0	0	1	0	0	0	0	0	0	0	0	0	0	0
Total.	3	1	6	2	0	1	8	4	1	1	18	9	0	0	7	2	1	5	11	5	8	7
Both sexes	4		8		1		12		2		27		0		9		6		16		15	
Mortality..	8.69%		10.52%		33.33%		23.54%		8.33%		13.50%		0.0%		8.82%		13.33%		27.58%		8.18%	

Pneumonias involving the right lung were more fatal than those involving the left, in the proportion of 13.50 to 8.18. Aufrecht also finds a difference, though his disproportion is not so great—15.3 per cent for right side and 12.8 per cent for left side. It is a striking fact that we have no fatal case of left upper pneumonia to report, though there were 36 cases in this site out of 325 cases (see Table II.). This does not support Juergensen's view that the prognosis is better when a lower lobe is involved.

TABLE V. (*a*)

HIGHEST TEMPERATURE, PULSE, AND RESPIRATION WITH RECOVERY IN A SERIES OF 183 CASES.

Temperature...... Number of cases...	97–97.9 0	98–98.9 6	99–99.9 3	100–100.9 8	101–101.9 8	102–102.9 22	103–103.9 30	104–104.9 66	105–105.9 32	106–106.9 7	107–107.9 1	108–108.9 0	Total, 183
Pulse.............. Number of cases...	60–69 0	70–79 1	80–89 7	90–99 11	100–109 36	110–119 36	120–129 50	130–139 21	140–149 19	150–159 1	160–169 1	170–179 0	Total, 183
Respiration..... Number of cases ..	20–23 2	24–27 10	28–31 18	32–35 22	36–39 31	40–43 37	44–47 19	48–51 19	52–55 13	56–59 2	60–70 7	80–100 4	Total, 183

TABLE V. (*b*).

HIGHEST TEMPERATURE, PULSE, AND RESPIRATION IN A SERIES OF 38 DEATHS.

Temperature... Number of cases ...	97–97.9 1	98–98.9 0	99–99.9 1	100–100.9 0	101–101.9 0	102–102.9 3	103–103.9 4	104–104.9 15	105–105.9 7	106–106.9 3	107–107.9 2	108–108.9 2	Total, 38
Pulse............. Number of cases...	60–69 0	70–79 0	80–89 0	90–99 2	100–109 1	110–119 5	120–129 3	130–139 5	140–149 9	150–159 7	160–169 4	170–179 2	Total, 38
Respiration...... Number of cases...	20–23 0	24–27 2	28–31 0	32–35 3	36–39 1	40–43 6	44–47 6	48–51 9	52–55 0	56–59 1	60–70 9	80–100 1	Total, 38

These tables give a general idea of the type of case we had to deal with in 183 recoveries and 38 deaths, at least so far as a record of pulse, temperature, and respiration can do so. The data do not include cases under 14 years of age, because of their less intimate relation in children to the type of disease.

In 183 cases of recovery, 40 had temperature of 105° and over—about 22 per cent.

In 183 cases of recovery, 92 had pulse of 120 and over —about 50 per cent.

In 183 cases of recovery, 100 had respiration of 40 and over—about 54 per cent.

By a study of Tables V. (*a*) and V. (*b*) we see that out of a total of 122 cases in which pulse ran to 120 or over, there were 92 recoveries to 30 deaths—in other words, a little less than 25 per cent of deaths. This result is more favorable than that of Griesinger (quoted by Juergensen). who, from a study of 72 cases, inferred that 33⅓ per cent of the patients die under these circumstances; but Juergensen objects to a generalization from so small a number of cases. There was similarly a death rate of about 26 per cent in which the temperature ran to 105° or over (14 out of 54), and a death rate of about 30 per cent in cases in which the respiration ran to 48 or over (20 out of 65). The following details of the tables are of interest: 8 recoveries with temperature of 106° and over, 4 recoveries with respiration between 80 and 100.

TABLE VI. (*a*)

TABULATION OF THE MORE FREQUENT COMPLICATIONS OCCURRING IN THE WHOLE SERIES OF 500 CASES.

Complication.	No. of cases.	Sex.		Cured.	Died.	Frequency in percentage.
		M.	F.			
Pulmonary œdema	29	21	8	3	26	5.80
Pleurisy with effusion	25	14	11	20	5	5.00
Empyema	18	12	6	12	6	3 60
General bronchitis	11	8	3	8	3	2.20
Acute conjunctivitis	5	5	0	5	0	1.00
Pericarditis with effusion	7	5	2	5	2	1.40
Acute endocarditis	5	3	2	4	1	1 00
Acute nephritis	5	1	4	3	2	1.00
Acute endocarditis and pericarditis with effusion	4	3	1	1	3	0 80
Pleuritis sicca	2	2	0	2	0	0.40
Colitis	5	2	3	2	3	1.00

Statistics from various cities show some differences with regard to frequency of various complications, though some of the differences may be accidental. In our own cases pulmonary œdema was both the most frequent and the most fatal complication, occurring in 5.8 per cent of the cases, and of these nearly 90 per cent ended fatally. Pleurisy with effusion comes a close second with a frequency of 5 per cent. Effusion statistics from other sources vary from 4 to 15 per cent. Aufrecht gives 5.5 per cent in 1,501 cases. He includes, however, the empyemas. If we add our own empyema figures to those of effusion we get a somewhat larger number, 8.6 per cent. Pericarditis occurred 11 times (4 with endocarditis)—2.2 per cent. Of these, 5 died—nearly one-half. In 1 of the 5 cases of conjunctivitis the purulent discharge was examined microscopically and the presence of pneumococci demonstrated. There were 4 cases of colitis. There has been some conflict of opinion regarding the relation of colitis to pneumonia. Some experiences with the Widal reaction in the past two years excite a suspicion that this type of case may belong to the masked typhoids, in the recognition of which in the future the Widal reaction will play a prominent rôle.

The small number of acute nephritis cases I am inclined to attribute to imperfections in the records as well as to the rigid exclusion of the simple albuminuria of fever.

TABLE VI. (*b*)

TABLE OF JAUNDICE CASES WITH REFERENCE TO SITE AND MORTALITY.

	Site of pneumonic process.	Cured.	Died.
1	Right upper lobe..	0	1
2	" lung entire	0	1
3	" upper lobe	0	1
4	" and left base	1	0
5	" lung entire	1	0
6	" lower lobe	0	1
7	" lung entire	0	1

Total number of jaundice cases in series of 325 cases.

In view of the many discussions regarding the nature and classification of cases complicated by jaundice, I have arranged them in a separate table. There were 7 cases out of 325 (2.15 per cent). In Vienna and Stockholm there were 53 cases out of 8,354 (0.62 per cent). Pye-Smith gives 4 cases out of 434 (0.9 per cent).

Aufrecht found 15 cases out of 1,501 (1 per cent). In Basle it was observed 65 times in 230 cases (28.3 per cent), which unusual frequency does not seem to be entirely explained by Juergensen's theory that the jaundice had been looked for more carefully.

Of Aufrecht's 15 cases 2 ended fatally (1 complicated with chronic nephritis), which is no more than his average mortality. In cases complicated by jaundice not due to obstruction, and which he believes are due to other infection than the diplococcus pneumoniæ, he believes the prognosis is much worse. It is an interesting fact that the right lung was involved in every one of our 7 cases and that in 3 of them the entire right lung was affected. Pye-Smith's 4 cases were also right-sided. Our mortality was high in these cases, 5 out of 7.

TABLE VII.

NUMBER OF CASES AND DEATHS, WITH PERCENTAGES OF EACH, OCCURRING IN THE DIFFERENT SEASONS, IN THE ENTIRE SERIES.

Season.	No. of cases.	Percentage of cases.	No. of deaths.	Percentage of deaths.
Spring—March, April, and May..	167	33.40	29	30.85
Summer—June, July, and August	83	16.60	8	8.51
Autumn—September, October, and November..	92	18 40	20	21.27
Winter—December, January, and February....	158	31 60	37	29.26
	500	100.00	94	

In this table the largest morbidity is shown in the winter and spring months, 65 per cent, and only 35 per cent for the summer and autumn. Aufrecht, from a study of 1,501 cases, gives for the first half of the year 66.9 per cent and for the second half 32.9 per cent of the cases. As was to be expected from the greater morbidity, the total mortality is also greater in the winter and spring than in the autumn and summer, our percentages being respectively 70.21 per cent and 29.79 per cent. Juergensen gives as a result of a study of the mortality tables in six large European cities 66.2 per cent for the winter and spring and 33.8 per cent for summer and autumn.

Our summer cases appear to have been more benign than those of other seasons, for, though they represent 16.60 per cent of the morbidity, they give only 8.51 per cent of the deaths.

TABLE VIII.

SHOWING THE FREQUENCY OF OCCURRENCE OF PREVIOUS ATTACKS OF ACUTE LOBAR PNEUMONIA IN A SERIES OF 325 CASES.

No. of cases, 30	Cured, 27	Died, 3
Frequency in per cent, 9%	Total cases in series, 325	Mortality, 10%

If Juergensen's view were true that "one attack probably increases the disposition to a recurrence," it would seem to me there would be a larger number of cases with previous attacks than our table shows—30 out of 325 (9 per cent). Pye-Smith gives 18 recurrences in 434 cases, which is a still smaller percentage (4.1 per cent). Aufrecht believes in a congenital predisposition, and quotes Ziemssen, who found recurrences 19 times among 201 pneumonic children; 14 had 2 attacks, 3 had 3 attacks, and 2 had 4 attacks. The believers in a specific causation of pneumonia may find some satisfaction in the fact that the percentage of deaths (10 per cent) in the recurrences is materially less than the mortality of all the cases (18.8 per cent). The recurrences, in other words, appear to be of a milder type, as is not infrequently the case with typhoids.

TABLE IX.

SHOWING NUMBER OF CASES AND DEATHS EACH YEAR IN THE ENTIRE SERIES OF 500 CASES.

Year.	No. of cases.	No. of deaths.	Mortality
1888	17	5	29.41%
1889	40	8	20.00%
1890	30	7	23.33%
1891	68	7	10.29%
1892	40	6	15 00%
1893	79	19	24.05%
1894	62	8	12 80%
1895	69	19	27.53%
1896	48	11	22.9 %
1897	47	4	8 51%
Total..	500	94	18.80%

This table is interesting as showing a mortality varying between wide limits in different years—8.51 per cent in 1897 and 29.41 per cent in 1888. Aufrecht's extremes (already referred to in Table I.) are 6.6 per cent and 25.3 per cent. These changes in mortality rate, so striking at Mount Sinai Hospital as elsewhere, are continually urged as a confirmation of their view by those who believe in a "status epidemicus" or in the varying virulence of the pneumococcus.

Treatment.—With reference to the treatment it may be said that there has been no single method in vogue at Mount Sinai. Stimulants, both alcoholic and medicinal (digitalis, sparteine, strychnine), have entered more largely as a factor than any other; for out of 284 cases stimulants were used in 250, either alone or combined with other measures (in 85 cases cold compresses on chest, tepid sponging, and, rarely, plunges). In 89 cases antipyretics were used, either alone or combined with stimulants and hydrotherapy.

It is extremely difficult to draw conclusions as to the influence of treatment on the result—first, because the treatment was rarely limited to a single active procedure; second, because of the varying severity of the disease.

Neither Petresco's method of using very large doses of digitalis, nor Aufrecht's of employing hypodermatic injections of muriate of quinine, has been used sufficiently to permit of any deductions.

The question of venesection in the treatment of pneumonia is still a mooted one. Some condemn it utterly, and Aufrecht thinks it has been positively proven that pericarditis is more frequent in cases thus treated. Others, again, like Pye-Smith, urge that it should not be forgotten or neglected, and believe venesection suitable at the commencement of the disease, or during its course "to relieve the overpressure in the right side of the heart and the systemic veins." In our own cases we have records of only four patients in whom venesection was practised: three of these died and one recovered. In none of them is there any mention of pericarditis. They were all severe cases; the area involved was extensive, and the three fatal ones were complicated by an acute nephritis. In other words, the prognosis was unfavorable irrespective of the treatment.

IV.

NOTES ON SOME INTERESTING RESULTS WITH THE WIDAL TEST.

By ALFRED MEYER, M.D.,

ATTENDING PHYSICIAN.

In view of the complaint in various quarters that the Widal reaction appears so late, in doubtful cases, as to be of little practical value in the very type in which it is most needed, the following cases, though few in number, may not be without interest. They are all cases that have been observed within a year on my own service, with the exception of the case of Benjamin K., for which I am indebted to Dr. M. Manges, on whose service it occurred. Only brief extracts from the histories will be given.

1. *Abortive Typhoid.*—Dina K., admitted December 22, 1897, æt. 26 years. Sick one week, last four days in bed; headache, lassitude, anorexia, nausea, no epistaxis, bowels regular, well nourished, tongue slightly dry. Physical examination: Heart, lungs, and spleen negative; a few erythematous spots on abdomen. Temperature on admission 99.6°, pulse 96, respiration 24. She had with her a report from the Board of Health that the Widal reaction was positive. Temperature, afternoon, 103.2°. December 24, temperature range 100.6° to 101.8°; tongue moist and clean; all evidence as bearing on a probable typhoid negative. December 26, temperature touched normal, did not go above 100°; Widal positive. December 28: Convalescence may be said to have commenced from this day; tongue moist and clean; no clinical evidence of illness; no roseola nor headache; feels perfectly well; Widal positive. Widal tests made daily to January 2, inclusive, were positive. January 4, soft diet. Discharged January 16, cured.

Here is a woman in whom convalescence was practically established in ten days or less after taking to bed; whose temperature touched normal on the fourth day after admission to the hospital; in whose case there was scarcely a symptom outside of the fever, headache, and anorexia: and in whom in former years the indefinite diagnosis of febricula would have been made, or possibly a suspicion of typhoid entertained, or the case might have been relegated to the class of intestinal toxæmias.

2. *Irregular Typhoid.*—Henry T., æt. 44, clerk, admitted September 27, 1898. Illness began about a month ago. Nothing ails him but sleeplessness, and can ascribe no reason for this trouble. Has no headache; talks peculiarly; says he was the "beauty of the family": has had no mental worries, except the care of an aged mother; appetite fair, bowels regular; has lost flesh and strength. House physician noted slight ptosis of left eyelid, and tongue deviates to right side; occasional tremor of right side of face and of tongue, and tremor of voice while speaking: speech hesitating, and tendency to repeat; some indistinctness of enunciation: marked tâche cérébrale; patellar tendon reflexes markedly exaggerated. Temperature 101.8°, pulse 126, respiration 30. Physical examination: Chest and abdomen negative In the evening, temperature normal; for the next three days, temperature ranged between 99° and 100.6°. October 1, temperature 100° to 101°; 2, 100° to 103°: 3, 100° to 102.4°: 4, 99° to 102°; 5, 99° to 103°; 6, 99° to 102.4°; 7, 99.2° to 101.2°. Partial Widal reaction. Has been having one movement of bowels daily, either by enema or spontaneously. October 8, 99.6° to 103.6°; positive Widal; no symptoms, subjective or objective, of any kind outside of fever; no headache, no muscular pains: tongue moist and clean; no roseola, no spleen, no diarrhœa, no tympanites. October 9, 101° to 102.4°: Widal positive, but less marked. From this date to October 25 these slight variations of temperature continued; otherwise patient was perfectly well. Daily inquiries elicited the reply that he was "first rate," that he had nothing to complain of except that he received nothing to eat. From October 26 to the date of discharge on November 9 his temperature remained normal.

Here the prominence of the nervous symptoms (sleeplessness for a month before admission, motor disturbances of face and tongue, exaggerated reflexes, etc.), with the almost complete absence of fever at the time of admission, did not even excite the suspicion of typhoid fever. As it was, the Widal test, taken in a routine way, disclosed the true state of affairs, and the patient convalesced after the fever had continued exactly four weeks.

3. *Typhoid Obscured by Pneumonia.*—Benjamin K., æt. 44, presser, admitted February 26, 1898. Owing to patient's poor mental condition and refusal to answer questions, history imperfect. Illness of eight days' standing. Began with a chill, followed by fever, cough, difficult expectoration, and pain in chest. General condition fair; fairly well nourished. Tongue dry and brown. Lungs: anteriorly, negative. Posteriorly at left base a dull note, crepitant and subcrepitant râles. All other organs negative. Slight general tenderness of abdomen. On admission, pulse 102, respiration 36, temperature 100.2°. February 27, temperature, afternoon, 105°; urine 22 ounces, 1020, albumin; trace of bile, few pus cells. Ehrlich positive. Next day albumin increased to 0.4, many casts present; urine involuntary in part. March 1, chill of ten minutes' duration this morning; temperature above 104° all day; physical signs unchanged. Widal positive. Treatment with plunges begun. With the exception of delirium, his condition continues about the same until March 4, when the pulse begins to intermit. In spite of rectal and hypodermatic stimulation, he died early on March 5.

Until the Widal reaction was obtained on the third day after admission, it would scarcely have been justifiable to make a diagnosis of typhoid; the pulmonary signs were prominent, and the fever, mental and renal conditions could very reasonably be explained as secondary to the pulmonary trouble, perhaps more reasonably than by a typhoid only in its tenth day. And yet the result of the Widal was decisively the other way.

4. *Typhoid Obscured by Pneumonia.*—Esther L., æt. 29, housewife, admitted October 15, 1898. Has been in bed two weeks with a cold. Prominent symptoms were fever, cough, pain on both sides of chest, and severe dyspnœa. No chills. Cough, fever, and dyspnœa persist. Great prostration and weakness. Eight days ago a crop of boils appeared on the body and right hip. Bowels regular On admission temperature 102.2°, pulse 118, respiration 48 ; lips pale bluish ; skin moist, showing a diffuse maculo-papular eruption with acne and furuncles. Spleen enlarged (?). Lung: anteriorly, resonance on right side ceases at fourth rib, dull note in right axillary line; also a few crepitant râles in both axillæ. Posteriorly : dull note below right midscapula and at left base; fine crepitant râles and diminished voice and breathing over right side; crepitant and subcrepitant râles over left base. Treated as a typhoid suspect.

First day had three stools. October 16, temperature 101° to 102.8°, respiration 40 to 48, pulse 108 to 118, Widal negative. The next four days general condition about the same, stools slightly more frequent (from 5 to 8 daily). Widal still negative. October 21, temperature 99.8° to 103.8°; October 22, temperature 99.2° to 103.6°. Partial Widal for the first time. This partial Widal continued daily with normal morning temperatures and slight evening rises until the 27th, when the Widal reaction was positive and continued so for several days. October 30, herpes labialis. Discharged cured November 11, 1898.

In this case it is true the Widal reaction did not appear until late (the twenty-second day); still it was not too late to be of material service in making the diagnosis of typhoid a certainty. In the ante-Widal days, the sudden commencement, the prominence of chest symptoms, the early dropping of the temperature to normal, and even the appearance of herpes labialis, would all have rendered the diagnosis of a primary pulmonary complaint justifiable. The long duration of the disease and the diarrhœa might have helped to confirm our suspicion of a typhoid even without the Widal, though the uncertainty would not have been entirely removed without the bacteriological test, in view of the occasional occurrence of severe diarrhœa with pneumonia.

5. *Ambulant Typhoid.*—Adolph K., æt. 19 years, shoemaker, admitted October 16, 1898. Was a volunteer soldier at Camp Black during August; had slight diarrhœa there. Afterward went to Camp Meade. Illness began there about six weeks ago. Was in hospital at Camp Meade one week during September, with malaise and fever, though he did not take to bed. Was treated for malaria, with quinine. Has lost twelve pounds during last three months. No definite complaint at time of admission. Looks pale and poorly nourished. Temperature 99.6°. Spleen enlarged and easily felt. Widal positive, Ehrlich negative. October 20, spleen still palpable. Widal positive on October 21 and 23, though gradually less marked. October 27, Widal negative. Discharged November 10.

Here is a patient who was proven by the Widal test to have been an ambulant case of typhoid through the entire disease. He was already in the apyretic stage when he reached the hospital, and was then merely suffering from malnutrition. The military diagnosis of malaria would very likely have been concurred in, had it not been for the bacteriological evidence. That the infection was recent was shown by the gradual disappearance of the reaction while the patient was under observation.

Regarding the technique employed in the Widal reaction in these cases, I would refer to the report of the pathologist and assistant pathologist of the institution.

V.

A CASE OF PERNICIOUS ANÆMIA WITH FATTY HEART OCCURRING DURING PREGNANCY.

By ALFRED MEYER, M.D.,

ATTENDING PHYSICIAN.

MRS. SARAH W., æt. 37 years, admitted January 28, 1898.

Family History.—Negative.

Previous History.—Has always enjoyed good health, no illness of any kind, in particular no inflammatory rheumatism or chorea. Has had four children, the last one eight years ago; is now pregnant over four months.

Present History.—Illness of about two and one-half months' standing, beginning with weakness and increasing pallor, and dyspnœa on the slightest exertion. There then followed swelling of the feet, slight headache and cough, increased on lying down. Appetite poor, bowels constipated. Also began to have sweats. During the past two weeks pallor, cough, sweats, œdema, dyspnœa, and weakness have become much worse, confining patient to bed. Passes her urine frequently. Chief complaints: great weakness and dyspnœa on slightest exertion.

General Condition.—Good panniculus adiposus, but intense anæmia; conjunctivæ perfectly white; mucous membranes very pale and resembling those of a patient dying of hemorrhage; no cyanosis; general anasarca.

Lungs—Slightly diminished resonance at both bases, in part due to œdema of soft parts. Coarse and fine râles diffused over chest. *Heart*—On the right, dulness extends about one finger's breadth beyond right border of sternum; large mammæ and œdema make this somewhat uncertain. Systolic murmurs heard over all the orifices and over the entire precordial region. The apical murmur audible to a point midway between apex and axillary line. Basic sounds not accentuated.

Auscultation difficult on account of the great dyspnœa. *Liver*—Left lobe apparently enlarged and extending a good four fingers' breadth beyond free border of ribs. Palpation hindered somewhat by the abdominal distension. *Spleen*—Enlarged to percussion and distinctly palpable beyond the free border of the ribs. *Abdomen*—Enlarged and contains free fluid. *Uterus*—Enlarged and extends more than half way to umbilicus. Marked œdema of feet, legs, and hands. On admission, pulse 100, respiration 48, temperature 100°. *Urine*, first specimen—Cloudy, acid, 1019, no albumin, no sugar, abundant urates, a few blood cells, uric acid crystals, no casts.

January 28 (first day): Temperature range, 100° to 103°; pulse range, 100 to 120; respiration range, 48 to 56. January 29: Temperature range, 102° to 103.4°; pulse range, 120 to 132; respiration range, 48 to 56; urine, 54+ ounces; two stools. Blood: hæmoglobin 20 per cent; no leucocytosis. January 30: Temperature range, 102.4° to 103.6°; pulse range, 120 to 132; respiration range, 54 to 60. Urine, 37+ ounces; morning specimen: 1009, negative, urea four grains to the ounce; twenty four hours' specimen: 1019 negative, urea eight grains to the ounce. Blood count shows: red blood cells, 1,090,000 to cubic millimetre. Reaction of perspiration on chest, forehead, and hands is decidedly acid; saliva ditto A drop of blood, however, does not redden litmus paper. Ophthalmic examination by Dr. Gruening on this date shows the presence of neuroretinitis and of extensive hemorrhagic patches in both eyes. January 31: Temperature, pulse, and respiration, as well as general condition, practically unchanged. Urine: total, 51+ ounces, 1016, negative, a few blood cells and epithelia, uric acid crystals. February 1 and 2: Urine on latter date, 59+ ounces, acid, 1016, clear, no albumin, indican present, urea nine and a half grains to the ounce. Microscopic examination negative. Marked Ehrlich. February 3: Condition unchanged. Urine, 62 ounces. Urea in twenty-four hours' specimen, nine grains to the ounce. Widal test negative. Canula introduced into outer aspect of each ankle to relieve the excessive œdema. February 4: No change in urine. Blood examination: No increase in number of leucocytes; a few neutrophiles and neutrophile granules; poikilocytes fairly numerous; nucleated red blood cells; micro- and macrocytes. Died at 7:45 P.M.

I append a report of blood examination made for me by Dr. Ewing, of the College of Physicians and Surgeons:

"The blood of Mrs. Sarah W. appears to fall in the class of primary pernicious anæmia on the following grounds: (1) The marked reduction in the number of red cells; (2) the extreme poikilocytosis; (3) the presence of some megalocytes with increase of hæmoglobin, although the chief character of the blood is the reduction of hæmoglobin; (4) the marked reduction in leucocytes; (5) presence of one megaloblast among many normoblasts; (6) the indications of the clinical history that the case was not one of purpura hæmorrhagica, which might prove fatal with blood of very similar morphology." (Signed) JAMES EWING.

During patient's period of observation of one week sleeplessness was a prominent feature, partly produced by the uninterrupted dyspnœa and partly by coughing. The last few nights were spent entirely in a chair. There was at all times a great deal of sweating, particularly marked upon the face, where the perspiration gathered in beads. At no time was there any diarrhœa; bowels were kept open by enemata. Stools contained nothing that might explain the intense anæmia; in particular, no entozoa were discovered. Rectal and vaginal examinations were negative, excepting, of course, the evidence of pregnancy. The patient was seen on the 30th of January by Dr. Mundé. The existence of pregnancy was confirmed and the propriety of bringing on labor was negatived by him, on account of the danger of profuse and possibly uncontrollable hemorrhage during the third stage, as well as the doubtful utility of such interference in producing a favorable change in the disease. Before she was seen by me she had received infusion digitalis and bitartrate of potash. Afterward the treatment consisted of Fowler's solution, carnogen, stimulants, enemata of defibrinated beef blood (received only one), washing out of bowels with one per cent saline solution by means of a long rectal tube, on the theory of pernicious anæmia being an intestinal toxæmia, or, as Bramwell has suggested, a gastro-intestinal hepatic anæmia.[1]

[1] See Bramwell: "Atlas of Clinical Medicine," vol. iii., p. 128.

The case herewith reported corresponds very closely in its main clinical features to five cases published by Gusserow in 1871,[1] and which have frequently been referred to in the literature of pernicious anæmia and of fatty heart. And still, in spite of the great lapse of time and the many studies in tissue metamorphosis, and great improvements in methods of blood count and examination, this affection still remains as mysterious as ever. Only two years ago Andry, of Lyons, referring to pernicious anæmia in general, wrote in Robin's "Traité de Thérapeutique Appliquée": "Nous devons reconnaître que nous sommes encore mal éclairés sur la nature et l'étiologie de l'affection." In an article on the relation of pernicious anæmia to spinal cord disease Dr. Paul Jacob[2] says: "Weder ist es gelungen das Wesen, die Aetiologie der perniciosen Anämie überhaupt zu ergruenden . . ."

An effort has recently been made to associate acute pernicious anæmia, in some cases at least, with traumatism.[3] Heretofore this has not been regarded as a possible etiological factor. Strange to say, in both of the quoted cases the injury was left-sided. In my own case there was no history either of injury or of shock.

Unfortunately it was not possible to obtain a postmortem examination in this case, although every possible effort was made to secure the consent of the relatives. The only other possible diagnosis would be a combination of cardiac disease with a chronic Bright's, but an analysis of the history, symptoms, and course forbids it. The anæmia was probably more intense than is ever seen in any form of chronic renal disease; it was also more sudden in appearance; the specific gravity of the urine was high for the cirrhotic type that might temporarily have shown no albumin:

[1] Arch. f. Gyn., Bd. ii.

[2] Berl. Klin. Woch., August, 1897.

[3] Bret: La Prov. Méd., Lyons, Dec., 1897; and James Herrick, of Chicago, Jour Amer. Med. Assoc., June, 1896.

albumin and casts were persistently absent in every specimen of urine examined; the daily amounts of urea were large, even for a person on full diet, and, in accordance with this fact, there were neither gastric nor nervous symptoms present to indicate a uræmic condition—not even a vomit, and only slight headache at time of admission; the dyspnœa could easily be explained on the score of the anæmia, the pulmonary congestion, and the fever. The ophthalmic picture might have been present in either primary pernicious anæmia or in the secondary anæmia of Bright's. The microscopic examination of the blood, however, seems to make the diagnosis of pernicious anæmia a certainty.

VI.

A CASE OF ABSCESS OF THE LIVER WHICH RUPTURED INTO THE LUNG.

By N. E. BRILL, A.M., M.D.,
ATTENDING PHYSICIAN.

Abscess of the liver is not a very common disease, nor is its presence readily recognized. The latter is especially true if the liver be the seat of multiple abscesses. It is not infrequent that an etiological factor for its production cannot be elicited, which renders the question of absolute diagnosis still more difficult. Where the liver is enlarged beyond the free border of the ribs, where the etiological moment of trauma, infection, hemorrhoids, dysentery, etc., can be ascertained, where the clinical picture indicates sepsis, the diagnosis may be made with a more positive assurance than when the liver is enlarged upward and no predisposing cause can be elicited. When the left lobe of the liver is the seat of the abscess—a very rare occurrence—the diagnosis is a matter of not much difficulty.

The following case is of interest from a diagnostic point of view and from the fact that recovery occurred without surgical intervention.

Jacob G., aged 33, born in Russia, married, and by occupation a musician, was admitted to my service on June 21, 1898. His family history was an unusually good one, both his parents being still alive and well; of his brothers and sisters all are living in good health. He himself is the father of a boy who has never been ill. With the exception of an attack of measles in childhood and an attack of gonorrhœa eight years ago, he had never had any illness. He uses alcohol in moderation, and has ceased the use of tobacco, to which he formerly was immoderately addicted.

About nine months ago he began to suffer with hemorrhoids, which were removed in this hospital five months ago. After the operation for hemorrhoids he had a diarrhœa, which persisted for three months, during which time he had from five to seven watery stools every day. During the two months previous to his recent admission he was free from the diarrhœa, but had a slight "hacking" cough; otherwise he felt fairly well, but noticed that he was growing weak.

His present complaint is of three days' standing, the result of what he called "catching cold"; it was characterized by headache and the *coughing* up of a considerable quantity of bright-red blood. This has continued until his admission to the hospital, his expectoration changing from bright-red blood to sputum streaked with blood. During the past few weeks he has become weak and has lost weight. He complains chiefly of pain in the right side of the chest, which is increased by coughing, shortness of breath, and weakness on exertion. He has noticed that he sweats a great deal. Before his admission to the hospital he had received medical treatment at home, which reduced the amount of perspiration, but which brought no relief to his general feeling of illness. He says that he has steadily grown worse; that he has completely lost his appetite; that he has become constipated. He complains also of a persistent pain in the pit of his stomach. He has not vomited at any time. He had no urinary disturbance.

Status præsens.—The patient is of medium stature, small frame, of poor muscular development, thin and emaciated. His face is sallow, of a peculiar muddy color, and indicates a condition of poor nutrition; he looks sick and debilitated. His body shows no eruption or scars of any sort. His temperature is 100° F., his pulse 112 and of regular rhythm. His arteries, though slightly tortuous and sclerotic, do not show a wave of high tension. His respirations are costal in type and 20 to the minute.

There is a retraction of the chest wall above and below each clavicle.

He shows no disturbed function of his nervous system.

His lips are pale and his tongue is slightly coated. His appetite is poor and he is occasionally thirsty. The stools are diarrhœal.

Palpation of his abdomen reveals an epigastric tenderness, sufficiently marked to occasion note.

There is no increased area of liver dulness below the free border of the ribs; an area of dulness extending upward in the axillary line to the fourth interspace and in the scapular line to the angle of the scapula is continuous with the liver dulness. Pressure over the region of the liver in the mammary, axillary, and scapular lines elicits tenderness in each.

The spleen cannot be felt, nor is it enlarged to percussion.

There are no resistant areas anywhere within the abdominal cavity.

The respiratory rhythm is regular; his thorax is long, rather broad, and somewhat flattened. The respiratory movements are costal in type, of fair expansion. There is some bulging on the right side at the lower aspect of the thorax, more noticeable in the axillary line. There is considerable cough and expectoration; the latter is bloody, prune-juice in color, profuse in amount (about twelve ounces in twenty-four hours), and of peculiar sweetish odor. The microscopical examination revealed a large number of blood cells, many pus cells, and some fat cells and granular detritus. No amœbæ coli were at any time found.

Percussion of the chest reveals an increase in pitch over the right apex in front and behind, and slightly diminished resonance over the left apex posteriorly. Dulness is distinct on the right side at the fourth interspace in the axillary line and at the angle of the scapula behind; it extends downward and becomes continuous with the liver dulness. Percussion of the remainder of the left half of the thorax reveals no abnormal deviation. The heart is not displaced.

There is broncho-vesicular breathing in front over the right apex, and normal pulmonary breathing over the left. Behind there is broncho-vesicular breathing over both apices. On the right side, beginning at the angle of the scapula and extending downward, there are absent voice and breathing, associated at the base of the right lung with some very coarse râles. There is increased pectoral fremitus over entire right lung.

The heart sounds are feeble, the apex one inch to the right of the left nipple in the fifth interspace. Superficial and deep percussion shows no abnormal changes in the size or position of the heart. There are no cardiac murmurs.

The urine is acid, has a specific gravity of 1025, contains no albumin, no casts, and no sugar.

The blood shows a reduction of hæmoglobin and a leucocytosis.

The weight of the patient is 104 pounds.

At our first examination of the patient an absolute diagnosis could not be made because the necessary data were not sufficiently determined. We required to know more about the fever, more about his previous hemorrhoids, more about the condition of the lung, about his cough and expectoration, about his pain and tenderness on the right side.

The symptoms which stood out prominently were the fever, the loss of strength and body weight, the sudden hæmoptysis, the pallor and muddy complexion, the large irregular distribution of dulness over the region of the right lung, the broncho-vesicular breathing above and diminished and absent breathing below, the coarse râles, the increased pectoral fremitus, the pain and tenderness over the hepatic and gastric regions. The leucocytosis and the prune-juice expectoration were no less important. Taking these data into consideration, the following conditions suggested themselves as the probable pathological process giving rise to the existing conditions:

1. Pneumonia.
2. Acute pneumonic phthisis.
3. Ulcerative pulmonary tuberculosis.
4. Empyema of the right pleural sac, or
5. Encapsulated empyema.
6. Tumor of the lung.
7. Abscess of the lung.
8. Abscess of the liver.

We were not inclined to regard it as an acute pneumonia, because there was no history of sudden onset with chill, no sharp pain in the side, no continuous high temperature. While it is true that pain could be elicited on pressure in the axillary line over the thorax, it was like a dull ache in his ordinary condition. The physical signs and the prune-juice expectoration might have justified, if considered alone, such a diagnosis. Again, a large hæmoptysis could not be explained on the basis of an acute inflammation of the lung. Even his general condition contraindicated a pneumonia and pointed rather to a septic process.

Acute Pneumonic Phthisis.—This could be excluded on the same grounds that we were inclined to exclude an ordinary pneumonia. The sudden onset, the hæmoptysis, the fever, the previous weakness and loss of weight, the dyspnœa, the expectoration, together with the physical signs, might have justified such a diagnosis, providing no microscopical examination of the sputum for tubercle bacilli had been made. In fact there are times when a pneumonia and an acute pneumonic phthisis cannot be differentiated even after repeated examinations of the sputum for tubercle bacilli, for it not infrequently happens that they may not be found in the sputum of the latter disease in its early stage.

One of the physical signs which existed in this case, and which is said by Traube to be an important diagnostic feature of acute pneumonic phthisis, was the absence of breath sounds over the area of consolidation.

Empyema.—A collection of pus in the pleural sac may give rise to the symptoms presented by this case, both in its clinical and physical aspects. The fever, the exhaustion and emaciation, the dyspnœa, the cough, were all present. Some of the local physical signs, such as tenderness on pressure, the bulging of the lower region of the thorax, the marked dulness extending to the fourth interspace in the axillary line, the bronchial breathing in the upper lobe and the absent breathing below, might be indicative of a collection of fluid in the pleural sac. Yet such a condition was excluded by reason of the irregular disposition of the dulness. The S-shaped line of dulness of Ellis when the patient was set upright was absent. There was no change in the line of dulness when the position of the patient was changed from upright to prone. There was increased pectoral fremitus over the area of dulness. The dulness extended higher in the scapular line than in the mammary. An aspirating needle was introduced in the seventh interspace behind, and in the sixth in the axillary line, and no fluid was obtained. The same means excluded the presence of

An Encapulated Empyema, whose presence was more suspicious than an ordinary empyema, owing to the irregular distribution of dulness which not infrequently is present in such conditions. The fact that the lower border of the liver did not extend beyond the free costal margin was likewise a factor which served to exclude the presence of fluid in the pleural sac.

Chronic Ulcerative Phthisis.—The progressive weakness, attended by the hacking cough, the fever, the gradually developing emaciation, the sweats, the sudden hemorrhage from the lungs, the bloody expectoration, the dulness posteriorly on the left side over the supraspinous fossa, the broncho-vesicular breathing and dulness over the right upper lobe, the loss of vesicular breathing on the same side in the lower lobe accompanied by the coarse râles, were clinical features which were all reconcilable with the presence of a tuberculosis of the lungs. In fact, in the absence, at the time of the first examination of the patient, of a bacteriological examination of the sputum for tubercle bacilli, the diagnosis of phthisis was one of the conditions which were assumed to have a more than probable basis. However, the fact that such a pathological condition began with great infrequency in the lower lobe of the lung was not lost sight of.

Tumor of the Lung.—The anomalous physical signs, the enlargement of the thorax, the cough, the prune-juice expectoration, the emaciation, the pallor and weakness, are features not uncommonly distinctive of pulmonary neoplasms. These were the early features in a case of primary carcinoma of the lungs which occurred in my service two years ago. That patient was a man of 36 years who had a primary carcinoma of the left lung, which subsequently involved the pleura, in whom there developed a large hemorrhagic effusion in the left pleural sac. In addition he had total left recurrent laryngeal paralysis. There were no glandular enlargements, nor distension of the veins of the face or thorax. He died in nine weeks after the beginning of his illness, from a perforation of the aorta, which became involved by the pressure of the rapidly growing tumor.

While the so-called distinctive features of pulmonary neoplasm were present, the presence of a new growth was excluded by reason of the absence of a pleural hemorrhagic effusion (hemorrhage in the pleura occurs rather infrequently in pulmonary neoplasm, according to Moutard-Martin in only 12 per cent of 200 cases collected by them), the absence of enlarged glands, the increased pectoral fremitus, the fever and sweats.

Abscess of the Lung.—This pathological condition occurs very infrequently. While it very rarely follows a pneumonia, it relatively more frequently attends general infective associated with embolic and infarctive processes. While this patient gave signs of sepsis, his history contraindicated the presence of a previous pneumonia. There were no general pyæmic abscesses, no signs of a breaking down of lung tissue. The expectoration was not like that of abscess of the lung, either in color or in general character; no elastic fibres were found in the sputum on microscopical examination. It might occur that breath sounds could be absent over a lung, which was the seat of an abscess, but on coughing, when the pus would be expectorated from the air cells, some breathing should be detected on auscultation over the cells which had been freed of their contents.

Abscess of the Liver.—From all the data presented we were inclined to believe that the weight of probability was in favor of the presence of this disease.

The individual features strongly indicative of this disease were the etiological factor of hemorrhoids. On inquiry we ascertained from the hospital records that this patient had been operated on by the clamp and cautery method some nine months previously, and that during his stay in the hospital at that time a "dysentery" had developed. The previous history of epigastric pain, of fever, his septic look, especially his muddy countenance, the loss of appetite, the cough, the subsequent pain over the lower portion of the right side of the thorax, the tenderness on pressure over the same region, were all indicative of a purulent collection in that region, whether it were a subphrenic abscess or one connected with the liver could not then be determined.

During the next few days examinations were made of the sputum for tubercle bacilli, for liver cells, and for amœbæ coli. The blood and urine were likewise subjected to clinical analysis. With the knowledge afforded by these additional data, as well as that obtained by daily observation as to the course of the disease, we concluded that this patient was suffering from abscess of the liver. An aspirating needle of fair diameter and rather longer than the ordinary aspirating needles was freely used, without obtaining the faintest sign of pus either above or below the diaphragm in the hepatic region. This, we concluded, was owing to the fact that the abscess was discharging its contents freely. The clinical diagnosis was, therefore, a large abscess of the right lobe of the liver, which had perforated the diaphragm, produced adhesion between the pleural layers, and ruptured into the lung, producing the hemorrhage, and emptied its contents through a bronchus.

Careful daily examination was made of the patient. During the first week his temperature remained almost constant, save a daily morning remission varying from 100.6° to 101.4° in the morning and 102.8° to 103.8° in the evening. His pulse was 104 to 112. His pallor and dirty hue increased, his weakness became more pronounced, and he lost three pounds further in weight. At the end of the first week he complained of severe, *agonizing* pain over the right chest. His cough became very troublesome and his sputa changed in color to a pink, resembling somewhat the color of strawberry ice-cream. The expectoration was more profuse, varying in amount from twelve to eighteen ounces in the twenty four hours.

Repeated examinations failed to reveal the presence of tubercle bacilli; pus cells were much more numerous, but no elastic fibres could be detected. Perspiration at no time was very profuse. His appetite did not improve. The pain in the epigastric region diminished. The patient could lie equally well on either side, and changing his position from the right to the left side did not produce, according to his statement, any increased pain or dragging sensation over the right hypochondrium, a usual feature of hepatic abscess.

During this period the urine showed nothing abnormal, the examination of the blood revealed the same change as on admission. No changes in the physical signs developed.

We were now fully convinced that the primary disturbance was not a tuberculosis nor a tumor of the lung, but that the disease was a very large abscess of the liver, by whose upward pressure the pulmonary signs were produced. The pressure of this large abscess had occasioned necrosis of the diaphragm, adhesive inflammation between the pleura and lung; it had then ruptured into the lung and involved the lower lobe in the necrotic process.

From the absence of amœbæ in the stools and in the expectoration we may conclude that the disease under consideration was the direct result of an infective process transmitted to the liver by the vessels of the gut, which had been the seat of the hemorrhoids. The liver was most probably the seat of numerous small abscesses, which had finally coalesced into one great abscess cavity, rather than the seat of a solitary abscess originally, because solitary abscesses are usually the result of amœbic dysentery, while multiple abscesses follow infections of the gut, operations for hemorrhoids, etc.

The subsequent course of the disease was unmarked by the development of any other noteworthy clinical features. Pain in the right shoulder first appeared six weeks after admission.

The fever remained of a remittent type for ten weeks, varying between 98.4° F. and 103.6° for a period of over ten weeks before the exacerbations began to diminish, which they did gradually. The temperature became subnormal thereupon for a period of four days before it assumed the normal type, which it did on October 7, 1898.

His subjective symptoms became less marked uniformly with the diminution of fever. He began to gain in strength about the end of September, and with this gain there came a change in his general appearance. The sickly, muddy hue of his countenance was the first objective sign to improve.

The expectoration became less profuse, its color gradually changing from pink to yellow. The cough persisted until a week before he left the hospital.

The pain in his chest and in the epigastrium gradually disappeared.

His weight, which had gone down to 98½ pounds at the end of the second week, where it remained stationary for eight weeks, then began to increase. When he left the hospital on October 12, 1898, it had reached 125¼ pounds.

On the day of his departure a careful physical examination was made, which demonstrated the fact that the physical signs in his lungs were still indicative of a considerably damaged right lower lobe. At no time was there any evidence of the formation of a pulmonic cavity of sufficient size to be detected by any of the means at our command. The breathing in the upper lobe became more vesicular, whilst in the lower lobe it was still absent. Dulness on percussion was still a marked feature over the lower aspect of the right lung. The bulging, however, which had been a prominent feature, had receded. The expansion was feebly perceptible on the right side of the thorax. The dyspnœa was no longer a prominent feature. The cough and expectoration had disappeared. His appetite was voracious.

When the patient was lowest and nearly moribund the question of surgical interference was seriously considered. It was borne in mind that the advances made in the surgery of the liver afforded, under ordinary circumstances of hepatic disease amenable to surgical treatment, great promise and hope of cure. But when we considered that the abscess involved the upper portion of the liver and had pushed itself upward into the thoracic cavity, that it had perforated through the diaphragm into the lung, the lower portion of which it had involved in the destructive process, that it had a free communication with the bronchus and was discharging itself at the rate of over a pint of pus *per diem*, it was but a justifiable conclusion to reach to permit the drainage established by natural means to continue rather than to subject the patient to the shock of a serious surgical operation. The site of the abscess could only have been reached with great difficulty, as numerous attempts to aspirate some of its contents from the exterior had signally failed, either because the cavity of the abscess was fully drained through the bronchus or because it was beyond the reach of a long aspirating needle. We further argued that if it was completely drained by natural means, surgical drainage could do no better, and that, if it were beyond the reach of a long needle, the technical difficulties in getting to its site, while not insuperable, would subject the patient, low as his condition was, to a more hopeless condition, with a chance, perhaps, of passing away while on the operating table. The fact that the patient left the hospital fully restored to health and strength was sufficient justification for the means employed to produce such a result.

VII.

A CASE OF ULCERATIVE ENDOCARDITIS INVOLVING THE VALVE OF THE PULMONARY ARTERY.

By N. E. BRILL, A.M., M.D.,
ATTENDING PHYSICIAN.

An acute endocarditis of the pulmonary valve belongs to the rarities of cardiac affections, and occurs almost invariably as the result of infective processes, such as staphylococcic, pneumococcic, and gonococcic infections. It has been so fully treated by Weckerle in a series of articles in the *Muenchener Medicinische Wochenschrift*, 1886, Nos. 32-36, on "Acute Ulcerative Endocarditis of the Pulmonary Valve," that it would be but tautological to premise anything further on this subject. This case is herewith recorded simply for the purpose of giving the data of another instance of this uncommon valvular affection, and to indicate the great difficulty of making a positive *intra vitam* diagnosis. The uncommon involvement of this valve in an ulcerative process is borne out by the statement of Osler in his "Gulstonian Lectures." He says that of 209 cases of *malignant* endocarditis the pulmonary valve was only affected in 15.

Mary B., aged 15 years, born in Russia, a tailoress, and single, was admitted to my service on June 21, 1898. Of her parents, her mother is suffering with "some heart disease." She has three sisters, who are well, and three brothers, two of whom died from causes unknown to her.

She herself has always been well, having had only measles in her childhood. She began to menstruate at 14 years, her menstrual period lasting from four to five days, the flow being very profuse. For the past two months she has not had her "periods." Her hygienic surroundings are very poor. She gives no history of any previous illness, save the measles, nor of having had any injury. She denies syphilis, but has a vaginal discharge which she says was absent before her present illness, which began seven weeks before her admission, with pain in her right knee, brought on, she says, by exposure. With this, for the first few days, she had chills and fever. She had two chills daily. The pain in the knee increased and was followed by a swelling of the joint. The chills disappeared four days afterward, but the fever remained and persisted up to this time without cessation. At times she suffered with general vague pains over the left side. For the past two weeks she had cardiac palpitation. During the past week a cough supervened, accompanied by mucous expectoration. She sweats profusely at night. She had no symptoms referable to the urinary apparatus. During all this period she had not left her bed; she states that her illness was at its height one week before coming to the hospital. She further states that her knee is not now as painful nor as swollen as it was then. She has vomited a number of times. She had been treated at her home with liniments, ice to the knee, and with a salve. She says she sleeps well, but her appetite is very poor; that she has lost flesh and strength, and that she has become extremely pale since her illness began.

Status præsens.—The girl is of medium stature, large frame, with poor muscular development and moderate adiposity. She has an enlarged thyroid gland. Her position in bed denotes a patient who is still active.

Her face is extremely pale, almost chalky in color. Her flesh is flabby. She has the expression of a very sick patient. Her skin is generally white and moist; no odor is apparent to its secretion; its temperature is 101.8° F., and over the forehead and face it presents an acne eruption.

Her pulse is regular and beats 128 to the minute. Her arteries are not tortuous, still slightly sclerotic, and of slightly increased tension.

Her respirations are abdominal and 30 to the minute.

The prominent symptoms are swelling of the right knee, fever, and extreme anæmia.

The patient's lips are very pale; her tongue is moist at the edges and dry in the centre, and is not furred. She has much thirst; vomits occasionally after taking food. She is constipated and her stools show nothing abnormal in character.

The abdomen presents a small umbilical hernia. There is slight enlargement of the liver on palpation, and her spleen may also be felt.

Percussion over the abdomen is generally tympanitic; liver dulness extends two fingers' breadth below the free border of the ribs, whilst that of the spleen also extends upward beyond normal limits, as well as below the eleventh rib downward. There are no resistant areas otherwise in the abdominal region.

Her thorax is flat, short, and broad. Her respirations are regular, of the abdominal type, and 30 per minute. There is fair expansion and resiliency of the chest walls. A cough is also present. The expectoration is moderate in amount, of no characteristic odor, and chiefly mucous. Percussion of the thorax anteriorly reveals in the axillary line on the left side dulness beginning at the fifth rib. On auscultation a few crepitant râles are heard anteriorly over the left lung, increased breathing over the right apex. Posteriorly there is dulness on percussion, beginning at the angle of the scapula on both sides, over which areas there are diminished breathing and diminished voice sounds. Pectoral fremitus is much diminished on both sides.

The apex beat is diffuse and forcible; the carotids pulsate prominently. Palpation shows the apex beat to be most forcible in the fifth interspace and in the mammary line. Percussion reveals the upper border of cardiac dulness to be along the fourth rib, the right border one-half inch to the right of the sternum, and the left border one half inch to the left of the nipple line in the fourth interspace. On auscultation a double murmur is heard over the aortic area, with almost an obliteration of the cardiac sounds; the murmur is transmitted up and down the sternum and to the vessels of the neck. Over the pulmonic area a loud, rough, rasping murmur is heard in the place of both sounds. There is a slight capillary pulse.

She has a profuse vaginal discharge, which on microscopical examination reveals *no gonococci*.

Her urine is pale, acid, 1018, and contains a trace of albumin, no casts, but a few epithelial cells.

Her blood examination reveals 2,800,000 red cells, 8,600 white, and hæmoglobin 25 per cent.

Her subsequent history in the hospital is one of great suffering and gradual decline to a fatal termination. It is as follows:

June 22, 1898: Patient complains very much of severe præcordial pain. The murmur over the pulmonic is loud and more rasping, simulating rather a pericardial friction sound than a valvular murmur, yet always synchronous with the cardiac sounds. No change in the aortic murmurs. Her pulse varied between 102 and 142, her temperature between 100.8° F. and 102° F.

June 24, 1898: Same condition as on previous examination. The vaginal discharge was examined again for gonococci, but none was found.

June 26, 1898: The anæmia has increased, as have the præcordial pains. The knee is still swollen and tender, and an œdema of the feet and legs has appeared.

July 1, 1898. Vomiting has been frequent since last report, her general condition is worse, the pulse and respirations have been the same, and the daily variations of temperature have been between 99.4° F. and 103.8° F.

July 5, 1898: Præcordial pain much less; sleeps much better. To-day a purulent discharge appeared from the right ear. The pain in the knee has become more severe and troublesome. Her general condition continues to retrograde, the fever being still the same. A blood examination showed a further diminution in red cells, they now numbering 1,760,000, the whites being likewise diminished to 4,000, and the hæmoglobin to 16 per cent.

July 12, 1898: There are no signs of improvement. The area of cardiac dulness has increased, the right border being one inch to the right of the sternum and the left the same distance to the left of the mammary line. The apex beat is now in the fourth space, indicating the development of some fluid in the pericardial sac. The pulse, respiration, and temperature are respectively the same as on last report. The color of the patient has become greenish. Over the left border of the heart the same loud, rough murmur is heard as is heard over the base at the pulmonic valve. She complains again of agonizing pain over the heart and in the side of the thorax. The patient has been vomiting a green fluid.

July 15, 1898: The patient's condition is extremely

low. The cardiac dulness has still further increased by one-half inch to the right and the left. A marked thrill on palpation appears to the right of the xiphoid process. She has an anxious expression, great dyspnœa and exhaustion. She vomits now continually. Her urine, which at the previous examinations showed an increasing amount of albumin, now presents blood and epithelial casts; it is much diminished in amount, to 8 ounces in the twenty four hours from 30 ounces. Her pulse is becoming feebler.

July 19: There is now retention of urine, which is relieved by hot stupes; the urine passed in twenty-four hours was 10 ounces, 8½ grains of urea to the ounce. Her general condition is even worse. She objects to being disturbed for the administration of medicine or food. Her mental state is becoming clouded. She has the appearance of one who has reached almost the end of the struggle.

July 20: With constant vomiting, increasing exhaustion, and stupor which lapsed into coma, the lethal exitus occurred.

The clinical diagnosis was ulcerative endocarditis with fluid in both pleural and in the pericardial sacs, and acute nephritis.

Autopsy.—Brain not permitted to be examined.

Heart.—The right ventricle is dilated. The heart muscle is pale. On the closure lines of the two flaps of the aortic valve are two small nodules. *The pulmonary valve is almost entirely destroyed;* part of one flap is converted into an aneurism-like sac. The mitral valve is normal. There are numerous ulcers on the wall of the pulmonary artery and on the endocardium near the pulmonary valve.

Kidneys.—Both are the seat of an acute nephritis.

Spleen.—Is very large and is affected by an acute inflammation.

Lungs.—Both are congested, œdematous, and present *no infarctions.*

Liver.—Is enlarged and moderately fatty.

There is moderate ascites, an increased amount of pericardial fluid, and a moderate general anasarca.

There were *no infarctions in any of the organs.* No bacteriological examination of the organs or of the blood was made.

The clinical history of this case was one of a malignant

endocarditis, the valvular lesions showing, clinically, aortic disease and a pulmonic disturbance. The murmur over the latter area was so rough and the area of cardiac dulness increased so rapidly, while the apex beat was being elevated one whole interspace, that we were inclined to doubt that the pulmonic valve might have been diseased at all and that perhaps a pericarditis had been superimposed upon an endocarditis. It occurred to us that the murmur over the pulmonic area might have been due to a transmission of the murmur of the aortic insufficiency, and that the rough character of the murmur arose from a pericarditis.

At best pulmonic disease is diagnosed with the greatest difficulty. Its distinguishing features, according to C. Gerhardt,[1] are:

1. Forcible and diffused apex beat.
2. Enlarged area of cardiac dulness.
3. Palpable pulsation of the right ventricular border between the right seventh costal cartilage and the xiphoid process.
4. Purring thrill on pressure in the same space.
5. Diastolic murmur, most marked at the left edge of sternum and to the left in the second intercostal space. The murmur is not transmitted to the vessels of the neck.
6. Audible capillary pulse, or a double murmur (analogous to the double murmurs occurring in peripheral vessels in cases of aortic insufficiency) in the capillaries of the lungs on auscultating the lungs. In addition one may hear, on auscultating a part of the lung removed from the heart, on slow, deep inspiration, that vesicular breathing is interrupted, becoming louder, then feebler, corresponding to the cardiac cycle. This is to be explained by the fact that variable resistance is opposed to the entrance of air into the lungs, owing to the extremely *variable* degree of distension of the lung capillaries.

[1] C. Gerhardt: Charité-Annalen, 1892, xvii., p. 255.

VIII.

ACUTE PANCREATITIS—DISSEMINATED FAT NECROSIS OF OMENTUM AND PERITONEUM; LAPAROTOMY; RECOVERY.

By MORRIS MANGES, A.M., M.D.,

ATTENDING PHYSICIAN.

SARAH B., 21 years old, German, housewife. Admitted February 20, 1898, to Female Ward III.

Family History.—Mother died of heart disease and asthma; father still living. No family illnesses.

Previous History.—Negative, except ordinary diseases of childhood; was well up to six years ago, when she had an attack of grippe. Five years ago was jaundiced for several weeks; the cause of this she does not know.

Has been married three years; bore a child after normal labor three months ago; lochia ceased in two weeks. Menstruation has returned since birth of child; usually menstruates every two weeks. Has never had malaria; denies alcoholism.

Present History is of six weeks' standing, the last five of which have been spent in bed. One morning, while still in bed, the attack began suddenly, a half-hour after drinking coffee, with very severe abdominal pain, which was especially marked in the epigastrium and was colicky in character. After a few hours the pains abated, when she arose and took another cup of coffee; this caused a return of the pain of the same character. She describes this as a severe burning, griping pain which "doubled her up," but which was stationary in the epigastrium. No vomiting. When the pain eased somewhat she went out to a neighboring physician and then returned to bed. The pains, after ceasing upon the taking of some medicine, returned upon drinking some hot milk, and became so severe that morphine had to be injected.

Thereupon she took nothing but cold milk and seltzer water. This attack of more or less constant pain lasted ten days.

After working about the house for a few days the same pain returned in the same place. There was no vomiting. During the first few days of this attack the stools were clay-colored. The pain never left her entirely, but she was better for a few days and then worse again. This kept up until ten days before admission; while out visiting a friend she was once more attacked with the intense epigastric pain, which again required the injection of morphine. No vomiting. The pain returned the next day at 11 A.M. Two days after that, after having been on a milk diet, she began to vomit everything, this being preceded by a pressing pain in the epigastrium. The vomit was white and at times greenish, and followed the ingestion of whatever she took. Soon after she also had pain in the right hypochon drium, which was less intense than the epigastric pain. After this, also had pain all over the upper abdomen and in the back at the same level, the pains being so severe that she could not take a long breath. Constipated throughout and had to take cathartics. During the past week had a little bleeding from the rectum. Movement of the bowels does not increase the pain. Two days later she entered the hospital.

On admission the chief complaints were: epigastric pain, vomiting, and constipation. The pain is always referred to the epigastrium a short distance above the umbilicus. At present she vomits everything. Has vomited many times this past week. There was never any blood in the vomit. Belches a great deal, and even this is painful. Bowels are very constipated and had not moved for three days, although she had taken castor oil, injections, etc. There is some difficulty in urination. Otherwise there are no other complaints.

General Condition on Admission.—Is a large, stout, flabby woman, quite anæmic, well marked acute vulgaris on face, expression anxious, tongue is slightly coated. Breasts well developed and contain milk. No œdema. Temperature (10 A.M.) 99.8°; two hours after admission it rose to 102°, respirations 36, pulse 116. Heart and lungs negative.

Abdomen is somewhat distended and shows signs of recent pregnancy. General tenderness on palpation all over, but is especially marked in the epigastrium: deep palpation is impossible. The percussion note is tympanitic all over the abdomen.

Liver is somewhat enlarged to percussion both upward and downward, extending in the mammillary line from the fourth rib to two finger breadths below the costal border. The lower border cannot be palpated.

Spleen: lower border can be percussed at the free border of the ribs. No glandular enlargement.

Pelvic organs negative. Urine: specific gravity 1034; trace of albumin, no sugar or indican; microscopic examination negative.

The condition which seemed to account for the patient's symptoms being some intestinal obstruction, she was treated on this assumption. After much difficulty the bowels were finally moved, but not until several high enemata of oil, ox gall, and water had been given through Kuehn's rectal tube—which, it may be said in passing, proved to be very useful for the purpose on this as on other occasions. The stool was large, yellowish, and unformed.

However, in spite of the fact that the bowels had been moved, the general condition did not improve. The stomach still remained very irritable, and vomiting followed almost immediately after taking any fluid. The pain and tenderness in the epigastrium persisted, although light ice bags were applied. The temperature varied between 100.5° and 102.5°, pulse between 104 and 120, respirations between 28 and 36.

On February 23 general condition somewhat better: less vomiting, bowels moved twice, the stools being formed and greenish. The pains and tenderness, however, remained, and now were referred more to the right of the epigastrium rather than to the lower part of this area, as she had formerly done. Urine negative. Intestinal obstruction having been eliminated, the diagnosis seemed to lie between some form of perforation peritonitis or an empyema of the gall bladder with or without impacted stones. The shifting of the pains toward the right made the latter seem the more probable. Still, any exact diagnosis was impossible on account of the difficulty of palpation of the epigastrium, which felt doughy, but beyond this nothing could be definitely determined. There was general tympanites, but the abdomen was not distended. Under these circumstances, with a view of having some surgical interference, Dr. Gerster was requested to see the patient and to operate if he saw fit. A careful examination by Dr. Gerster did not reveal anything beyond what has been stated above, and, as the general condition demanded something to be done, laparotomy was agreed upon.

She was accordingly transferred to Dr. Gerster's service and operated upon on February 25. A vertical incision was made in the right hypochondrium, exposing the top of the gall bladder in its lower angle. The liver and gall bladder appeared quite normal, the gall bladder being flaccid. The greater omentum, however, was studded with numerous small, whitish, plaque-like spots, varying in size from a small pea to a bean. There was no inflammatory zone about these spots, which were not elevated; if anything, they were a little depressed. The incision was prolonged downward and exploration continued. A large number of similar plaques were found on the omentum and parietal peritoneum. The common bile duct, as well as the cystic and hepatic ducts, were normal; duodenum and stomach apparently normal. Behind the stomach a nodular mass of very considerable size was felt; several large nodules were discovered below and a smaller one above the mass. Operation concluded by removing a piece of the infiltrated omentum for microscopic examination. Wound closed completely with silkworm gut and button sutures.

General condition after operation good. The vomiting ceased and the patient was much more comfortable in spite of the narcosis and operation. The pains ceased. The course of the temperature, etc., reported on appended chart. It will be noted that the patient's condition was decidedly improved by the operation, as evidenced by the drop in the temperature, pulse, and respiration. Although the temperature rose to 102° on the day following the operation, yet it gradually fell and remained very moderate with afternoon exacerbations.

February 26: A series of calomel and salts given, followed by enema, which was effectual. Urination voluntary. Urine negative. Morphine for pain.

February 28: Dr. F. S. Mandlebaum, Assistant Pathologist, reported that the piece of excised omentum contained characteristic area of fat necrosis. This report, together with the presence of the large mass behind the stomach, at once revealed the diagnosis of acute pancrea-

NAME Sarah B.

Operation

titis with disseminated fat necrosis of the omentum and parietal peritoneum.

March 1: Wound dressed. Primary union; three button sutures removed.

March 2: Full diet allowed. Urine negative.

March 4: All sutures removed. Wound healthy; good union; dry dressing.

March 18: Mural abscess developed in the lower portion of the scar; incision evacuated a considerable amount of pus. There was nothing abnormal about this pus. Two drainage tubes inserted and wet dressing applied.

March 29: Only small sinus left, which soon healed, and patient was transferred to the medical side on April 8. General condition has been excellent throughout; no fever or any complaints; repeated examination of the urine for sugar negative.

Soon after her transfer back to the medical service she again began to complain of pain coming on immediately after eating. The pain was of a different character, being a dull aching located in the epigastrium and lasting for several hours after meals, when it gradually disappeared, to return again after the next meal. Regulation of the diet in every possible way made no marked difference in the occurrence or character of the pain. Test meals given at different times revealed normal gastric juice. Distension of the stomach did not show any abnormality in the size or position of the stomach. The appetite was good: the stools were regular and did not contain any fat. Repeated examinations of the urine failed to show any albumin, sugar, or indican.

The fact that the pains came on immediately after eating precluded the possibility of their arising in the intestines. Careful examination of the abdomen, with an empty stomach, failed to reveal anything except a vaguely defined, deeply seated mass which was sausage shaped and which extended across the lower part of the epigastrium. This mass was undoubtedly the enlarged pancreas.

The only explanation which could be advanced to explain this pain was the presence of adhesions between the stomach and the pancreas. That these pains might be due to the areas of fat necrosis was considered, but was dismissed because there were no localized areas of tenderness over the abdomen. That the pains were not due to a chronic pancreatitis may be seen by comparing the symptoms with those which occur in the latter condition :

"The digestive disturbances, epigastric pain and tenderness, progressive loss of flesh and strength, are the symptoms which occur in fibrous pancreatitis, and may precede death for months or years. The digestive disturbances consist of loss of appetite, nausea, vomiting (rarely), belching, pyrosis, and a sense of epigastric fulness and weight. These symptoms, usually attributed to gastric catarrh, in rare instances may be absent. Diarrhœa frequently exists ; the dejections are sometimes fatty, and may be colorless even when there is no jaundice. Jaundice occasionally occurs, and is persistent if the common bile duct be compressed by the contracted head of the pancreas. The epigastric pain is deep seated, dull, burning, or boring in character, perhaps paroxysmal ; and, if severe, is associated with extreme anxiety, restlessness, and a sensation of faintness."[1]

With continued use of potassium iodide in doses of 0.3 gramme after meals, occasional courses of tincture of belladonna, counter-irritation, and Priessnitz compresses, these pains gradually abated, and the patient left the hospital in excellent condition on July 28, 1898. The reports I have had since then have been good as regards her general health, but at irregular intervals she has attacks of pain of the same character as above described, which are brought on by errors in diet.

This case is of interest apart from the fact that thus far but three other cases have been reported in which recovery has followed operative interference in acute pancreatic disease. These cases of Osler, Koerte, and Thayer will be referred to later on.

Acute pancreatitis is rare in women, as is shown by

[1] Fitz: Albutt's System of Medicine, vol. iv., p. 269.

the fact that of the forty-one cases collected by Koerte,[1] but four have occurred in women. The vast majority of cases have occurred in persons over 50 years of age; this patient was only 21 years old. That it may occur at any age is shown by the case reported by McPhedran, whose patient was an infant of nine months.

As to the etiology, traumatism, obesity, abuse of alcohol, and antecedent attacks of gastro-intestinal catarrh are the most important. Of these obesity and antecedent gastro-intestinal catarrh were present in this patient. It is also to be observed that one of the forty-one cases collected by Koerte occurred six weeks after labor, the details of which are briefly as follows:

A woman, 33 years of age, primipara, during pregnancy had frequent attacks of gastric pain and headache. From the seventh to the tenth lunar month had frequent attacks of abdominal pain, with at times mild peritonitic irritation, so that impending labor was suspected without any discoverable cause. March 24, 1883, was delivered with forceps on account of inertia; the convalescence was slow but normal. Afterward had two mild attacks of epigastric pain.

April 30, five and a half weeks after labor, was suddenly attacked with very severe pain in the pyloric region, with attacks of vomiting, which were relieved by hypodermatic injections of morphine. No fever; pulse 100-104 and regular. Epigastric tenderness, but no evidence of peritonitis; no icterus. Patient looked collapsed. In the evening collapse increased; pulse 110 to 120; vomiting ceased; flatus did not escape, no stools, moderate abdominal distension; pyloric region very sensitive. Uterus normal.

On the next day temporary improvement; epigastrium less tender; free passage of flatus. Later on the tenderness in the epigastrium increased and so did the meteorism. Collapse deepened, and death occurred within ninety-six hours after the onset of the attack.

Autopsy showed absence of peritonitis; a little bloody

[1] Die chirurgischen Krankheiten und Verletzungen des Pancreas. Deutsche Chirurgie, 1898, Lieferung 45d.

serum in the dependent part of the peritoneal cavity. The only discoverable lesion was in the pancreas, which was enlarged, deeply engorged; there was also some injection of the neighboring omentum.

Microscopic examination showed acute hemorrhagic pancreatitis with round-celled infiltration. No etiological factors could be discovered.[1]

It will be noted that the first symptoms from which my patient suffered also appeared six weeks after delivery. That the latter had anything to do with the onset of the disease can only be a matter of conjecture.

The early history of the attack is also exceptional and differs from the majority of those reported, which were nearly all quite rapid in their course. To explain these early attacks is difficult, except, judging from the subsequent course of events, to assume that they were due to small hemorrhages in the pancreas.

The relations of the fat necrosis to the pancreatic process are of very great interest, but, inasmuch as this subject has been so fully worked up elsewhere, it need not be discussed here. Worthy of especial attention are the researches of Flexner[2] and Williams.[3] A full discussion may also be found in Oser's recent monograph on "Pancreatic Diseases."[4] The views which are now generally accepted are that the fat necrosis is due to the escape of the fat-splitting ferment from the pancreas into the adjacent and distant fatty tissue. It is surprising how rapidly this lesion occurs and how extensive it may be, and to what distant organs its action may extend. This is exceedingly well shown in the case which has been recently published by Warthin,[5] in which fat necrosis was found even in the pericardial and peri-

[1] Heydlen: Centralbl. für Gynäkologie, 1884, p. 609.

[2] Journal of Experimental Med., 1897, p. 413.

[3] Bost. Med. and Surg. Jour., April 15, 1897; Jour. of Exp. Med., 1898, p. 585.

[4] Die Erkrankungen des Pankreas. Nothnagel's Spec. Pathol. und Therapie, 1898, Bd. xviii., p. 326.

[5] Philadel. Med. Jour., Nov. 19, 1898, p. 1067.

renal fat, although the disease had lasted less than three days. In the same paper an excellent description of the minute pathology of the lesions which occur in these cases may also be found.

On the other hand, fat necrosis is not found in all cases of pancreatic disease, a number of examples of which have already been published.

Furthermore, fat necrosis has been found in other conditions than pancreatic disease. Thus, cases of ovariotomy have been reported in which disseminated fat necrosis was present without any gross evidence of pancreatic disease. However, in spite of these facts, the occurrence of fat necrosis is so preponderating a symptom of acute pancreatic disease that its presence may be considered pathognomonic of the latter.

The absence of glycosuria and fatty stools throughout the course of the disease agrees with the reports of nearly all the cases of acute pancreatitis. Hence, although their presence strengthens the diagnosis, yet their absence may be disregarded.

Whether the operation had anything to do with her recovery, or whether she would have recovered without it, must remain an open question. I would, however, emphasize the fact that the whole clinical picture was at once changed after the operation; the vomiting and constant severe pain ceased at once, and the temperature gradually fell, and the pulse and respirations did likewise. That patients can recover without operation is proven by the fact that apparently healed pancreatic lesions and fat necrosis are not infrequently found at autopsies, and by the celebrated case of Trafoyer, whose patient lived seventeen years after the gangrenous pancreas had been passed per rectum. Chiari also reports two cases of the same kind. Koerte[1] reports a case in which the diagnosis of chronic pancreatitis was apparently justified, recovery following symptomatic treatment. Very recently a case of recovery after probable acute pancreatitis under

[1] Deutsch. Arch. für klin. Chirurgie, Bd. xlviii.

symptomatic treatment has been published by Edwards, of Chicago.[1]

Recovery after operation is exceptional, the present and the three cases above mentioned being the only ones thus far. Possibly another case may be included, this being another patient of Koerte,[2] who for two months survived laparotomy for omental bursitis due to suppurative pancreatitis, but died subsequently from marasmus, the result of a pyloric cancer. At the autopsy the correctness of Koerte's diagnosis of the pancreatic disease was confirmed.

Two additional cases operated upon by Koerte died. I have been able to collect nearly twenty cases which have been operated upon with fatal results within the past three years.

And yet, in spite of this gloomy showing, I would emphasize the importance of operation in these cases, and am in full accord with Stockton,[3] who also recommends it. The prognosis is exceedingly grave if the patient is left alone to nature and to the only means at our disposal—rest, morphine, and the ice bag—and his chances are certainly not lessened by this interference on the part of the surgeon.

The best time to operate is not at the beginning of the attack, but a little while after the acute onset. It is scarcely necessary to make this suggestion, for the diagnosis is rarely made so early, since few of us can hope to repeat the brilliant diagnoses made by Fitz and Thayer, the former's correct diagnosis being ante mortem, the latter's before operation. Besides, the majority of operations were performed for other conditions (impacted gall stones, intestinal obstruction or perforation, etc.), the pancreatic disease being revealed after the abdomen had been opened. Unfortunately in quite a large number of these cases the onset and course of the disease are so fulminating that nothing can be done, since the patient's

[1] Phila. Med. Jour., April 9, 1898, p. 652. [2] Loc. cit.
[3] Loomis and Thompson's System of Medicine, 1898, vol. iii., p. 654.

death follows within too short a time to allow any correct appreciation of the conditions which might exist. Where the disease is less fulminating the indications for operation may be said to exist. That these cases occur less rarely than is usually supposed is a fact which is being more clearly shown year after year by the large number of reports which are being published by surgeons and pathologists.[1] With a clearer conception of the nature of the disease and its various clinical forms, we may trust to a larger number of successful operations in the near future.

The three cases of Osler, Koerte, and Thayer in which operative interference in acute pancreatic disease has been successful are appended.

Osler's case is thus briefly reported by him:[2] A man (age not stated) was admitted to the Johns Hopkins Hospital.

"Symptoms of obstruction of the bowels had persisted for three or four days; the abdomen was distended, tender, and very painful. I saw the patient on admission, concurred in the diagnosis of probable obstruction, and, as the condition was serious, ordered him to be transferred at once to the operating room. (Operation by Halsted.) The coils of intestines were distended and injected, and the peritoneal cavity contained a small amount of serum. No obstruction was found, but in the region of the pancreas and at the root of the mesentery there was a dense, thick, indurated mass, and there were areas of fat necrosis in both mesentery and omentum. The patient recovered." He was readmitted four years afterward on account of a similar attack. Operation

[1] Since the above was written a most striking corroboration of the frequency of pancreatic disease has been furnished in the report of the meeting of the Clinical Society of London, Dec. 9, 1898 (Brit. Med. Jour., Dec. 17, 1898, p. 1815), at which no less than seven cases of acute hemorrhagic and suppurative pancreatitis and two cases of pancreatic calculi were presented. All but one were fatal, the result of one not being stated. Two of the fatal cases were operated upon.

[2] Practice of Medicine, 1893, p. 459.

was proposed and refused, and he left the hospital soon afterward and was lost sight of.

Koerte's patient[1] was a stout married woman of 47 years, who had had seven children and two abortions, the last seven years previously. In 1888 cholelithiasis for four months with icterus; since then had been well. On June 2, 1893, was suddenly taken ill with severe pain in the epigastrium and vomiting. Was admitted to hospital next day. The tongue was dry, expression anxious; temperature 38.2° (C.), pulse 128, breathing rapid. Abdomen distended and very tender, with dulness in the pendulous portions. Any especial resistance could not be made out on account of the tense abdominal walls. Frequent eructations and vomiting. Inguinal and femoral rings free. Vaginal examination negative. Heart and lungs negative. Stool followed high enema. Urine free from albumin or sugar.

Treatment consisted of ice bag to abdomen, opium, and high enemata. Vomiting relieved by lavage of stomach.

Diagnosis : peritonitis, probably due to former cholelithiasis. June 7, general abdominal pain less; abdomen softer; no resistance on palpation. Patient complains of pain radiating from epigastrium to the back. Liver dulness from fourth rib to free costal border, behind up to eighth rib. Gall-bladder region free. Multiple puncture of liver, on account of suspected abscess, negative.

The patient's condition continued thus, with irregular fever, great weakness, occasional paroxysms of epigastric pain, up to the beginning of July without any clue as to the real site of the disease. On July 4, on the left side of abdomen, a large area of resistance could be made out, extending from the free border of the ribs down to the iliac crest and backward to the region of the kidney; there was indistinct fluctuation. Percussion note over the area was dull. Puncture over the iliac crest revealed pus. Free incision liberated a large quantity

[1] Deutsch. Arch. für klin. Chir., 1894, Bd. xlviii.

of pus, which came from a retroperitoneal cavity which extended up the kidney and behind colon. Here there is a narrow opening into which a probe could be passed 15 centimetres. The pus was yellowish, non offensive, and contained numerous dirty brownish particles of broken-down tissue. Later on, washing out this cavity brought down yellowish-brown, tallowy and calcareous particles, as well as large pieces of necrotic tissue which proved to be structureless on microscopic examination.

There was frequent vomiting, stools normal, urine negative.

August 18: Status idem. Acinous gland structure could now be recognized in some of the fats of tissue.

September 4: Normal temperature, wound smaller.

September 15: Fistula discharges alkaline secretion which contains fat-splitting ferment, but no diastasic ferment.

November 10: Wound healed. Only complaint is frequent migraine.

November 27: Fistula opened. Finally healed completely, and was discharged in good condition January 6, 1894. Urine was always free from albumin or sugar.

Thayer's[1] case of acute pancreatitis, parapancreatic abscess, occurred in a man 34 years of age, of alcoholic habits. For the past two years suffered from alcoholic gastritis, and during the past one and one-half years had had three or four attacks of very severe epigastric pains, located in the median line near the umbilicus, and which were so severe that large hypodermatic injections of morphine were required. Vomiting often present, but no jaundice. June 15, 1895, had an attack of very severe pain and vomiting; swelling noticed just above umbilicus. Constipated. Continuous fever for a week; at times delirious. His physician diagnosticated abscess of liver. Admitted to Johns Hopkins Hospital June 25. The examination showed quite a corpulent man, with moist tongue, dull mental condition, some fever. It

[1] Amer. Journ. Med. Sciences, 1895, vol. cx., p. 396.

was found that the liver was enlarged, the lower border reaching to the umbilicus. The epigastrium was tympanitic. Below this tympanites, and between it and the umbilicus at the point of maximum protuberance, one could feel a deep-seated mass, over which there was marked tympany. The outlines were vague, and it was not tender on ordinary palpation; it did not move with respirations. No albumin or sugar in urine. Leucocytosis.

After careful consideration of all the various factors (for which see p. 398, loc. cit.), Thayer made a diagnosis of acute pancreatitis with disseminated fat necrosis, with possible sequestration of the pancreas, and advised an exploratory laparotomy.

Operation by Dr. Finney on June 27. In the median line, adjoining the liver and stomach, and adherent to them, a mass of adherent fatty tissue was found; this was filled with numerous discrete and confluent nodules of disseminated fat necrosis. The transverse colon was also adherent. The general abdominal cavity was packed off with gauze and an opening left for drainage.

For the next few days general condition was fairly good, but the temperature remained somewhat elevated. Was restless, nauseated, and delirious at times later on. On July 7, while examining the wound, a large cavity was opened into at the upper angle of the wound. The cavity contained thick pus with large masses of necrotic tissue; the finger could be pushed far backward into what appeared to be a cavity in the pancreas. The discharge from the cavity consisted of pus cells, large numbers of bacteria, fatty acid crystals, and small masses of necrotic fat. The cavity was drained freely, healed slowly by granulation, and the patient left the hospital on September 23 in fairly good condition.[1]

[1] Full bibliographies will be found in Oser's monograph and Warthin (loc. cit.)

IX.

MULTIPLE CARCINOSIS OF BONES SECONDARY TO CARCINOMA OF BREAST.

BY MORRIS MANGES, A.M, M.D.,
ATTENDING PHYSICIAN.

MARY B., age 37; housewife; Russian; admitted March 4, 1898, to Female Ward III.

Family History.—Father had tuberculosis.

Previous History.—Has had scarlet fever, measles, typhoid fever, and malaria. Has been married seventeen years, but has never been pregnant. Three years ago had a cough for several months; since then has had a cough each winter.

Present History.—Two and a half years ago first noticed a swelling in the right breast, which was subsequently amputated at the German Hospital seven months ago. Before the operation she had fugitive pains throughout the body, which have become worse since then. While convalescing she fell out of bed, striking on the left foot, which has since been especially painful. On account of these pains and increasing weakness she enters the hospital. These pains are sometimes dull, at others lancinating, and are aggravated by sitting up. They are most marked over the neck, right side of head, chest, and left leg. Does not cough at present, but has frequent attacks of palpitation. Occasional nausea; constipated. At times incontinence of urine.

Examination.—General condition fair; 99.8°. Scar of amputation of right breast. A prominence in median line of back, extending from fourth cervical to second dorsal vertebra ; is tender on percussion; does not fluctuate. She does not know how long this mass has been there.

Thorax and abdomen negative. No œdema, but there is some thickening of the subcutaneous tissues, which gives the skin a doughy, elastic feel. This is especially marked over the abdomen.

Patellar reflexes absent; left pupil contracted. Some flatness of the left side of face: tongue deviates slightly to the left. No other changes in the face. Diminished power on the right side; some atrophy of the muscles of the right hand. All muscles react well to faradic current.

Urine has trace of albumin and a few granular casts and bacteria; reaction acid; fifty ounces daily. After admission her general condition became worse. She ran a temperature which was constant and reaching up to 102°. Must be catheterized. Pains unimproved, save such temporary relief following phenacetin, etc.

A few weeks after admission, began to complain of pain in the scar, which became slightly ulcerated. Also had pain in the right chest, at the base of which posteriorly a few fine crepitant râles can be heard. The fever, which had disappeared for a short time, again returned. Coughed, and lost weight quite rapidly.

April 10: Severe pain in the abdomen, and the liver was found to have increased considerably. Both pupils contracted and do not react to light. Daily quantity of urine diminished to thirty ounces; specific gravity 1010; still contains albumin and granular casts, but no distinct tumor elements. Low fever continues and general condition progressively poorer. Night sweats. She continued thus until the early part of May, when it was observed that the angles of the ribs of the right side were unduly prominent and painful. This deformity gradually increased and was found to be due to subperiosteal tumors. In the meantime the margins of the ulcer at the site of the operation scar had thickened so that there was now a hard ring about it. In the beginning of June a hard tumor appeared in the right groin, which was also evidently a subperiosteal growth. Small carcinomatous growths also appeared in the skin of the back, and the general hard, œdematous condition of the entire skin became more marked than ever. The patient's condition was now deplorable, the pains being constant and all movement on her part impossible. Almost complete paraplegia. Sensation could not be completely tested on account of the somnolence of the patient. Anæsthesia of the lower extremities; no patellar reflexes; no ankle clonus. Blood count shows

3,600,000 red cells; 19,580 white cells, the polynuclear cells being increased. The carcinomatous involvement of the bones was especially marked in the second rib and the right ilium and upper part of the right femur.

June 15: Deposits in both humeri and femora; considerable deformity of the right buttock. A few days later deposits were found in the inner portion of the right clavicle, and the swelling in the right ribs increased. Has great difficulty in swallowing.

June 20: Numerous brownish-black pigment spots, about the size of the head of a pin, appeared on the face, neck, and chest. Deposits in the right internal condyle of the femur and in the head of the tibia.

The comparative measurements of the two sides will show how extensive was the deformity caused by the numerous secondary deposits in the bones:

	RIGHT. Cm.		LEFT. Cm.
Circumference of arm around tip of acromium	31		28
Circumference of upper arm	23		20
" " " thigh	48		45
" " calf	23		26
" " chest, pit of axilla		73	
Circumference of chest below mammæ		78	
Circumference of body above crest of ilia		81	
Circumference of body at greater trochanters		89	
Distance from anterior superior iliac spines to internal malleoli	69		67

July 1: Patient's condition becoming progressively worse. Incontinence of fæces and death on July 4.

The essential features of the report of the autopsy, ten hours after death, by Dr. E. Libman, Assistant Pathologist, are as follows:

Scar from breast amputation very closely adherent to ribs and infiltrated for an area an inch broad with hard, carcinomatous tissue, part of which is ulcerating. Sternum bent back at its centre, with convexity backward. Ribs on right side much distorted, especially at angles, where they are bent inward, so that looked at from within they seem to be tumors on the ribs.

Thyroid Gland.—Normal in size; indurated. Microscopic examination negative.

Lungs.—Left bound down by adhesions; œdema of both lungs; numerous small, white, flat nodules under pleuræ. Microscopical examination of these revealed carcinoma from lymph spaces.

Bronchial Glands.—Enlarged; no tuberculosis or metastases.

Heart.—Fatty; moderate atheroma of aorta.

Liver.—Congested and fatty. *Spleen.*—Normal in size, firm on section. Microscopical examination showed marked splenitis with much new connective tissue. *Pancreas* negative. *Stomach and Intestines* negative. *Mesenteric Glands* enlarged, but not infiltrated.

Kidneys.—Capsules slightly adherent; markings indistinct; cortex thinned. Numerous small, whitish nodules in lower pole of right kidney. Microscopical examination of these nodules showed them to be areas of round-celled infiltration. Parenchymatous nephritis.

Bones.—The ribs are very flexible. The marrow is infiltrated with carcinoma (confirmed microscopically) and in places is almost bony in consistence. The upper ribs are bent near their necks. Subperiosteal thickening, especially of the upper ribs, due to carcinomatous infiltration. Similar condition in the upper part of right humerus, which is broken at its upper third. Left femur fractured at its neck. Marrow of the left femur infiltrated with carcinoma in its upper third; the remainder of marrow is red. On right femur, in upper third, is a large carcinomatous tumor.

The skull and spinal column could not be examined, as permission to do so was refused.

So extensive and rapid an involvement of the bony system with so few metastases in the viscera makes this case worthy of being reported, as such cases are rather infrequent. It is to be noted that the flat bones nearest the site of the original neoplasm were first involved, the growth of the metastases being at first quite slow. The long bones, first of the upper and then of the lower extremities, were the last to be involved, so far as the physical examination showed. Yet the process must have been of much longer duration, and was probably first located in the marrow long before the subperiosteal growths were detected, as proven by the spontaneous fractures which were found. These fractures are due to infiltration both from within the medullary canal and from the periosteum; the shaft of the bone gradually becomes so weakened that the slightest untoward movement will suffice to fracture the bone.

While it is to be regretted that the skull and spinal column could not be opened, so that the interesting nervous phenomena could have been explained *de visu*, yet they can be explained by analogy from the report of a case of Brunon[1] which is the exact counterpart of the present one. The patient was a woman, 68 years old, who had had a cancer of the breast; this was amputated; recurrence after eighteen months. Left facial paralysis developed soon after, together with mild continuous headaches. She fell out of bed and fractured her left femur. After this accident she had paraplegia with anæsthesia of the lower extremities; retention of urine and fæces. Examination of spine and skull did not explain symptoms.

After her death, one and a half months later, it was found that the only metastases were in the pleuræ and the bones, exactly the same conditions as in the present case. In the skull, at various parts, there were found a number of cancerous plaques, extending from the external surface through to the internal table, the dura mater and brain being adherent at the superior angle of the occipital bone. The vertebral column was also involved at the first lumbar vertebra, the bony tissue being replaced by the new growth without changing the external contour or without any deformity of the spinal column.

One is, therefore, justified in assuming that the nervous phenomena in the present case were also due to carcinomatous deposits in the skull and vertebral col-

[1] Bull. Soc. Anat. de Paris, 1883, lviii., p. 282.

umn, and that the swelling in the upper part of the back was probably of a carcinomatous nature.

Pieces of the skin which presented the peculiar hard, doughy feeling, almost like that of myxœdema, were excised and examined microscopically, without, however, revealing any pathological changes. I wish to direct attention to this change in the skin, which I also observed in another case of multiple visceral carcinosis which was under observation about the same time. It was most marked in the skin of the abdomen, and at first sight it looked like œdema. There was, however, no pitting on pressure, and the absence of œdema elsewhere, together with the general emaciation, at first led me to believe that the abdominal panniculus had been well preserved. The absence of any definite changes in the microscopic sections of the skin was, therefore, a disappointment, and no explanation can be offered for this phenomenon in these two cases.

X.

STUDY OF A CASE OF ECHINOCOCCUS CYST OF THE LIVER WITH DISCHARGE OF DAUGHTER CYSTS THROUGH THE COMMON BILE DUCT.

By HENRY W. BERG, M.D.,
ADJUNCT ATTENDING PHYSICIAN.

Echinococcus cyst of the liver is hardly of sufficient rarity to warrant the devotion of a paper to the study of its occurrence in an individual case, but there are points of especial diagnostic interest in the following history of a case of this disease, which must be my excuse for its presentation.

On September 18 I was sent for to see A. M. E., designer of clothing, 30 years of age, who had been confined to his bed since August 27, 1898, and who gave the following history: Three years ago he began to complain at intervals of a distressing feeling of pressure over the epigastrium. This feeling was generally relieved by the action of an emetic or cathartic. In the early spring, about April, of this year, these attacks became more frequent, and were accompanied by severe pain in the right hypochondriac region, which would come on suddenly, last for a few hours, and cease. August 26 he had an especially severe attack of this sort, pressure over the stomach, and pain in the right hypochondrium and right side of the back, which was not relieved by emetics, and which caused him to take to his bed and send for his family physician. The pain continued and he began to have fever, not preceded by a distinct chill, however. The bowels were constipated, and when a passage occurred from cathartics the stools were clay-colored. August 30 jaundice was noticed. These symptoms—that is to say, fever, constipation, pain at intervals as described above, and jaundice—lasted about a week. During this time the stools were at first colorless, later on brown. At this time also slight pressure in the axillary region, about on a level with the ninth and tenth ribs, was painful. Later on he suffered from diarrhœa, the movements then being lightish yellow in color, mingled sometimes with a muco-purulent material. The fever now became more marked, especially after a rigor, the temperature rising as high as 105° and then falling suddenly to a little above the normal. The temperature, however, was lower in the morning and higher in the evening, irrespective of the sudden rise following a chill. He was first seen by me the evening of September 18, 1898, and a careful physical examination elicited the following objective symptoms: Patient emaciated; pulse rapid and weak; respirations shallow, about 28; rectal temperature 103° F.; well-marked jaundice of the cutaneous surface and conjunctivæ. I was told that this jaundice had been more marked some days before and had never been present before August 29. Heart: No organic murmur; slight accentuation of the second aortic sound. Percussion of heart showed outer border at nipple line, upper border at the third rib, lower border indefinite, right border about at middle line, apex beat normal. Lungs negative; marked bulging of right chest as compared with the left. Intercostal spaces less marked on right side. Liver: Anteriorly flatness begins at the fifth rib and extends in the nipple line to two inches below the free border of the ribs; dulness extends across the epigastric region and fades into splenic dulness on the left and extends downward, up to two inches above the umbilicus. The edge of the liver can be felt through the abdominal walls; gall bladder cannot be felt. No tenderness or abnormality observed in any other part of the abdomen. Posteriorly on the right side the liver dulness extends up to two inches above the angles of the scapula. No general œdema, no anasarca, no enlarged glands; rectal examination negative; urine 1010, no albumin, bile pigment present, reaction acid. Sputum negative. Owing to the size of the liver I supposed that an abscess of the liver was present, to which the septic temperature curve could be ascribed. The history furthermore seemed to give evidence of the passage and lodgment of gall stones in the common bile duct. I therefore ordered the nurse to examine the stools carefully, after an attack of colic, for gall stones. The night following quite a severe attack of colic occurred, and at my subsequent visit, upon inquiry, I was told that although the stools had been carefully washed no gall stones were found. The wife showed me, however, five or six opalescent whitish bodies, about the size and appearance of white grapes, which she said she had found in the stools. On examining the grape-like bodies I recognized them as daughter cysts of the echinococcus. Two days later similar white-grape-like bodies were shown me, again passed after an attack of colic. These had been passed in a mass of muco-purulent material which had been observed in the stools of the patient for several weeks. Indeed, the wife of the patient assured me that she had noticed such grape-like bodies some weeks previous, but did not think that they were of any importance to a diagnosis of the disease. A microscopic examination of the walls of the cysts confirmed the opinion of their character made when seen with the naked eye. My diagnosis of simple abscess of the liver was changed, therefore, to one of large echinococcus cyst of the liver with discharge of daughter cysts through the rectum. Furthermore, these daughter cysts appearing only after an attack of hepatic colic, I was led to believe that the cysts got into the bowel through the common bile duct, and that the colic was produced in a manner similar to that which occurs from the passage of gall stones. The patient thereupon, at my request, entered Mount Sinai Hospital for the purpose of operation. He was operated on the 30th of September, in the afternoon, by Dr. Howard Lilienthal. It was decided to make the opening into the cyst posteriorly, because the greatest enlargement of the liver was in the backward direction. An aspirating needle was passed into the seventh interspace in the axillary line to a depth of three inches, when a clear fluid was withdrawn. Needle, left *in situ*, moved with the diaphragm. An incision was then made five inches long in post-axillary line, and the seventh and eighth ribs were resected in the usual manner; that is to say, the periosteum having been peeled back, about two inches of rib were resected from each. Then the intercostal arteries were tied off by passing around a ligature on hæmostatic needles. The costal pleura and diaphragmatic pleura having been retracted, an incision through the diaphragm into the liver was made. A large cavity about one inch from the surface of the liver was entered, and, the opening having been enlarged, a great quantity of echinococcus cysts were evacuated, also considerable clear fluid. Cavity held about fourteen to sixteen ounces of fluid. Cysts varied in size from a pea to a walnut. The cavity was thoroughly cleaned out, then filled with peroxide and this washed out. Probe went in six inches the greatest depth of the cavity. No communication found with gall bladder, gut, stomach, or thorax. Afterward the cavity was thoroughly cleaned, walls curetted freely and cleaned of all cystic material. One large piece of iodoform gauze was put in, filling out and lining the cavity, and this then filled with gauze strips. Pleura packed well away with gauze and then a large dry dressing and binder applied. Patient slept three hours after a hypodermatic of Magendie; later felt nauseated and complained of pain on the left side; vomited green fluid.

October 1: Temperature, 101.8° to 100°; respiration, 28; nourishment, 48 ounces; urine, 35½ ounces in twenty-four hours. Pulse, 92; respiration, 24. General condition: Very weak; slept some; perspired occasionally. Complains of pain in side and nausea.

October 2: Considerable yellow discharge from the wound. Series of calomel given every fifteen minutes for eight doses, followed by salts; later by enema; effectual. Complains of pain around wound. Drowsy most of the time. Superficial dressing changed; considerable discharge of bile. Wet dressing applied Nourishment, 52 ounces: urine, 27 ounces.

October 3: Complaining of burning sensation in chest. Had another series of calomel and salts—effectual.

October 4: Temperature below 100°. Has hiccough. Expectorates profusely. Severe pain in the abdomen. Vomited. Strychnine $\frac{1}{100}$ grain, whiskey 4 drachms, every four hours. Soft diet. Wound: Some packings removed and renewed; considerable greenish discharge; packings bile-stained; wet dressing applied.

October 6: Given spirits of nitrous ether, 1 drachm every two hours. General condition: Very weak; looks badly. Dressings changed daily.

October 8: Nitrous ether stopped. Vomits occasionally.

October 10: Eruption on arms noticed. General condition: Improving. Ox-gall pills given, 2 grains every three hours Stools not quite so gray. Temperature normal. Wound dressed. Profuse discharge of bile. Cavity four inches deep, but it gradually is filling;

washed out with salt solution. Two tubes put into bottom, then cavity packed with plain gauze. Wet dressing and moss cushion applied. General condition: Patient very much improved; appetite good; is brighter; temperature normal.

November 1: Wound has been dressed daily; twice large, hard sloughs resembling cartilage have come away, followed by decided contraction in the size of the cavity; now holds about two ounces only. Patient becoming very much stronger. A single tube is now in the wound. Discharge still quite considerable and tinged yellow.

November 15: Patient was discharged. A small sinus remaining, which could be followed inward three or four inches, discharging thick, yellow fluid.

Apart from the rarity of a case of this disease, the fact that the daughter cysts were discharged with the stools, and thus became the factors in a recognition of the character of the "abscess" in the liver, lends this case great interest. How did these cysts get into the bowel? There are four possible ways by which these small cysts can have passed from the liver into the gut.

1. By adhesion, ulceration, and subsequent perforation between the cyst in the right lobe of the liver and the hepatic flexure of the colon.

2. By the occurrence of a similar process between the cyst and the duodenum.

3. By the occurrence of a similar process between the cyst and the gall bladder.

4. By adhesion and ulceration followed by perforation into the hepatic, cystic, or the common bile duct.

It does not appear probable that these cysts perforated directly into the bowel either at the duodenum or the colon, for the reason that the discharge of these daughter cysts was always preceded by distinct attacks of biliary colic followed by jaundice, simulating exactly the passage of biliary calculi through the ducts. Were any further proof needed that there was in this case no direct communication between the intestine and the cyst in the liver, it would be given by the fact that at the time of the operation no fæcal odor was to be detected in the liver cyst at the evacuation of its contents. This certainly, as Dr. Lilienthal remarked at the operation, would not have failed had there been any direct communication between the abscess and the colon.

Perforation into the gall bladder, while a much more plausible theory as far as the history of the case is concerned, is not the most probable supposition. For while the biliary colic and subsequent jaundice might correspond with the passage of a daughter cyst from the gall bladder through the cystic and common bile ducts into the duodenum, the fact that the gall bladder was not found to be dilated, and could not be mapped out or recognized notwithstanding the emaciation of the patient, is almost absolute proof that the daughter cysts found no lodgment in this viscus.

The remaining possibility, that in this patient ulceration between the echinococcus sac and the hepatic, cystic, or common bile duct took place, is certainly the most probable. As to which of these ducts was the seat of communication with the hydatid sac is questionable. The fact, however, of the presence of bile pigment in the fæces several days after an attack of biliary colic, which I observed, would seem to indicate that the cysts did not perforate into and occlude the hepatic duct, for then the pain would have been followed by colorless stools almost immediately. The same might be said of perforation into the common bile duct. With perforation into the cystic duct, however, and slow passage of the daughter cysts through the duct, the discoloration of the fæces would not occur until the cyst had reached the point of junction with the hepatic duct. It is not necessary to conceive that the pain should have lasted during the whole of the passage of the daughter cysts through the duct. The cysts which appeared in the stools of the patient were flaccid, like white grapes which had had their contents pressed out. This was exactly what occurred to the cysts when they entered the duct. The pressure to which they were subjected in the passage through the duct burst the cysts and was followed by a very great diminution of the pain. The considerable discharge of bile which is noted as occurring from the wound on October 2, 4, and 10 would also seem to argue a communication with the bile passages very near to that reservoir of bile, the gall bladder. The persistent gray color of the stools for weeks after the operation might possibly be due to the lodgment of a daughter cyst or shreds of membrane in the common bile duct at about the time of the operation, which slowly passed through into the intestine. The patient now passes normally colored fæces.

It may be interesting to recall in this connection some facts concerning echinococcus cysts in man. As you know, a species of tapeworm, known as the tænia echinococcus, inhabits the small intestine of some of the carnivora, especially the dog and wolf. This worm is about five millimetres long and is composed of three or four segments, the anterior of which, the head, is the smallest. The largest segment is the terminal one, and this contains the ova. When the tænia has reached maturity these ova are discharged into the intestines of the dog and passed per anus. In this way these microscopic eggs lodge in the hairy integument of the animal, especially at the anus and mouth. They enter the stomachs of human beings by being eaten with food such as lettuce, salads, or with drink contaminated with the fæces of dogs, or brought directly in contact with the lips by unclean hands after fondling domesticated dogs. When these ova have reached the human alimentary canal the digestive ferments dissolve the external membrane and albuminous contents, setting free the minute embryo with its six hooklets. This embryo bores its way through the walls of the alimentary canal into the blood vessels, and is carried by the blood current to any part of the body where it reaches a terminal capillary, where it lodges. From the anatomical connection of the portal circulation within the alimentary tract it is natural that these embryos pass most frequently into the radicles of the portal vein and are thence carried to the liver, where they become arrested in the terminal portal capillaries. This explains the frequency with which the hydatid disease affects the liver. Some authorities state that more than sixty per cent of the reported cases of hydatid disease affect the liver. Other organs of the body are frequently affected. Thus echinococcus cysts are found in the lungs, pleura, heart, brain, abdomen, uterus, and even in the bones and muscular system. Indeed, it would be difficult to mention any organ of the body in which hydatid disease has not been found. When the embryo has thus been lodged in a terminal capillary of the liver, for instance, it begins to develop. Leuckart[1] has described its development. Soon it appears as a small capsule or cyst, the outer wall of which is composed of a thick, pearly, transparent material. At this stage the contents of the cyst have a granular appearance. This cyst grows so that in about half a year it has attained a diameter of about five millimetres. In the meantime small buds have appeared upon the inner surface of the wall of the cyst. Each bud is known as a brood capsule and contains the head and neck of a tænia echinococcus, with its four suckers and rostellum with a double row of hooklets. These suckers, rostellum, and hooklets can be protruded from the brood capsule and retracted into the capsule by the tænia. The brood capsules are continuous with the cyst wall and with each other. If the worms become separated from the cyst wall they die. A brood capsule generally contains more than one head or scolex. The brood capsules generally occur on the inner surface of the wall of the parent cyst in groups. Sometimes they grow to a size of one or two centimetres, and generally in these cases develop on the inner surface of their walls other brood capsules or daughter cysts, and these in turn may develop granddaughter cysts.

Cysts which produce upon their inner surface large

[1] "The Parasites of Man," 1886.

numbers of brood capsules become enormously increased in size. But even cysts that grow no brood capsules, and hence no scolices, and which are termed acephalocysts or sterile hydatids, may grow to quite a large size. A hydatid cyst growing in the liver, more especially, irritates the surrounding structures to such an extent that a secondary capsule is formed. This capsule is then found encompassing the cyst wall proper. In the large majority of cases hydatid cysts of the liver in human beings are single. In the herbivora, however, they are frequently found multiple. These multiple cysts must not be confounded, however, with multilocular echinococcus of the liver, which is an affection found much more frequently in man and very rarely in the lower animals. In multilocular echinococcus the daughter cysts, instead of developing from the inner surface of the parent cyst wall into the cavity of the mother cyst, are localized offshoots from the external wall of the parent cyst. Some of these become separated and develop as independent echinococcus cysts. In other cases they retain their connection with the parent cyst, forming secondary daughter cysts connected with, but outside of, the mother cyst. The prognosis of the latter variety of cysts is very much more grave even than that of unilocular echinococcus cyst. The fluid contents of an echinococcus cyst, when withdrawn with the aspirator through a needle of fairly large calibre, are found, when microscopically examined, to contain characteristic booklets and sometimes shreds of cyst membrane. The fluid itself has an opalescent appearance, a specific gravity of 1006 to 1016, and a neutral reaction. It is composed of about ninety-eight per cent of water and two per cent of solids. The solids are chiefly sodium chloride and phosphates, sulphates, and carbonates, and partly albuminoid material. A ptomain has also been isolated from the fluid, which is supposed to account for the urticarial eruption which occurs when the fluid is absorbed upon spontaneous or traumatic rupture of the cyst. Echinococcus disease varies in frequency in different countries, depending upon the familiarity of the relation existing between the inhabitants and the domesticated dogs. Thus in Iceland the disease causes a large percentage of the deaths. In Australia, also, it is said by Waring, in his excellent work on diseases of the liver, to be quite common. In this country and in Europe the disease is uncommon, if not rare.

The chief interest in a case of this sort is its value from a diagnostic standpoint. Echinococcus of the human body is situated in the liver in more than sixty per cent of the cases. Its differentiation from other diseases of the liver, therefore, becomes a matter of considerable importance. The diseases from which hydatid disease of the liver must be differentiated are those in which there is considerable increase in the real or apparent size of the liver. These are malignant disease of the liver, abscess of the liver, subphrenic abscess, pleural effusions, both serous and purulent, and aneurism. Malignant disease of the liver has for its characteristic more or less constant pain in the region of the liver. The portion of the liver which can be felt presents a hard and uneven surface. The tumor can generally be felt at the free margin of the liver in front. There is usually malignant disease of other portions of the digestive tract or of the abdomen present. This is not by any means intended as an enumeration of all the symptoms of malignant disease of the liver, but only of such symptoms as are not present in hydatid disease of this organ. Abscess of the liver is by far most frequently diagnosed when hydatid disease is present. Physical examination, apart from extreme sensitiveness of the liver present in abscess, yields little that is distinctive. When a hydatid cyst of the liver undergoes suppuration, as was the case in our patient, owing to infection by pus organisms brought from a distance, the difficulty of differentiation from simple hepatic abscess becomes even greater. But the subjective symptoms of hepatic abscess are more distinctive. There is pain; almost constantly there are rigors followed by high fever. Some increase of temperature is always present, and finally abscess develops rapidly. Hydatid disease, on the other hand, is of slow growth. There is no pain, or very little pain, until the cyst is very large. There is no fever. In abscess there is frequently disease of the heart as a causative agent. Should suppuration involve a hydatid cyst, the history of a slowly enlarging liver with no fever and no pain, followed by a period of fever with rigors, pain, and very rapid increase in the size of the previously slowly growing liver, would cause one to suspect an abscess of a hydatid cyst of the liver. This was the case in our patient. Pleural effusions should be readily differentiated from hydatid disease of the liver by a physical examination, unless the pleural effusions are encapsulated posteriorly. A highly probable diagnosis of pleural effusion may at least be made and confirmed by the aspirating needle. I have purposely avoided the use of the aspirating needle to differentiate the diagnosis between hydatid disease of the liver and abscess, malignant disease and simple cyst of the liver, for the reason that I do not think that either in hydatid disease or in abscess should the aspirating needle be used unless all the preparations for opening the cyst or abscess are ready at the time of aspirating. In other words, such aspiration should only be done as the first step in the radical operation. For diagnostic purposes such aspiration is unwarranted, for the reason that it is apt to be followed in these cases by a discharge of pus or hydatid fluid into the peritoneal cavity with a resulting fatal peritonitis. Some authorities do, however, puncture hydatid cysts, not only for diagnostic purposes, but with therapeutic ends in view. In subphrenic abscess the liver posteriorly is not enlarged upward, but the whole organ is pushed downward, its anterior contour being normal to the touch. Here the aspirating needle, when used, will withdraw pus. The history is that of an acute suppurative disease. It is important to remember that a subphrenic hydatid cyst sometimes occurs. When the aspirating needle is used at the time of the radical operation or previous to it for diagnostic purposes, the fluid withdrawn from a hydatid cyst has the positive characteristics described above when examined with the microscope, which enables us positively to affirm the presence of hydatid disease.

The vomiting of daughter cysts or pieces of cyst wall with the characteristic hooklets from the stomach, or, as in our case, the passage of these cysts or strips of membrane from the bowel, generally indicates an echinococcus of the liver. The limitations to the growth of an echinococcus in this organ render it highly probable that adhesion with organ and structures occurs sooner or later, followed by ulceration and the discharge of cysts or portions of cysts. Indeed, echinococcus cysts of the liver may burst and discharge their contents in any direction. Thus they may burst into the peritoneum and terminate fatally; into the pleura, giving rise to empyema; into the stomach, bowels, and ureters, and discharge their contents through these passages. They may even ulcerate through the abdominal wall and discharge their contents, and thus undergo a spontaneous cure. The latter result may also occur when these cysts discharge through the stomach or bowels, provided the opening is sufficiently large to empty the cyst cavity before suppuration occurs. When suppuration occurs in the cavity of the cyst, either before or after ulceration into the stomach or bowels, the patient may die of septicæmia or pyæmia, unless the cyst is promptly laid open and thoroughly evacuated.

Treatment.—So few of these cysts undergo spontaneous evacuation and cure as detailed above that the expectant treatment, after a diagnosis has been made, is never warranted. Although formerly medicinal treatment having for its object the destruction of the parasite was attempted, the location of the echinococcus in the liver certainly precludes any hope that medicinal treatment can be effective. It is curious, in this connection, to note that bile is supposed to be fatal to the life of this parasite. And yet the case I report proves that even when a communication between the bile passages and the cyst exists the growth of the scolex is not hindered.

We practically have to consider only the surgical treatment. And there are only two procedures which should be considered in any given case of hydatid disease, and they are incision with evacuation of the contents of the cyst, and puncture.

Taking up the latter first. Puncture consists in plunging into the cyst either an aspirating needle and withdrawing a part of the contents, or passing a trocar into the cyst and permitting it to discharge its fluid contents through the trocar. Both of these methods are dangerous, owing to the liability of leakage into the peritoneal cavity and a resulting fatal peritonitis. Still, Thomas,[1] after a study of the statistics, reports 54 per cent of cures, 19 per cent of deaths, and 27 per cent of failure to cure, the patient not having succumbed to the treatment.

The operation of incision is the only proper operation for hydatid disease of the liver, resulting, when favorable, in absolute recovery, as far as freedom from the parasite is concerned, and subjecting the patient to no risk as a result of the operative procedure, as is the case in puncture. It is the only proper surgical procedure The opening into the cyst is made either through the chest wall, as in our case, at the site nearest to the location of the cyst as shown by physical examination and aspiration, or through the abdominal wall in one or two stages. The technique of various operative procedures to accomplish these results is not within the province of this paper, but I cannot refrain from expressing, as I have done, my conviction that the only proper therapeutic procedure in these cases is incision and evacuation of the cyst.

[1] "Hydatid Disease," 1894.

XI.

DEPARTMENT OF DISEASES OF CHILDREN.

BY BARNIM SCHARLAU, M.D.,

ATTENDING PHYSICIAN.

Number of cases from December 1, 1897, to December 1, 1898, 383. Of these were cured, 246 cases; improved, 41 cases; unimproved, 15 cases died, 81 cases. Death rate, 21 per cent, which must be considered a good result for a special children's service, more so still considering the many cases which came for treatment in an already hopeless condition.

DISEASES.

Disease	Cases
Acute pharyngitis	1
Gastritis	2
Gastro-enteritis	22
Peritonitis	1
Colic	1
Colitis acuta	1
" chronica	1
Dysenteria	8
Dyspepsia	1
Entero-colitis	7
Nephritis chronica	4
Sarcoma renis	1
Chronic valvular heart diseases	23
Open ductus Botalli	1
Palpitatio cordis	1
Tachycardia	1
Laryngitis acuta	1
Bronchiectasis	2
Bronchitis acuta	13
" chronica	1
Broncho-pneumonia	64
Emphysema	2
Hydropneumothorax	1
Pneumonia lobularis	10
" tuberculosa	1
Tuberculosis acuta miliaris	4
Empyema acutum	50
" chronicum	7
Pleuritis serosa	6
" sicca	2
" chronica	2
Diphtheria	12
Tonsillitis follicularis	2
Malaria	4
Morbilli	2
Parotitis	2
Pertussis	4
Febris typhosa	82
Poliomyelitis anterior	3
Meningitis cerebro-spinalis	5
Chorea	13
Hysteria	2
Imbecility	1
Sclerosis, multiple	1
Neurasthenia	1
Paralysis post-diphtheritica	2
Poliencephalitis	1
Spasmus nutans	1
Paraplegia spastica	1
Meningitis tuberculosa	1
Thrombosis cerebralis	1
Anæmia	5
" perniciosa	1
Epistaxis	1
Eczema	1
Erythema nodosum	1
Hæmophilia	1
Heat prostration	4
Leukæmia	2
Myxœdema	1
Rheumatismus acutus	3
Rachitis	1
Trismus et tetanus	1
Atresia ani	1
Arthritis coxæ tuberculosa	1
Combustio	14
Foreign body in stomach	2
Lymphadenitis tuberculosa	1
Labium fissum	1

OPERATIONS.

Empyema:		Atresia ani	1
(*a*) Primary exsection of rib	47	Angioma congenitale	1
(*b*) Intercostal incision	3	Abscess of leg	1
(*c*) Secondary exsection of rib	5	Skin grafting	1
(*d*) Delorme's operation	7	Excision of tubercular glands	1
Sequestrotomy	3	Labium fissum	1

DEATHS.

Colitis	2	Pneumothorax	1
Dysenteria	1	Typhoid fever	4
Enteritis	9	Meningitis cerebro-spinalis	2
Nephritis chronica	1	Poliencephalitis	1
Sarcoma renis	1	Meningitis, tubercular	5
Heart disease	5	" traumatic	1
Broncho-pneumonia	11	Thrombosis cerebralis	1
Tubercular pneumonia	1	Anæmia perniciosa	1
Acute tuberculosis	4	Hæmophilia	1
Empyema	6	Leukæmia	1
Empyema and broncho-pneumonia	9	Atresia ani	1
Diphtheria	6	Burns of body	5
		Harelip	1

XII.

CASES FROM THE CHILDREN'S DEPARTMENT.

By BARNIM SCHARLAU, M.D.,

ATTENDING PHYSICIAN.

SIX CASES OF CHRONIC EMPYEMA OPERATED AFTER DELORME'S METHOD.

THE treatment of chronic empyema has gone through different phases. When, after the evacuation of pus, the lung either did not expand or the ribs did not sink in sufficiently to allow of the formation of adhesions between the pulmonary and the costal pleura, a cavity persisted which required the constant use of a drainage tube; if left alone these cases were hopeless and terminated fatally after months or years. It was, therefore, a great progress when Simon, Küster, Estlander, and others recommended the extensive exsection of several ribs, thus lessening the rigidity of the chest wall and allowing the now more movable parts of it to come in closer contact with the pulmonary pleura; under favorable conditions adhesions formed and the patients got well. But there remained a number of cases in which the operation was no success, because the costal pleura had become so much thickened that it remained convex even after the exsection of half a dozen ribs. It was obvious that the total removal of the ribs with the intercostal muscles and the costal pleura might be beneficial. Schede operated in this way; granulations sprang up from all sides, gradually closing the deep cavity. It is to be wondered that he did not, at the same time, try to free the lung from the exudate over the pulmonary pleura, for the lung cannot expand as long as it is bound down by the fibrinous, more or less organized exudate. Delorme, in Paris, improved Schede's operation in this way by what he called "décortication pulmonaire." I say he improved it, because it is only necessary to exsect as many ribs as to give free access to the pleural cavity, and not all the ribs overlying the cavity, as Schede demands. In discussing Dr. Curtis' paper on chronic empyema in December, 1897, at the New York Academy of Medicine, Dr. Robert F. Weir spoke highly in favor of Delorme's modification of Schede's method. It has since been our good luck to try its merits six times in the children's service of Mount Sinai Hospital. When I operated my first case I had not read the original publication of Delorme, and therefore had to follow my own inspiration. The method proved successful and was consequently carried out in all the following cases. I make first Schede's operation in the usual way, but I do not (as many do) remove the soft parts with the scissors, at the same time securing all bleeding vessels with the artery forceps, but I ligate in sections *en masse*, with strong pedicle silk, the soft parts close to the exsected ribs before using the scissors, thus making the operation almost bloodless. After exposing the pulmonary pleura to view I tear off parts of the exudate with a tenaculum, avoiding to insert it deeply, but rather removing layer after layer. When I come down to the pulmonary pleura I slip a blunt instrument under the exudate and enlarge the opening until I can introduce my index finger; the exudate could mostly be easily loosened by gentle manipulations, and necessitated only in two cases the cutting of strong bands over the apex with the scissors. Sometimes the tenaculum enteredthe lung itself, as could be demonstrated by the little gas bubbles; in another case the lung was superficially torn, when the finger had to remove the exudate with some force, but at no time was this of any consequence, the tle wounds invariably healing up by the next morning.

Out of the 6 cases, 5 were discharged cured, 1 child only dying, not from the effects of the operation, but from scurvy.

CASE I.—Julie Loewy, 6 years old, had measles one year ago; seven weeks ago she had pneumonia on the right side and was sick in bed for five weeks; two weeks ago she came home with severe cough and dyspnœa, and it was noticed that the right side bulged out. After admission to the Hospital, on March 29, 1898, she was in a very bad condition, body greatly emaciated. The physical examination showed all signs of considerable effusion into the right pleural cavity; pulse 120–140; respiration 40 to 60; temperature 101.6°. After withdrawing pus with the exploratory syringe, the right seventh rib was exsected and an enormous amount of pus evacuated; the lung, however, did not expand at all. On the following day the general condition was much improved—pulse 112, respiration 28, temperature 99.4°—and continued to remain so. On April 12, was allowed to be out of bed, having gained in weight; there was continually a profuse discharge of pus, but the lung remained unexpanded; the introduced finger could run around the whole upper part of the thorax without coming in contact with anything but the spine and the ribs. When no change for the better had taken place until April 28, I operated for the second time by enlarging the wound and exsecting the fifth, sixth, and eighth ribs, and some newly formed bone of the seventh rib, followed by Schede's operation. A large cavity presented itself; the lung was entirely bound down to the diaphragm and the mediastinum; the exudate over the pulmonary pleura exceedingly firm and tightly adherent, and it was only with great difficulty that I could gradually loosen it by using the tenaculum and mouth-toothed forceps and afterward my index finger. Having accomplished the decortication, the cavity presented about half the size as before, the lung having considerably expanded; this was loosely covered with iodoform gauze and the dressing finished. From this date the patient recovered uninterruptedly, though the closing up of the wound was slow owing to the general poor condition of the child. On July 4 patient was up and about, temperature, pulse, and respiration normal. On August 1 the general condition was good, wound small, with almost no discharge. On September 4 the wound was completely healed, all functions normal, vesicular breathing over the whole right chest; discharged cured.

CASE II.—Willy Zamoire, 10 years old, was admitted to the Hospital on June 11, 1898; family history good; has had measles and varicella; three weeks ago he became suddenly sick with fever, dry cough, dyspnœa; after ten days he seemed to be better, but five days ago fever returned. On admission his temperature was 103.6°, pulse 130; all symptoms pointed to an effusion into the right pleural cavity. Pus was withdrawn by exploratory needle, the seventh rib was exsected, thirteen ounces of pus evacuated, but the lung did not expand; the examining finger could not enter between the lobes, but the three lobes formed one single mass tightly bound down by a thick exudate. Therefore, on June 22, I exsected the fifth and sixth ribs, followed by Schede's operation; I loosened the exudate with tenacula, slipped my index finger between the pleura and the exudate, and loosened the latter one completely: the boy coughed a few times, and the lung filled almost completely the whole thorax. The reaction was very slight; temperature was never higher than 102°, and became and remained normal after a few days. On July 4 his weight was forty-two and one-half pounds; on July 14, forty-eight and one-quarter pounds. On July 30 his general condition was very good, the wound almost healed. On August 15 all dressings were left aside, and on September 2 he was discharged cured.

CASE III.—Lena Grossmann, 2 years old, admitted to Hospital on July 30, 1898, has been sick for about three weeks with pneumonia followed by empyema; the general condition of the child very poor, temperature 103.4°. After exsection of the seventh rib eighteen ounces of pus were evacuated, but the lung did not expand well. On the following day the child looked much better, but there was a profuse discharge of pus, and the lung did not present any tendency for expanding. Therefore, on August 10, Schede-Delorme's operation was performed after exsecting the sixth and seventh ribs; a thick layer of exudate was removed from the pleura, whereafter the upper lobe rapidly expanded. From this date the little patient constantly improved; temperature remained normal; granulations sprang up from all sides. The wound was closed on September 4 and the child discharged cured, having gained considerably in weight.

CASE IV.—Harry Rothstein, 3 years old, has a purulent discharge from both ears two years since; had measles a year ago, varicella six months ago, scarlet fever four months ago; tubercular glands of the neck were removed one year ago. He was admitted to the Hospital on August 9, 1898, having been operated for empyema a week ago by intercostal incision and insertion of a drainage tube. We found the chest full of pus, and exsected the seventh rib; twelve ounces of pus were removed, but the lung did not expand. For the next five days the purulent discharge continued to be very large; the temperature ran up at times as high as 105°, though generally not over 103°; weight of child, twenty and one-quarter pounds. From August 17 a general improvement set in, the fever subsided, and on September 6 the child had gained two pounds in weight. The lung, however, having remained unexpanded, Schede's operation was performed on September 12; the fifth, sixth, and eighth ribs were removed, and the exudate over the pleura was easily loosened; only the upper lobe was kept down by a dense constricting fibrous band, which necessitated the cutting with the scissors. The effect of the operation was instantaneous. The reaction was great; temperature rose to 104° in the afternoon, but came down to 102° on the following day; was normal on September 14. From this date the improvement was uninterrupted, the child gaining constantly in weight. On October 21 he was discharged cured, weighing twenty-six pounds, a gain of six pounds since his admission six weeks ago.

CASE V.—Morris Stone, 4 years old, had pneumonia in March, 1898; in July a swelling appeared on the left side of the thorax as large as a hen's egg, which after bursting has discharged pus ever since; has had no fever and no complaints except pains in side. Admitted to the Hospital on September 27 in a fair condition and pretty well nourished. On the left seventh rib in the mammillary line was an old scar and a sinus; the physical examination revealed a considerable effusion into the pleura. On September 29 the seventh rib was exsected and twenty-four ounces of pus with large clots evacuated. The lung, however, did not expand a particle, being bound down toward the diaphragm and the mediastinum by an exudate covering the surface of both lobes, so that the examining finger could nowhere be passed between the upper and lower lobes. No reaction set in after the operation; the purulent discharge was very considerable, but the lung remained in the same compressed condition, leaving the whole upper part of the thorax empty. Therefore, on October 3, Schede's operation was performed by exsecting the fifth, sixth, and seventh ribs, followed by the removal of the exudate, which could easily be loosened by the finger with the exception of a thick, tough fibrous band over the apex which required the cutting with the scissors. As soon as the child coughed, the whole lung expanded and filled the thorax completely. There was no reaction; the temperature remained normal, rising only once to 101°; the discharge was greatly diminished, granulations sprang from all sides, and the cavity became visibly smaller from day to day. Weight of child, October 8, twenty-seven pounds. On November 10 the wound was closed with the exception of a small sinus which required repeatedly the use of a scoop before it closed, on November 30.

CASE VI.—Samuel Morris, 22 months old, was admitted to the Hospital on June 18, 1898, after having been sick with cough, fever, and diarrhœa for some time; he was fairly well nourished, had signs of rickets and slight scurvy; the heart beat in the epigastrium to the right of the median line, no murmur, action regular; the left chest gave signs of considerable effusion into the pleural cavity; the liver is enlarged, the spleen palpable; abdomen tympanitic; pus was withdrawn with the needle from the left pleura. On June 19 the left seventh rib was resected and a great deal of pus removed; the heart came back to its place, but the lung did not expand. On June 20 the child did not rest well, the pulse 136, temperature 99.6°, profuse discharge from the wound; the mouth looks worse, the gums swollen and bleeding. For the next ten days particular attention was paid to the treatment of the scurvy. The lung remained unexpanded and a profuse discharge of pus continued. Therefore Delorme's operation was performed after the scurvy was greatly improved. The operation was successful, allowing the lung to expand; but the scurvy grew worse again and the little patient died four days later.

ACUTE LEUKÆMIA—PERNICIOUS ANÆMIA.

I. S., 8 years of age, admitted to Children's Ward April 23, 1898, with the following history: Two weeks previously he was struck by a playmate in the right temple; the parents attributed the boy's symptoms to the blow, although there were no marks of violence apparent. He began to have fever, general malaise, vomiting, and rapid emaciation. His feet became swollen; there was some abdominal pain and headache. The physician who saw the case stated that the child had a large spleen. During the ten days preceding his admission he had bleeding from the mouth and gums, and numerous red and bluish spots appeared on the skin of the entire body. The vomiting persisted; he retained very little nourishment. Cardiac palpitation, dyspnœa on exertion, and extreme weakness were the latest symptoms.

On admission his general condition was very poor, emaciated, markedly anæmic. There was œdema about the eyes; the face was swollen; numerous new and old subcutaneous hemorrhages were present on chest, back, arms, and legs. The gums were bleeding; teeth were absent, others falling out. The lungs were negative. Heart action was rapid and regular; a loud, soft systolic murmur was heard at the apex; the second pulmonary sound was accentuated; apex beat was in the fifth space in the nipple line. Liver extended two finger breadths below the free border of the ribs. Spleen was enlarged to percussion, extended about a hand's breadth below the free border of the ribs and to within two finger breadths of the median line; it was easily palpable, hard and tender. The abdomen was negative; slight œdema of legs and feet. Glands in the neck, groins, and axillæ were enlarged; the bones were tender to pressure.

A blood spread was taken; the following report was made: Examination of a thin spread, with a Zeiss one-twelfth immersion and a 6 ocular, showed on an average twelve leucocytes in a field. Red cells showed poikilocytes, numerous microcytes and macrocytes, a moderate number of normoblasts and megaloblasts. In a count of 1,000 leucocytes the following were noted:

Poly-nuclears	31
Medium-sized mono-nuclears...........	941

The remainder were either very large or very small mono-nuclears. A blood count next day showed 900,000 red blood cells, 2,200 whites. During the night the entire blood picture had changed; there was on the average but one leucocyte to the field; the changes in the red blood cells, with the exception of poikilocytosis, had disappeared. Hæmoglobin was 17 per cent. On the 25th white cells numbered 2,200, reds 977,500. About eight-elevenths of the whites were mono-nuclear, three-elevenths polynuclear. The spleen diminished rapidly in size, so that just before death it reached only to the free border of the ribs; the liver, on the contrary, increased in size, and in two days its edge could be felt at the level of the umbilicus.

Fundus examination showed numerous large hemorrhages in both eyes. Urine examination showed blood cells and a few casts, specific gravity 1022, reaction acid.

During the five days at the Hospital his temperature hovered between 102° and 104° Far. until just before death, when it became slightly subnormal. He was restless and delirious, vomited frequently, the bleeding from the mouth and gums was uncontrollable, the subcutaneous hemorrhages increased in extent and in number. Dyspnœa became quite marked: there was evidence of pneumonic trouble in the left lower lobe.

Postmortem Examination. Lungs.—Left showed small amount of clear, pinkish fluid in pleural cavity. There were numerous subpleural hemorrhages. The lower lobe contained an area of beginning consolidation, the upper lobe was emphysematous. Right showed subpleural and parenchymatous hemorrhages, a few small areas of consolidation secondary to the hemorrhages. *Heart.*—Reddish effusion into pericardium; numerous small hemorrhages under the visceral pericardium, and under the endocardium of all the chambers. *Bronchial Glands.*—Moderately enlarged; non-tubercular. *Thymus.*—Reached to fourth rib; very pale. *Spleen.*—Measured twelve by eight centimetres; weight, 250 grammes; dark red; pulp moderately soft. *Adrenals.*—Pale, otherwise negative. *Kidneys.*—Small hemorrhages on surface; capsules not adherent; cut sections pale; markings indistinct. *Liver* contained few hemorrhages on upper surface, and *Stomach* a few into the mucous membrane. *Pancreas.*—Negative. *Intestines.*—Pale; hemorrhages into mucosa in places; the entire lymphatic apparatus, especially in ileum and transverse colon, enlarged. *Glandular System.*—All glands moderately enlarged. *Marrow of Radices.*—Pinkish and jelly-like in consistence. *Head* showed small hemorrhagic extravasations under the periosteum and pericranium. *Brain.*—Pale; slight œdema of pia; petechiæ beneath pia and over cerebellum and olfactory tracts.

Microscopical Examination.—Kidneys show cloudy swelling; spleen, congestion, hypertrophy, and swelling of Malpighian bodies, increase of connective tissue; intestine, hyperplasia of lymphatic apparatus; thymus, marked lymphoid infiltration; liver, round-cell infiltration around vessels, and fatty infiltration.

Blood cultures remained sterile.

TYPHO-MALARIAL FEVER.

S. M., female, aged 13, was admitted to the Children's Ward August 11, 1898, with a history of two weeks' illness at home, the symptoms being headache, general malaise, fever, higher in the evening, diarrhœa, and recently cough and expectoration. Her sister was admitted at the same time with similar symptoms. Physical examination showed enlargement of the liver and spleen, roseola eruption on abdomen and back, pneumonic areas in both lungs. She was delirious and restless, and had frequent involuntary evacuations of bladder and bowel; the temperature was persistently high, often above 105°; the urine gave a marked Ehrlich reaction; the blood showed a positive Widal reaction on the 17th. She improved somewhat during the next few days. August 20, at 8 A.M., temperature was 104°, at 11 A.M. it was 103°, at 2:30 P.M. it had dropped to 98.6° and was followed by a profuse perspiration. Fresh blood specimens were taken and examined, and plasmodia were found. The organism was found in abundance, was situated near the periphery of the red blood cells; about one third its size. Its shape was almost circular; large, brownish pigment occupied its centre; the number of granules was small. Repeated examinations after this failed to show them. The fever reappeared and did not strike normal until September 20, even after attempts to reduce the temperature. After this day her temperature remained normal. The course of the fever was interrupted once by a hemorrhage from the bowel. Convalescence was good. Widal reaction persisted.

XIII.

ON ERYTHROMELALGIA.

BY B. SACHS, M.D.,
CONSULTING NEUROLOGIST.

(With three illustrations.)

RARE diseases are not necessarily interesting, but they become of the greatest possible value to medical science if the study of them, in spite of their rarity, lead to a clearer understanding of one or several morbid conditions. From this point of view the disease in question may well claim attention, for its discussion necessarily involves the consideration of disorders to which it is more or less closely allied. Does erythromelalgia constitute a disease *sui generis*, or is it a mere complex of symptoms which may be associated with a number of other diseases? Is it of peripheral or central origin? Is it always due to the same cause? Is it, indeed, a nervous disease, within a liberal interpretation of that term? These are a few of the questions which I have kept in mind in the present research.

For many years after Weir Mitchell[1] had published his first studies on the subject, the condition which he so ably described seemed to arouse but little interest. In 1878 it received its formal baptism, the oddity of its name serving to call attention to an affection which few had a chance of observing. In 1880 Lannois[2] published an exhaustive treatise on erythromelalgia, but little was added, except in a purely statistical sense, to the conclusions of Weir Mitchell. The presentation of three typical cases of the disease by Gerhardt,[3] Senator,[4] and Bern-

[1] Weir Mitchell: Phila. Med. Times, 1872.

[2] Lannois: Thèse de Paris, 1880.

[3] Gerhardt: Berliner klinische Wochenschrift, 1892, p. 1125.

[4] Senator: Berliner klinische Wochenschrift, 1892, p. 1127.

hardt,[1] at a meeting of the Berlin Medical Society in 1892, gave renewed interest to the subject, as is shown sufficiently by the relatively large number of contributions which have appeared since that day. I need mention only a few of these, for the purely historical data may be gathered from the paper of Lewin and Benda,[2] and the value of the majority of the writings has been critically analyzed in the last excellent contribution of Mitchell and Spiller.[3] It may be worth while to select for special mention the contribution of Heyman,[4] who reported two acute cases of this disease, and that of Eulenburg,[5] who reported three cases. The first patient of the latter was afflicted with a form of progressive muscular dystrophy ; in the second, the symptoms appeared in conjunction with a cerebral neoplasm—the same patient, by the way, who formed the subject of Gerhardt's paper; and in the third patient the condition appeared to be hereditary. Eulenburg was much impressed by this association of erythromelalgia with a variety of diseases, and therefore concluded that the disease was not an independent affection, but represented a sensory vasomotor group of symptoms which he was inclined to attribute to some lesion of the gray matter of the spinal cord. Facts are preferable to theories ; it is evident that the origin of the disease could not be determined satisfactorily except by microscopical studies.

Dehio[6] has described an interesting case ; from his patient a portion of the ulnar nerve and a piece of the ulnar artery were removed and examined. No change was found in the nerve ; in the artery only slight changes in the elastic membrane were discoverable, and the intima was thickened so that the lumen of the vessel was reduced to half of its normal size. In view of these

[1] Bernhardt: Berliner klinische Wochenschrift, 1892, p. 1129.

[2] Lewin and Benda: Berliner klin. Wochenschrift, 1894, p. 53.

[3] Mitchell and Spiller: American Journal of Medical Sciences, January, 1899.

[4] Heyman: Berliner klin. Wochenschrift, 1896, p. 1135.

[5] Eulenburg: Neurologisches Centralblatt, 1893, p. 657; Deutsche medicinische Wochenschrift, 1893, p. 1325.

[6] Dehio: Berliner klin. Wochenschrift, 1896, p. 817.

slight findings in the peripheral nerve and artery, Dehio was of the opinion that the condition was due to a lesion in the posterior and lateral horns of the cord. It is not wise to base the morbid pathology of any disease upon the examination of such a slight amount of tissue, and I agree with Mitchell and Spiller, that the relief following the excision of a portion of the artery and nerve above the wrist in Dehio's patient, and the fact that the patient lost pain after this excision, militate against the supposition of a central origin of the trouble, and would, at least, render the theory of a peripheral neuritis possible.

The last-named authors have shown, by the examination of the tissues taken from an amputated toe, that the nerves were considerably degenerated and that there was most marked disease of the arteries. As their case was not complicated by symptoms pointing to any central affection, their findings seem to me to be of great value as showing the plausibility of Mitchell's view that, while the disease might possibly in some instances be of central origin, it may be due to a nerve-end neuritis.

Auerbach[1] is the only one who thus far has been fortunate enough to report a case with a complete autopsy, but the value of the findings is lessened by the consideration that the suspicion of tabes arose some years before the patient's death, and that the disease of the upper sacral and lower lumbar posterior roots may have had some relation to tabes, but not necessarily to the complicating erythromelalgia. To be sure, Auerbach, assisted by Edinger, found no changes in the nerves of the lower extremities; but this examination does not seem to have been made with exhaustive thoroughness, and he too is bound to acknowledge that the media and the intima of the blood vessels were somewhat thickened. Both Dehio and Auerbach have made much of the relations of the vasomotor fibres to arterio-sclerosis, and, as vasomotor fibres are known to be present in the posterior roots, some support appeared to them to be lent to the view that the

[1] Auerbach: Deutsche Zeitschrift für Nervenheilkunde, vol. xi., 1897, p. 143.

posterior roots have a direct relation to the appearance of the symptoms of erythromelalgia. But if they be directly dependent upon the posterior roots, it is strange that the symptoms of erythromelalgia should not appear more frequently in the course of tabes, of syphilis of the spinal cord, and, above all, in cases of compression of the cord by extra-dural neoplasm. The trophic and vasomotor disturbances, as I have observed them in connection with tumor of the spinal cord, differ widely from those observed in erythromelalgia. Auerbach has felt this objection, for he closes his paper by postulating the question as to the nature of the disease of the posterior roots which produces erythromelalgia, without, however, being able to answer this question satisfactorily. The vasomotor disturbances which are so frequently associated with neuralgic affections would lead one to suppose that there is an intimate relation between the innervation of the blood vessels and the subsequent arterial changes. But it is still a matter of doubt whether the peripheral nerve affections or the arterial changes are the primary factors.

The first case which I am about to relate, and which I have studied with Dr. Alfred Wiener, seemed to be of unusual promise, for the symptoms were very typical of the disease as laid down by Weir Mitchell, and there was no suspicion of any central nervous affection. The necessity for amputating the thigh gave us unusual opportunities for extensive microscopical studies of the tissues of the leg; and while these studies were not as thoroughgoing as they would have been if we had had a complete autopsy, it is an advantage to have been able to examine nerves and arteries in a tolerably recent period of the disease, and it is a further satisfaction to be able to report that the patient has been entirely relieved by the operation. The history[1] of the case is as follows:

M. S., male, aged 36 years, born in Russia, was admitted to my department at the New York Polyclinic in

[1] I am indebted to Dr. Lederman for his kind assistance in keeping a careful record during this patient's stay in the Hospital.

April, 1898. At that time he stated that he had been in good health until August, 1897, when he began to be troubled by pains in the left calf, shooting from there into the groin and into the foot. As far as he knew, he had been free of syphilis and of every tubercular and rheumatic taint. Before his present illness he had been able to attend to his work as a tailor. He lived in unwholesome quarters and used a sewing machine for ten to twelve hours each day. During the first few months of this illness he was much annoyed by what he considered "rheumatic" pains, but continued to walk and to use the leg as before. He experienced great pain, however, in standing and in sitting; in bed he was more comfortable. He noticed no swelling or redness of the foot until the beginning of 1898, when the pain increased to such a degree that it became almost intolerable. At the time of my first examination (April, 1898) there was no doubt of the reality and intensity of the pain. When sitting on a chair for a few minutes, with the feet touching the floor, the left foot turned a deep violet red, the color spreading from the toes upward several inches above the ankle. The skin was dry and glossy. After a few minutes the whole extremity became so sensitive that he could not bear the touch of the finger, and an electrical examination of the dorsal or plantar surface of the foot was forbidden by the pain. According to the patient's statements made at these visits he was not free from pain at any time. All forms of sensation were present, including the muscular sense; but the tests had to be made quickly, as the slightest handling of the affected limb was excessively painful. The records of the clinic also show that the arteries in the leg and foot pulsated distinctly, and that there was a flaccid condition of the muscles of the thigh and a marked atrophy of the anterior tibial group. The faradic response was present in the nerves and muscles of the thigh and in the upper portion of the leg, but even in this part only feeble responses were obtained with the currents which we were able to use, the patient resisting because of the pain. In the thigh muscles the galvanic reactions were not altered. Both knee-jerks were present. The other extremity was entirely normal in all respects.

Other details need not be recited here as they are substantially the same as those elicited at a later examination. The condition of the patient became steadily worse, and he sought admission to the Hospital, where he was seen by me again October 23, 1898. At this period one other symptom had been added—a sore on the

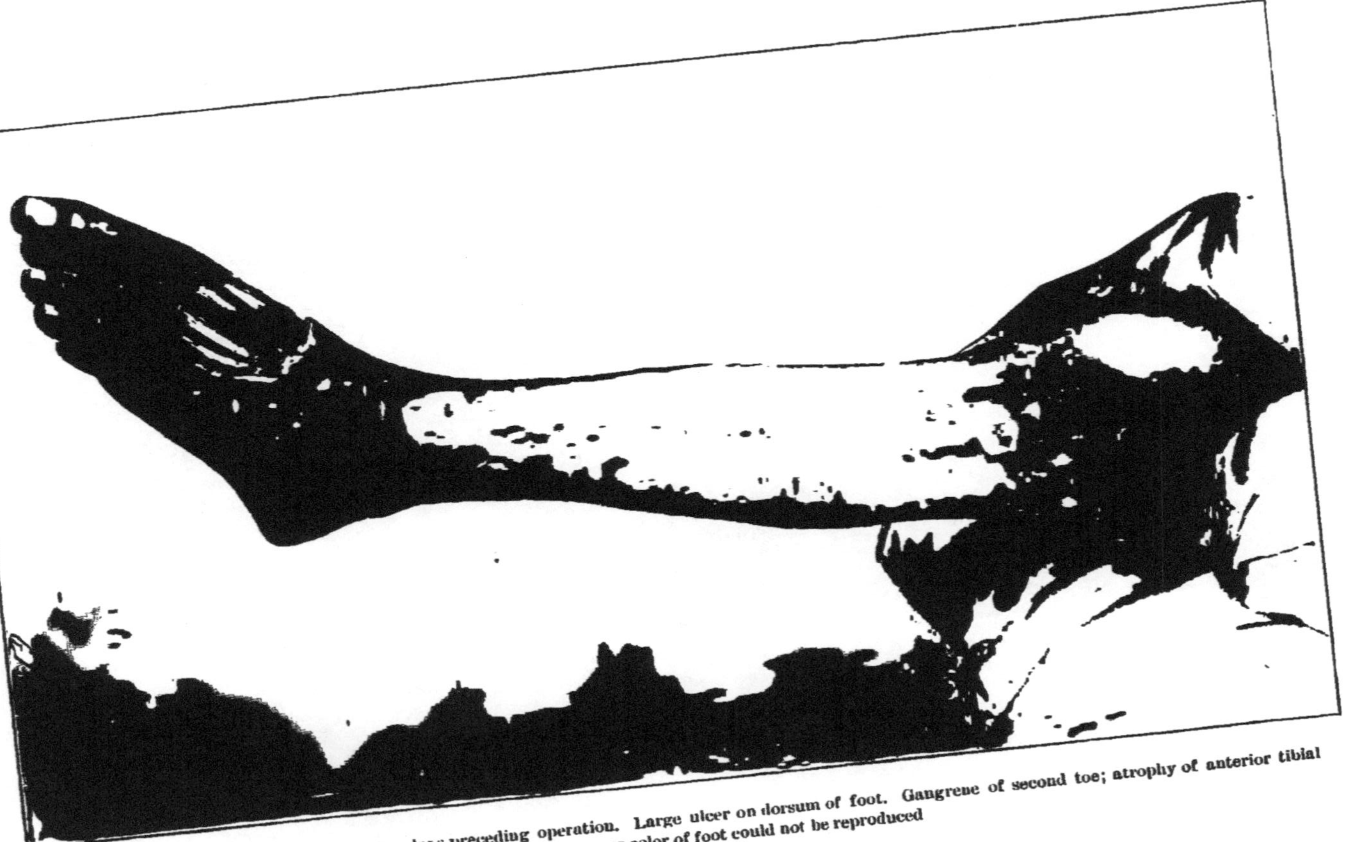

Fig. 1.—Condition of lower extremity a few days preceding operation. Large ulcer on dorsum of foot. Gangrene of second toe; atrophy of anterior tibial group. Violaceous color of foot could not be reproduced

dorsum of the foot, the patient stating that a small red pimple had appeared nine weeks previously, which was soon followed by an area of black tissue (gangrene). A slough came away, leaving a small sinus discharging pus. The ulcer gradually increased, and in the course of time the tendons became exposed and the patient was bedridden (Fig. 1). His general health remained good. From the records of the Hospital I quote the following:

Physical Examination.—General condition fair; complexion sallow; tongue coated and breath foul; slight gingivitis; gums soft and retracted; the skin of the body of normal softness; no hyperidrosis; ears slightly red and warm, the color returning promptly after pressure; the eyes are normal, and the pupils react promptly to light and during accommodation. *Thorax.*—Frame is large, chest broad; slight retraction above and below clavicle. There is some dulness on percussion over left apex. Sibilant and sonorous breathing is heard all over the chest, especially on the left side. The pulse is soft and regular. There is no evidence of arterio-sclerosis. Heart sounds are feeble, and a faint change of first sound is audible at the apex. The heart is not enlarged, and all other organs are normal. *Hands and fingers.*—There is no abnormality, except a slight redness of the phalanges, which disappeared on pressure and returned with moderate rapidity. *Examination of the spine* shows entirely normal conditions. *Lower extremities.*—Atrophy of all muscles of the left leg, as shown by the measurements of both lower extremities:

Circumference of right thigh, . .	40	centimetres.
" of left thigh, . .	36	"
" 2 inches above right-knee,	32½	"
" 2 inches above left knee,	32½	"
" of right calf, . .	29	"
" of left calf, . . .	23	"

Motion at the hip and knee were normal on both sides. No external abnormalities were noticed in either extremity, with the exception of the atrophy of the left leg, and of the redness beginning about three inches above the ankle. There is a slight pressure "sore" over the sacrum and a distinct atrophy of the left gluteal region. Both knee-jerks lively and cremasteric reflexes equal. All superficial reflexes were active, possibly a little exaggerated. A rectal examination showed that there was no loss of sphincteric power, and the prostate was of medium size. The left foot is distinctly cyanotic as soon as it is allowed to be in a pendent position, but even when lying in bed it is distinctly redder than the right. There is a swelling over and below the internal malleolus. The toes are red and cold. The heel is sensitive to the touch, but its color is normal. Over the dorsal surface of the foot, extending from the metatarso-phalangeal articulation of the second toe, is a circular ulcer 6 centimetres in width, extending outward, but not beyond the space between the fourth and fifth metatarsals; it has involved the entire thickness of the skin, and the tendons are exposed. The borders of the ulcer are sharp, even, and not undermined. The gangrenous tissue is surrounded by a zone of redness, disappearing on pressure, the color returning slowly. The base of the ulcer is sloughy, but there is no odor. On any attempt to change dressing, or when the foot was allowed to hang down, there was free venous hemorrhage from the ulcerating tissue. The nails of the toes were normal and there are no blebs or corns.

Temperature on admission was 100.2° F., pulse 108, respiration 28. Urine was clear, acid, specific gravity 1020, no albumin or sugar.

The patient was put to bed and given potassium iodide, 10 grains three times a day, and alternately Magendie solution and codeine for extreme pain. The ulcer was dressed with orthoform, protective strips, and wet dressing.

From October 24 to October 31, when he was transferred to the surgical clinic, every possible attention was given to the ulcer, which continued, however, to increase in size and depth, bled frequently, and was the seat of intense pain. As the second toe had become completely gangrenous, and all the other toes had already lost sensation and were threatened with gangrene, the question of operation had to be considered. The propriety of performing simple excision of the peripheral nerves, according to the suggestion of Weir Mitchell, was considered, but, as the gangrene was advancing rapidly, nothing was to be expected from this procedure, and amputation was decided upon. Dr. Gerster, to whom the case was referred, was of the opinion that if the amputation were to be made below the knee the stump might become gangrenous. He decided, therefore, that the leg should be removed above the knee. Of this there seemed to be all the more urgent need, as the patient's general condition was less satisfactory and he was running temperatures varying between 100° and 102° F. The operation was undertaken November 15, 1898. From the notes of the surgeon I quote as follows:

"After proper antiseptic precautions, a circular skin incision was made about 2½ inches below the knee joint;

a cuff of skin and subcutaneous tissue were reflected; then with large amputation knife, divided all the muscles down to the bone at lower third of the thigh. These were retracted, periosteum was peeled off, and the bone cut through a little higher up; the sciatic nerve was pulled out two inches and cut through; all vessels ligated; the femoral artery and vein were tied separately. After constrictor was removed, pressure was made on femoral artery near the groin; hot sponges were put in stump; pressure on the artery gradually released, and the bleeding points were caught and ligated. The wound was thoroughly irrigated, and the skin flap was sutured anteriorly and posteriorly by a running catgut suture. The lower angle was drained by two drainage tubes and a large dry dressing applied. From this time on the patient made a slow but steady recovery. The stump healed up satisfactorily, and the patient was discharged cured January 4, 1899."

After the operation I visited the patient repeatedly, by the courtesy of Dr. Gerster, and found that he was entirely free from pain and much relieved by the operation. Two weeks ago, nearly four months after the operation, the patient again presented himself at my clinic, at my request, when he was found to be entirely free from pain—a fact which it is well to bear in mind in connection with the suspicion of the central origin of the disease. The stump was of good color, entirely normal in every respect, and the patient was distinctly elated over the fact that, with an artificial leg, he would be able to walk about as before.

The main features of this case can be summed up in a few words. A man in middle life, without any evidence of other nervous or arterial disease, free of every specific and alcoholic taint, is seized with extreme pain in the left lower extremity, radiating from the calf into the groin and into the left foot. Swelling and redness were soon superadded. Both of these, as well as the pain, were increased when the foot was pendent. Several months after the appearance of this "red neuralgia" a slight sore appeared on the dorsum of the left foot, which developed into a large gangrenous ulcer, followed by dry gangrene of the second toe and with a threatening gangrene of all the other toes. Because of this condition and of the fact that the redness had extended for some distance above the ankle, and on account of the persistent pain, amputation of the thigh was considered necessary. The operation was performed, and the patient made a thoroughly satisfactory recovery.

Of the diagnosis in this case there can be little doubt. It was fortunate, however, that the patient was under my observation some months before he was admitted to the Hospital and before the ulcer appeared. During this first period of observation the symptoms were thoroughly characteristic, the only feature of special note being the marked atrophy of the anterior tibial group ; but such atrophies had been noted in other cases, and would not militate against the supposition of the peripheral or central origin of the disease.

From one of Weir Mitchell's [1] latest descriptions of the disease I take the following characteristic points :

The disease is much more common in men than in women. Little or no difference of color is seen until the foot hangs down in an upright posture. when it becomes rose-red. The arteries throb and the color becomes dusky red or violaceous in tint. Pain is usually present and is worse when the part hangs down or is pressed upon. In bad cases there is more or less pain at all times, which is also worse in the summer and from heat, and is eased by cold. Sensations of all kinds preserved. There is distinct hyperalgesia. Temperature greatly above normal ; dependency causes, in some cases, increase of heat, in others lowering of temperature ; there is no gangrene : the disease is asymmetrical.

It will be seen from the above that the case here described agreed in every particular but one with the description given by Mitchell, the only exception being the appearance of gangrene, which Mitchell distinctly states does not occur in erythromelalgia, and which he utilizes as a point in differential diagnosis between erythromelalgia and Reynaud's disease. It would not be wise, on account of the absence or the addition of any one symptom, to exclude a case from so well established a type, if all

[1] S. Weir Mitchell : Clinical Lectures on Nervous Diseases, p. 179 et seq Philadelphia, 1897.

other symptoms are entirely typical. Minor trophic changes have been noted in cases reported by others, and in the one herewith described you will remember that for months preceding the formation of the ulcer there could not have been a shadow of a doubt as to the clinical diagnosis. I have seen two other cases in which gangrene of the toes was associated with other typical symptoms of erythromelalgia. We must therefore modify Weir Mitchell's account and claim that in extreme instances of this disease gangrene may occur. The gravity of the disease in our patient has also been proved by the very marked changes in the arteries, yet the results of the histological examination are so much in accord with those reported by Mitchell and Spiller, that there is an additional reason to claim that. in spite of one atypical symptom, the case was an instance of genuine erythromelalgia.

It is with this morbid condition, as with so many others, that no one patient ever presents all of the possible symptoms. Several authors have reported hyperidrosis, œdema, and falling out of hair. I trust that it has been established to the satisfaction of all that this case may be considered to be typical of the disease in question, and, if so, we may well claim that the microscopical examination has revealed indisputable results.

After the removal of the leg a careful dissection of the parts was made by myself. The ulcer had assumed such proportions that it was impossible to make any satisfactory examination of the tissues in the foot. I contented myself, therefore, with removal of the anterior tibial artery, of the anterior tibial nerve, of the peroneal nerve, of the posterior tibial nerve, of the popliteal artery, and of a small portion of the sciatic nerve. A few veins were removed, and muscular tissue was taken from the various parts of the anterior tibial group of muscles and from the gastrocnemius. The nerves, as well as the arteries, were hardened in a four per cent formalin solution.[1] The nerve sections were stained by the Van Gieson and Wolter's modification of Weigert's method. It was not

[1] I am indebted to Dr. Alfred Wiener, who undertook kindly to prepare the specimens for me.

practicable to make an examination of fresh nerve tissue. The most marked changes were discovered in the anterior tibial and popliteal arteries and their ramifications.

It will be seen from the accompanying plate (Fig. 2) that there is a marked arteritis affecting all the coats, but more particularly the intima. The change is often so great as to lead to an occlusion of the larger as well as of the smaller branches. This arteritis is specially noticeable in the branches accompanying the nerve bundles, the occlusion of the arteries often being complete. But most marked of all is the change found in one of the larger branches of the popliteal, from which it is also evident that the disease is of old standing, for there has been time for the formation of well-developed connective tissue. Let me direct your attention to the facts that not a single normal artery was found, and that this arterial disease has been revealed not only in the immediate vicinity of the affected foot, but in the upper portion of the leg. This finding will persuade every one of the wisdom of the surgeon in insisting that amputation shall be performed above the knee. The nerves showed a slight degeneration of the nerve fibres altogether out of proportion, as it seems to me, to the marked arterial disease. Yet this degeneration is evident enough in the anterior tibial and peroneal nerves, while the sciatic and popliteal are almost normal (Fig. 3). The nerves chiefly affected are, therefore, those which have their blood supply from arteries given off below the seat of greatest arterial disease. No single bundle is completely degenerated, but in each there are some fibrils that are distinctly diseased. In some nerve bundles the degenerated fibres are replaced by connective tissue. It is worth noting that there is no evidence of any cellular infiltration of the nerve sheath, no evidence of any perineuritis, and that the changes in the nerves may, therefore, be said to be of a purely degenerative order. The veins showed a very slight thickening of their walls. The muscular tissue was carefully examined. The striation was normal and there was no increase in the muscle nuclei. A portion of the skin near the ulcer was removed, but the examination revealed

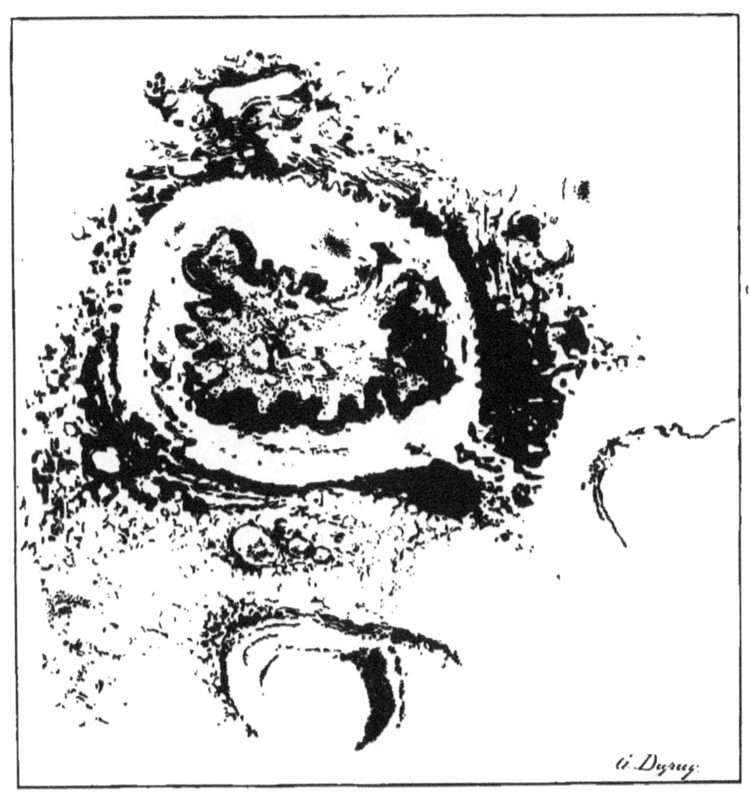

Fig. 2.—Cross section of a branch of posterior tibial artery. Thickening of fenestrated membrane. Van Gieson stain. +40.

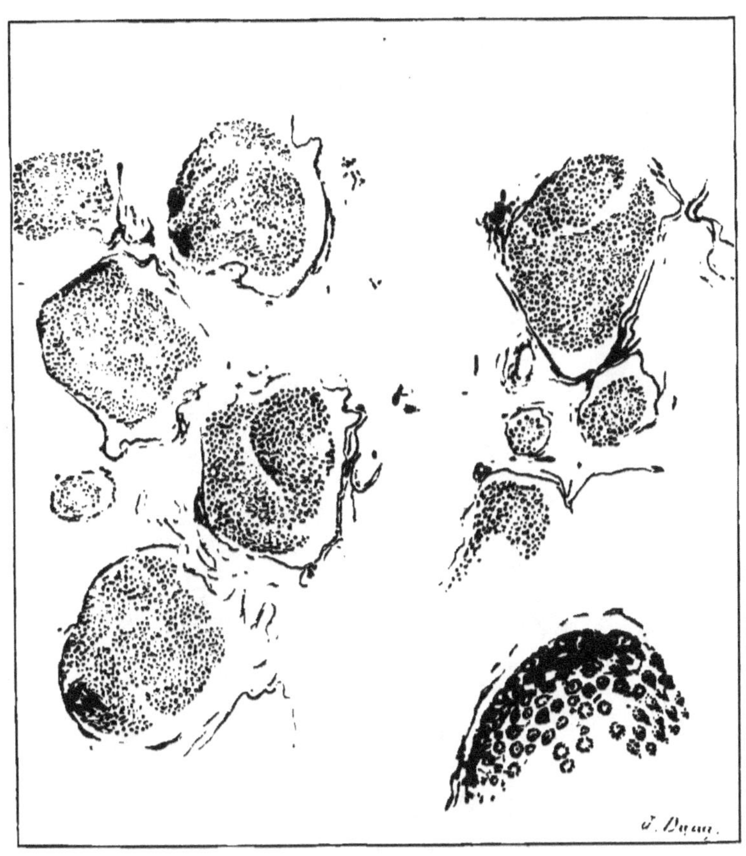

FIG 3.—Cross-section of a portion of sciatic nerve, showing only a few degenerated nerve fibres. Modified Weigert stain. Middle power.

nothing abnormal, except a marked hyperæmic condition and a total lack of hair development. The bone tissue was not altered.

In attempting to interpret these pathological findings, we are struck by the fact that the most marked changes are in the arteries and that the nerve changes are relatively slight. It is particularly noteworthy that the smaller arteries supplying the nerves were completely occluded, and, comparing the relative amount of disturbance in the nerves and arteries, it is scarcely probable that the changes found in the nerves were sufficient to cause the arterial disease. It is much more probable that the arterial disease was the cause of these nerve changes. But. we do not wish to assert that the question of the origin of the arterial disease can be determined by the findings of this case. This might possibly be due to some disease of the central nervous system, but such origin is rendered somewhat improbable by the fact that the patient presented no other symptoms pointing to any disease, however slight, of the spinal axis. The complete answer to this question can, of course, be given only in a case in which a thorough postmortem examination shall have been made: but it seems to us to be of some value to have found these marked arterial changes. for they are surely sufficient to account for the nerve symptoms present in erythromelalgia.

As was intimated above, the microscopical examination in this case would tend to corroborate Mitchell and Spiller's view of a peripheral origin of the disease. but it would lead to the opinion that the arterial condition is of greater importance than the changes in the nerves, and that, indeed, the latter may be due to the former. The theory of the arterial origin of erythromelalgia would also appear to us to obtain further corroboration from the occurrence of this symptom-group in cases of marked arterial degeneration, and from the fact that a very similar group of symptoms. barring the pain, occurs in connection with marked cardiac and arterial disease. It is surprising how little aid can be got on this subject from works on heart and arterial diseases, but some evidence is supplied by two cases, to which I shall briefly refer, which seem to me to support the close connection between arterial affections and erythromelalgia. Both these patients were examined in the Montefiore Home.[1]

W. G., aged 52 years, a tailor, was admitted June 6, 1898. His family history is negative. Three years ago he was in a hospital on account of pain in the right foot. The only points of interest to us are the symptoms of marked dilatation of the heart and of a widespread arterio-sclerosis. There were no sensory defects and no vasomotor anomalies in the upper extremities. In the right thigh there were large and small red patches; these areas were painful to touch and had been so for some seven months; the red areas were not constant. On the leg below the knee there was unusual sensitiveness to deep pressure, not merely along the course of the peripheral nerves; sensation was undisturbed and electrical conditions were entirely normal. A month later it is stated in the records of the Home that the areas of redness would recur in various parts of the right lower extremity; these would last about three to four days, would fade away, and then the redness would recur or would appear in other parts. When these red areas were fully developed the entire extremity would appear hot to the touch and the patient could not bear the contact of the bedclothes. In October there was œdema of the right foot, and the redness became more persistent, growing more marked as the foot was lowered. Elevation of the extremity gave some relief. In November the right big toe became very cyanotic, and, after slight superficial suppuration, gangrene was rapidly developed. In the course of a few days all the toes became gangrenous, the pain was persistent and excessive, the gangrene spread to the foot, and amputation was decided upon. Unfortunately, the patient died upon the operating table before the amputation was begun. No doubt the condition of the heart and of the peripheral blood vessels makes chloroform or ether narcosis particularly hazardous in this condition. Weir Mitchell seems to have had a similar experience. To my great regret, no autopsy was permitted by the relatives of our patient. In this instance the erythromelalgia was associated with marked arteriosclerosis. The symptoms were so typical of the conditions as described by Mitchell that we must allow its close

[1] The members of the house staff of the Home have kindly copied the records for me.

relationship to arterio-sclerosis, however anxious some writers appear to be to eliminate arterio sclerotic cases from the list of typical erythromelalgias. In view of our findings, the relationship between the two conditions, or rather the occurrence of the symptoms of erythromelalgia with marked arterio-sclerosis, is altogether natural.

The second patient is a man, S. S., 66 years of age, still at the Home. He complains of general weakness, cough, some expectoration, and dyspnœa on slightest exertion. Heart figure is enlarged in longitudinal direction. Apex beat faintly palpable in sixth intercostal space in mammillary line; two murmurs are audible over apex, and a double murmur over the aorta. Auscultation of peripheral arteries reveals nothing. This patient is of especial interest because of the discoloration of all peripheral parts, including the ears and the tip of the nose The purple discoloration of the hands is sharply defined, extending about two fingers' breadth beyond the wrists; the fingers are glossy; the nails do not show any nutritive disturbances; the lower ends of the forearm bones are swollen. The patient states that the discoloration of the right hand began fully ten years ago. Later on the fingers became *numb and painful.* When the hands were elevated for a long time, cramp set in in fingers and in forearm. Similar symptoms appeared in the lower extremities only a year ago. The feet are œdematous, the toes glossy and purplish, and during the last year the ears and tip of the nose show the same purplish discoloration. Sensation is not disturbed in any part of the body, except for a slight perversion of temperature in hands and feet, and there is no tendency to gangrene.

I do not claim this as a typical case of erythromelalgia, for the vasomotor disturbances preceded the pain by many years; but the patient's condition showed the closest possible resemblance between symptoms evidently due to arterial disease and those of the conditions under discussion. Previous writers have referred to erythromelalgia as being closely allied to the vasomotor neurosis of Nothnagel, to the condition of arterio-spasmus of Martin, to the chronic diffuse erythema of Senator, to the akroparæsthesia of Schultze, and so on; but I am impelled to look for its analogon among the sequelæ of cardiac and arterial diseases. The essential point in the development of the condition appears to be the obliterating endarteritis; and when this endarteritis occurs without central symptoms and with only very slight changes in the peripheral nerves, it is almost self-evident that the arterial disease, if not the primary factor, is at least the immediate cause of the typical symptoms as described by Mitchell. The acceptance of this view does not preclude the theory that in some instances the symptoms of erythromelalgia may be due to disease of the blood vessels—spasm or paralysis—following upon posterior root or peripheral nerve affections. Conclusive evidence of this should, however, be given by the advocates of this view, and I cannot agree with those who insist that the disease is always of central origin, or that the symptoms associated with syringomyelia, with Morvan's disease, etc., are identical with those characteristic of erythromelalgia.

It is puzzling to account for the fact that sensory and vasomotor symptoms predominate in a condition which we would ascribe to an obliterating endarteritis; that they are not the only symptoms, however, is evident from the atrophy present in our first case. Studies on peripheral neuritis, of toxic and traumatic origin, have shown conclusively that the sensory and motor fibres in the peripheral nerves are not always affected equally; that, following injury, motion is more seriously impaired than sensation, while in toxic forms of neuritis the reverse is sometimes the case. On the other hand, obliterating endarteritis may lead at times to a development of motor symptoms to the exclusion of sensory disturbances, as Erb[1] has shown in his recent charming study on intermittent claudication. The anatomical evidence of this is not complete, but the disappearance of the arterial pulses in the foot gives support to the view that the changes in the blood vessels with temporary or permanent occlusion causes this sudden arrest of motor functions. From the viewpoint of pathology, intermittent claudication may be contrasted with erythromelalgia; motor-paralytic symptoms with sen-

[1] Erb: Deutsche Zeitschrift für Nervenheilkunde, Bd. xiii., p. 1, 1898.

sory and vasomotor disturbances—both due to peripheral nerve disease or at least to peripheral nerve disturbance following upon an obliterating endarteritis.

As a result of our studies, imperfect as they are, the questions put at the beginning of this paper may be answered thus: Erythromelalgia cannot be considered a *morbus sui generis;* it is a complex of symptoms which *may* be associated with diseases of central origin, but has been shown to be due to disease of the peripheral arteries. It cannot be denied that this obliterating endarteritis may be caused by central or peripheral nerve disease, but the findings in one of our own cases render this unlikely, and comparison with conditions closely resembling erythromelalgia following upon marked cardiac and arterial disease leads to the inference that this symptom-group may be developed in the presence of arterial disease without any preceding nervous affection. Surely erythromelalgia is as much an arterial as a nerve disease.

XIV.

REPORT OF THE DEPARTMENT OF GENERAL SURGERY.

By ARPAD G. GERSTER, M.D.,
ATTENDING SURGEON.

INTRODUCTORY REMARKS.

Roughly speaking, Mount Sinai Hospital consists of five buildings—two pavilions, of four stories and a basement each, one containing four wards of twenty beds each for the accommodation of male patients, and the other one containing also four similarly equipped wards, three of which are occupied by female patients and the fourth one by children. Between these two pavilions, and serving as a communicating link between them, is situated the administration building. In the rear of the grounds are found the laundry and an isolating pavilion for infectious patients, both being detached and two-storied buildings.

Localities. — The surgical department of Mount Sinai Hospital is situated as follows: Two male wards are in the two upper stories of the South Pavilion, each calculated comfortably to hold twenty beds. In addition to this there are four small rooms adjoining these wards, in which six more patients can be accommodated. This would make the number of available surgical beds for males to be forty-six. But in Male Ward III. ten must be deducted from this number as belonging to the genito-urinary department. On the other hand, it must be said that, as urgent cases of strangulated hernia, intestinal obstruction, and appendicitis are never turned away if it can be helped, the press of important material is constantly so great that from four to six cots are placed in the open spaces of each ward for the berthing of convalescents during the night-time.

In the North Pavilion the second ward is reserved for twenty (20) female surgical patients. Adjoining the ward there is additionally a small room for one patient, and another somewhat larger room for six children suffering from surgical maladies. As on the male side, so here also from four to six cots are introduced nightly for convalescents.

From these statements it will be seen that there are at the disposition of the general surgical service altogether sixty-two beds, that is, thirty-six beds filled with male and twenty-six beds with female patients. This does not, of course, include the additional fourteen cots, the use of which has become sanctioned by usage, which again was rendered unavoidable by the necessities of an over-crowded service. The actual number of surgical patients is rarely less than seventy-six. Even then convalescent patients have frequently to be discharged before their cure is fully accomplished, in order to yield their beds to others urgently needing life-saving operations.

On the second floor of the middle—that is, the administration — building there are fourteen rooms for the housing of private patients. Our two operating rooms, with the adjoining room for anæsthesia, are on the third floor of this building, communication with which and the wards is maintained by corridors and three elevators. The older operating room was never meant to be an operating room, and lacks almost all modern requirements, especially proper lighting. It is used for the operation of septic cases. The new aseptic operating room is better; yet it is too small, cramped, and also lacks proper light, but is fitted out according to modern ideas. In the hallway connecting the operating rooms stand the distilling tanks for hot and cold water (Kay-Sprague), of indifferent quality. A large apparatus

(Lautenschlager), used for the sterilizing of dressings, gowns, towels, etc., is placed in the basement of the North Pavilion and yields very satisfactory results. The sterilizing of the instruments is done in each operating room by means of a Schimmelbusch apparatus. There is no provision made for a room in which dressings can be made and properly stored, none for the recovery of operated patients from anæsthesia, none for the dressing and undressing of surgeons and nurses. The most serious of these defects, however, are the first two, and of these especially the second one. There are constantly in each ward from two to six recently operated laparotomy patients, more or less noisy and restless, and a great trial to all the other sufferers in the ward.

Personnel.—The government of the Department of General Surgery was, since October, 1896, entrusted to a visiting surgeon aided by two adjunct surgeons. The term of service of the visiting surgeon was ten months of every year, allowing two months for his summer vacation. One of the adjunct surgeons is constantly on duty with the visiting surgeon, each of the former devoting five months to this service alternately. During the vacation of the visiting surgeon the adjuncts act as visiting surgeons, evenly dividing the beds of the department between themselves.

The simultaneous service of the visiting and of one of the adjunct surgeons offers many important advantages and deserves special mention. Both adjuncts being, though younger, yet thoroughly competent and experienced surgeons, one of them always sharing the clinical work of the department, a temporary or longer detention of the visiting surgeon by illness or any other cause can never occasion delay or interruption of current business—an immense advantage to patients and to the institution. The burdens are fairly and properly distributed among the visiting and adjunct surgeon and the members of the house staff, but direction and responsibility are concentrated in one hand, insuring harmonious and orderly co-operation without clash or conflict of authority. Unstinted credit and praise are due to Adjunct Surgeons Dr. W. W. Van Arsdale and Dr. Howard Lilienthal for the unflagging zeal and high efficiency displayed by both of them, especially under the trying conditions of the ever-increasing emergency and night work, which rested entirely on their shoulders.

Assistance is performed by a surgical house staff composed of seven men, three of whom, the house surgeon and his senior and junior assistants, are residents. Of these men, five are composing the house staff proper, being in regular line of promotion, their term of service comprising two years and a half. Thus it is seen that before entering upon his arduous and responsible duties, the house surgeon must have served two full years in the department. It must be stated that this prolongation of the service of the house staff has borne excellent fruit in every way, insuring to the Hospital, on the whole, an efficient and fairly trained corps of assistants. The ancient abuse, according to which the house surgeon monopolized all the work, being followed about at rounds by a train of idle assistants, has been abated in so much, that the after-treatment is now equally distributed among all the assistants. The house surgeon now reserves personal care only of the most important cases, controlling, however, and supervising the work of his subordinates in a systematic manner.

In addition to the five members of the house staff, there are attached to this service two provisional assistants, or dressers, whose term of service is one year, and who furnish needed help in emergencies as well as in the regular routine work of the department.

With the knowledge of the fact that a well-ordered and intelligently executed routine insures a tremendous saving of time, eliminates friction, resulting in a prompt and thorough despatch of the work in hand, the following time schedule has been adopted and invariably carried through since October, 1896:

Monday. Operative clinic, 2:30 P.M.

Tuesday. Operative clinic, 2:30 P.M.

Wednesday. General visit, 8:30 A.M.

Thursday. Operative clinic, 8:30 A.M.

Friday. Operative clinic, 2:30 P.M.

Saturday. Cystoscopic examinations and examinations under anæsthesia, 8:30 A.M.

Sunday. General visit, 9:30 A.M.

The hours were carefully selected so as not to interfere with the work of the aural and eye surgeon, the genito-urinary surgeon, or the gynæcologist; the visits timed in the early morning, so as not to lead to the unnecessary annoyance of the patients caused by a second change of dressings, which becomes unavoidable if the surgeon's visits fall in the afternoon or are irregular. The coincidence of morning rounds with the visit of the attending surgeon favors a much deeper scrutiny of the conduct of the bedside service, than irregular and erratic afternoon visits, when operations are going on, and the full house staff cannot be present. A number of other extremely important advantages, too well known to every clinician to require special mention, accrue to all concerned from this sacrifice of personal convenience and time, made by the attending surgeon. The chief advantage is reaped by the patient.

Histories.—The greatest stress was laid on the careful compilation and preservation of the histories, the most essential part of our routine being the rule that facts to be recorded are to be written down immediately at the time of observation, the writing of histories being thus done currently in the wards.

EXTRACT FROM RULES GOVERNING THE CARE OF HISTORIES IN THE GENERAL SURGICAL SERVICE.

1. The house surgeon must ascertain twice weekly whether all the histories are written up to date.

Notes are to be entered in the ward and preferably during the visit, and at the time of the observation of the phenomena to be noted.

2. The senior assistant surgeon shall be responsible for the care, fulness, and accuracy of histories of patients in, or discharged from, the wards during his tenure of seniorship, and shall hold himself ready at all times to produce for the house surgeon or attending surgeon any of such histories.

3. The histories of patients on admission are to be taken by the senior surgeon.

4. The descriptions of operations shall be immediately entered on the history sheets, in the proper place, by the senior surgeon.

5*a*. The house surgeon shall assign to each of his junior assistants a certain number of beds, the histories of the patients occupying which, it shall be the duty of the junior assistant to inscribe from time to time, so as to have all the histories of the service written up to date for the visiting surgeon's visits on Sundays and Wednesdays.

5*b*. The junior surgeon and the two provisional assistant surgeons shall enter on the history sheets all notes recording the progress of a case other than those mentioned under (3) and (4). These notes shall include the physical examination of the patient on admission, dictated by the house surgeon, together with a dictation of the *status præsens* of a patient whenever the house surgeon deems a change in condition worthy of special note.

During the stay of a patient in the hospital, notes as to his general condition, the progress of the wound, etc., shall be entered on the history sheets at frequent intervals, at least twice a week, and, in important cases, oftener.

6. The senior surgeon shall exercise a supervision over the entering of history notes. He shall twice a week inspect the history sheets and order the entering of any notes, not at variance with those dictated by the house surgeon. He shall see that all notes are neatly, accurately, and promptly recorded, and that any mistake in the entries is rectified by the assistant responsible for it. He may, in his discretion, require the rewriting of a history or a portion thereof.

8. At intervals of not more than a week the senior surgeon shall collect from the various wards the history sheets and clinical records of patients discharged, or of those who have died since his last collection.

9. After the histories of patients discharged have been collected by the senior, he shall distribute them to the junior assistants for the entry of the final notes by them.

These final notes shall be entered without delay, and the histories and clinical record returned to the senior within a week after their distribution to the junior assistants. The diagnosis is to be written plainly at the top of the first history sheet. Where the history occupies more than one page, each successive page shall be labelled in small letters, at the top, with the name of the patient and the number or letter of the page. Postmortem findings, if there be any, are to be recorded at the end of the history. Fever charts or diagrams are to be pasted to the history sheets in their proper places, and all the sheets are to be pinned together in order.

The last sheet of each clinical record shall be marked "O. K.," with the name or initials of the junior assistant, as an indication that all the requisite entries have been made, and that all the history sheets are intact and in order.

10. At intervals of not more than one month the senior is required to page, index, and sign all completed histories, and to file them away in such a manner that they may at any time be consulted.

11. The indexing is to be both by names of patients and by their diseases. The indexing by diseases is to be so arranged that it shall be a ready guide to the histories of patients suffering from those diseases. Thus "fracture of femur" is to be indexed under the headings of "femur" and of "fracture," etc.

12. Promptly at the end of his term of office the senior shall turn over the histories of patients discharged during the past six months, with accompanying indices, to the clerk of the Hospital, from whom he shall take a receipt for the same.

Where convenience of form requires it, the histories shall be turned over to the clerk quarterly, each quarter of histories to be bound in a separate volume with separate indices.

13. Where the junior assistant makes the final entries in a history not yet distributed to him by the senior, he shall leave the history in the ward in the care of the head nurse. Nor shall the head nurse allow histories or clinical records to be removed from the ward by any

one except the senior surgeon or his superior officers, or by such persons as they may direct.

16. Where the nurse in charge discovers the loss or mutilation of any clinical records or history sheets, she shall report such loss or mutilation to the senior without undue delay.

Where any record or portion of a record is missing, the senior shall institute a search for it, report its absence to the house surgeon, who, in his turn, must report it to the visiting surgeon.

17. When a patient is transferred to another service (medical, gynæcological, children's, or eye and ear), the senior surgeon shall direct the transfer with the patient of a copy of the history of the case written up to the time of the transfer.

Similarly, when a patient is received in a general surgical ward from another service, the senior surgeon shall require that a copy of the history of the case, written up to the time of the transfer, shall accompany the patient.

18. The senior shall keep a record of the number of histories received from each ward, with the date of their receipt, and of the number of histories distributed to, and returned by, the junior surgeons with the dates of the distribution and return. Such record must tally with the record of discharges and deaths as kept in the books of the Hospital.

19. In all the regulations above laid down, the senior surgeon and the junior surgeons shall be in all respects subject to the orders of the house surgeon.

Nursing.—Both the male and female wards of the surgical service are in the charge of female nurses supplied by the Training School connected with the Hospital. In the male wards their labors are lightened by an appropriate number of male orderlies; but the functions of nursing proper are exclusively performed by nurses. In important cases demanding special care, the management has always liberally provided as many extra nurses as were required.

Operating Rooms.—The operating rooms are in the exclusive care of a reliable and well-trained orderly, who is aided by two assistants. He has the care of the instruments, has to prepare sponges, suture and ligature material, superintends the sterilizing and distribution of the dressings, and is responsible for the orderly and clean condition of the entire plant. The plumbing being all freely exposed, the maintenance of scrupulous cleanliness is not difficult, though, on account of the vast amount of active work, very laborious and never ceasing. In addition to the regular staff of orderlies, two female nurses, not on duty in the surgical department, are detailed in turn to the service of the operating room, where they assist at operations for four weeks each, thus gaining experience and steadiness through the strict schooling of operating room discipline. The head nurse of the wards from which the patient is brought to the operating room has to stand by and assist the anæsthetizer.

REPORT OF ANÆSTHESIAS

IN THE SURGICAL, GYNÆCOLOGICAL, AND EYE AND EAR SERVICES, FOR YEAR ENDING NOVEMBER 30, 1898.

General Anæsthesias..................... 1,388.

Chloroform	631	Ether to chloroform	12
Ether	94	" " Schleich No. 3	1
Schleich No. 1	33	Schleich No. 3 to chloroform	25
Schleich No. 2	23	" " 1 " Schleich No. 3	1
Schleich No. 3	391	" " 3 " ether	3
Nitrous oxide gas	84	" " 2 " chloroform	1
Chloroform to ether[1]	48	Nitrous oxide gas to ether	7
Chloroform to Schleich No. 1	4	Nitrous oxide gas to chloroform	1
" " " " 2	8	Eucaine to chloroform	3
" " " " 3	18		

Local Anæsthesias..................... 133

Cocaine, 2%	18	Eucaine, 10%	1
" 4%	22	Ethyl chloride spray	35
" 6%	17	Ether spray	6
Eucaine, 1%	1	Cocaine spray	17
" 6%	16		

[1] The word "to" placed between the names of two anæsthetics indicates that a change was made from the first-mentioned to the second, before or during an operation.

For many years the number of chloroform administrations in this Hospital has greatly preponderated over the number of anæsthesias induced by ether or other general narcotic. The reasons for this are set forth below.

A comparison of this year's report with that of 1897 shows both a relative and an absolute diminution in the number of chloroform anæsthesias. This has not been because of any loss of faith in chloroform for general adaptability in hospital surgical work, but because chloroform was, to a considerable extent, temporarily abandoned in order to make an experimental and comparative study of other anæsthetics.

Schleich's General Anæsthetics.—Schleich's anæsthetic mixtures were given an almost exclusive trial in all the surgical departments of this Hospital for seven months, from December 1, 1897, until June 30, 1898. After that they were abandoned completely.

During those seven months nearly five hundred anæsthesias were administered by all three of the Schleich mixtures.

Briefly stated, our observations during those trials were as follows:

Schleich's mixtures of chloroform and ether, without having the advantages of either ingredient, possess, by very reason of their admixture, the dangers of both.

In those cases where chloroform should have the preference the bad effects of ether were not eliminated, and *vice versa;* and, withal, the anæsthetizer was ever at a loss to appreciate—which is the vital point in all anæsthesias—how much chloroform, how much ether, his patient was absorbing.

It may be said that the Schleich mixtures are more pleasant to inhale than either chloroform or ether. But this advantage is more than counterbalanced by the following disadvantages: Schleich anæsthesias are slower to induce; the eye reflexes are usually lost early and frequently are entirely unreliable; for these reasons a patient unexpectedly reacting during an operation may strain and struggle for several minutes before again reduced to complete relaxation; vomiting after operation is just as frequent and prolonged as after the administration of ether or chloroform.

The claim that the administration of the Schleich mixtures requires less care and less watchfulness than the use of chloroform or ether is, to say the least, vicious in purpose and result.

Ether.—This anæsthetic is given the preference by the heads of the genito-urinary and eye and ear departments. By the head of the gynæcological division, where no special indication exists to the contrary, ether is preferred for long operations, chloroform for short ones. For operations in the general surgical department ether is occasionally administered when a cardiac lesion of bad type contraindicates the use of chloroform.

A comparative study of the effects of ether and chloroform upon the kidney secretion was recently completed here, with the view to supplementing from the clinical standpoint the experimental work of Drs. Thompson and Kemp at the College of Physicians and Surgeons.

A hundred anæsthesias, with complete data, were recorded—about 50 being chloroform narcoses, 45 ether, and 5 nitrous oxide gas.

Without printing here the elaborate tables prepared, it will suffice to say that the results were negative. That is, there was no change observed in the urine, either immediate or remote, after the administration of chloroform or ether, with the following exceptions: a diminution in the total amount of urine excreted during the first twenty-four hours after operation, which diminution was as noticeable after chloroform as after ether; occasional excess of urates; one brief glycosuria after chloroform.

In none of these 100 cases was there a pre-existing renal complication.

Chloroform.—As above stated, this is the anæsthetic

most frequently employed. It is administered almost as a matter of routine for our general surgical operations. Just as renal or pulmonary lesions contraindicate the use of ether, so in the presence of a cardiac disease of severe type chloroform is abandoned. An old endocarditis of mild type, especially one without marked circulatory disturbances, does not here interfere with the administration of chloroform, however.

That chloroform is a depressant to the heart, and therefore a dangerous anæsthetic when incautiously administered, is recognized in spite of its free use in this institution.

Nevertheless it has been noticed repeatedly that respiratory paralysis, on the table, is far more frequent during chloroformization than is cardiac failure.

Anæsthetics are administered by members of the house staff, but no man is trusted to narcotize alone until he has watched others repeatedly and until he has administered frequently under the guidance of one more experienced.

For general surgical operations a hypodermatic injection of one-fifth or one sixth of a grain of morphine is frequently made just before the operation is begun, where the latter is apt to be prolonged, or where the quantity of the narcotic required to produce anæsthesia should be for any reason minimized. The same thing is done as a matter of routine in patients who are habitual users of alcohol.

The administration of stimulants before or during an operation is reserved for special occasions.

Artificial respiration for respiratory and strychnine for cardiac weakness are the first means employed in those emergencies. Stimulating enemata are occasionally exhibited before, during, or after an operation, to bolster a flagging heart.

Intravenous saline infusion (the quantity varying) is similarly administered for, or as a prophylactic against, collapse. Infusions of that nature are made by one or two of the house staff during an operation without interfering with the progress of the latter. [See Report of Infusions, page 220.]

There occurred two deaths from the administration of chloroform this year. These deaths were both of patients with cardiac disease of advanced type, where ether was considered ineligible on account of bronchitis in one case, and nephritis in the other.

1898, vol. i., page 325. *Dorsal-iliac Dislocation of Hip: Endocarditis; Chloroform Anæsthesia; Death.*—Moritz S., 72 years old, admitted February 21. Had been thrown to the ground by cable car twenty-four hours previously; carried home, where doctor diagnosed fracture of shaft of femur and applied temporary side splints. No other injuries or symptoms.

Patient complained of severe pain from the splints and begged that they be removed. Right lower extremity found in typical posture of dorsal-iliac dislocation. General condition of patient good; loud systolic murmur heard at apex of heart; arteries atheromatous. Patient requested an anæsthetic to relieve pain from examination of hip. Under chloroform narcosis crepitus was detected in the joint. When relaxation of the patient had just been accomplished, the pulse, suddenly and without warning, ceased, and, despite every effort to restore it, the patient died. Cardiac paralysis preceded respiratory failure by several seconds.

Postmortem.—Heart not enlarged, but walls flabby; atheroma of all aortic cusps; insufficiency of both aortic and mitral valves; coronary arteries atheromatous. Lungs: congestion and some œdema of both. Kidneys: capsules slightly adherent. Liver: chronic congestion. Spleen: small. Hip-joint: dorsal-iliac dislocation and fracture of edge of acetabulum.

1898, vol. ii., page 395. *Mammary Abscesses; Bronchitis; Nephritis; Operation; Chloroform Anæsthesia; Death.*—Sophie H., 26 years old. Admitted September 15. Four weeks ago confinement at full term. One week later pelvic inflammation developed, and shortly after mastitis on the right side. Abscess developed in right breast. Fever, chills, and moderate prostration.

Both breasts the seat of extensive suppuration. Sibilant and crepitant râles heard at both lung apices. Heart action tumultuous. Slight systolic murmur over aortic valve. Pulse, 108; respiration, 28; temperature, 99°. Urine contained albumin and a few hyaline and granular casts. During the night temperature rose to 104°. September 16: In the morning both breasts freely incised under chloroform narcosis. While the dressings were being applied, and fully ten minutes after the withdrawal of the anæsthetic, pulse became weak and face cyanotic. Stimulation, etc., immediately resorted to, but the heart did not respond. Cessation of respiration appeared an appreciable time after cardiac failure. No autopsy.

No death from ether has occurred during the past year, but there has been a noticeable number of cases of bronchitis and broncho-pneumonia following its use (cases which occasionally, in the past, have terminated fatally).

Nitrous Oxide Gas is administered in the usual manner. It is worthy of record, however, that an amputation of the thigh was performed under nitrous oxide anæsthesia on an old woman whose other thigh had been similarly amputated during the previous hospital year. [See case of H. S., page 163.]

Nitrous Oxide to Ether.—After administering nitrous oxide to a degree of moderately deep narcosis, ether can be substituted for the laughing gas, the anæsthesia being continued, as a rule, without a break and without a struggle. This is a saving in time; avoids the choking sensations inseparable from the first ether inhalations; and, for nervous patients especially, robs the etherization of much of its terrors.

Local Anæsthesias.—Eucaine was employed by Dr. Lilienthal in preference to cocaine, being non-toxic when used freely. He employs it in strengths of 6 per cent, 10 per cent, and 15 per cent. Several major operations have been performed under eucaine local anæsthesia. Of these a number were laparotomies. One, for example, was an inguinal colostomy for intestinal obstruction from carcinoma recti in an old man. Herniotomies, gastroenterostomies, etc., have been similarly performed. Under the heading of general anæsthesia will be found "eucaine to chloroform, 3." These represent three major operations which were undertaken under eucaine, but where general anæsthesia had to be substituted. Of these three operations one was a herniotomy performed on a demented man in poor physical condition, who could not be instructed to lie quiet. The second was an inguinal colostomy performed upon a woman with specific stricture of the rectum and syphilitic cachexia. She likewise suffered little or no pain from the manipulations under local anæsthesia, but was too hysterical to submit to them. The third operation was a Murphy-button resection requiring complete relaxation in order to permit of more extensive intestinal manipulation than was anticipated. One laparotomy was performed under cocaine for intraperitoneal abscess. The patient was a boy operated upon before for appendicitis, abscess, general peritonitis. After two weeks of apparently excellent convalescence the child had a relapse of fever, pain, and vomiting; pain and tenderness on the left side; pulse rate, 190; condition of collapse. General anæsthesia being inadmissible, an exploratory incision under cocaine was made in the left iliac region. Free collection of pus found, evacuated, drained. Twice after the operation an intravenous infusion of normal salt solution was made. Discharged cured. Eucaine, cocaine, etc., render the superficial (injected) tissues anæsthetic. Manipulation of the deeper parts (liver, intestine, etc.) is for the most part painless. It has been repeatedly noticed, however, that the ligating of blood vessels not lying within the anæsthetized area is quite painful.

WALTER M. BRICKNER, *House Surgeon.*

DISEASES TREATED IN THE DEPARTMENT OF GENERAL SURGERY.

TOTAL.......... 898

	Operation.			No operation.			Cured.			Improved.			Unimproved.			No treatment.			Died.			Totals.		
	M	W	C	M	W	C	M	W	C	M	W	C	M	W	C	M	W	C	M	W	C	M	W	C
Scalp—5.																								
Cellulitis of..	..	..	1	..	..	..	..	..	1	..	..	..	..	..	..	..	..	..	..	..	..	..	..	1
Contusion of, and lacerated wound of face	..	..	..	..	1	..	..	..	..	..	1	..	..	..	..	..	..	..	..	..	..	..	1	..
" " and rupture of tympanic membrane	..	..	..	..	1	..	..	1	..	..	..	..	..	..	..	..	..	..	..	..	..	..	1	..
Lacerated wound of	..	..	..	1	..	..	1	..	..	..	..	..	..	..	..	..	..	..	..	..	..	1	..	..
Sebaceous cyst of	1	..	..	..	..	..	1	..	..	..	..	..	..	..	..	..	..	..	..	..	..	1	..	..
Cranium—3.																								
Fracture of	..	..	..	..	..	..	..	..	..	..	..	..	..	..	..	..	..	1	..	..	..	..	..	1
" ", erysipelas	..	..	..	..	..	1	..	..	..	..	..	..	..	..	..	..	..	..	..	..	1	..	..	1
Mastoid, empyema of	1	..	..	..	..	..	1	..	..	..	..	..	..	..	..	..	..	..	..	..	..	1	..	..
Brain and Cranial Nerves—5.																								
Gunshot wound of, Jacksonian epilepsy, hemiplegia	..	..	..	1	..	..	..	..	..	1	..	..	..	..	..	..	..	..	..	..	..	1	..	..
Ophthalmoplegia externa	..	..	..	..	1	..	..	1	..	..	..	..	..	..	..	..	..	..	..	..	..	..	1	..
Trifacial neuralgia	1	1	..	..	..	..	1	1	..	..	..	..	..	..	..	..	..	..	..	..	..	1	1	..
Inferior dental neuralgia	1	..	..	..	..	..	1	..	..	..	..	..	..	..	..	..	..	..	..	..	..	1	..	..
Face and Mouth—38.																								
Face—11.																								
Burns of, and arms	..	..	..	..	1	..	..	1	..	..	..	..	..	..	..	..	..	..	..	..	..	..	1	..
" " " hands	..	..	..	1	..	..	1	..	..	..	..	..	..	..	..	..	..	..	..	..	..	1	..	..
" " " head	..	..	..	1	..	..	1	..	..	..	..	..	..	..	..	..	..	..	..	..	..	1	..	..
Hæmatoma of, hæmophilia	..	..	..	..	..	1	..	..	..	..	..	1	..	..	..	..	..	..	..	..	..	..	..	1
Parotitis, suppurative, chronic cystitis	..	1	..	..	..	..	..	..	..	..	1	..	..	..	..	..	..	..	..	..	..	..	1	..
Phlegmon of	1	..	..	..	..	..	1	..	..	..	..	..	..	..	..	..	..	..	..	..	..	1	..	..

	Operation.			No operation.			Cured.			Improved.			Unimproved.			No treatment.			Died.			Totals.		
	M	W	C	M	W	C	M	W	C	M	W	C	M	W	C	M	W	C	M	W	C	M	W	C
Face and Mouth—*Continued.*																								
Face—Continued.																								
Abscess of	1						1															1		
Phlegmon of	2						1												1			2		
Cellulitis of nose	1						1															1		
Carbuncle of lip	1	1					1	1														2		
Nose—5.																								
Epistaxis				1			1															1		
Epithelioma of	1	1					1	1														1	1	
Septum, deflection of	1									1												1		
Specific ulcer of		1						1															1	
Oral Cavity—8.																								
Alveolar abscess		1						1															1	
Harelip, cleft palate, marasmus			1																		1			1
Lacerated wound of lip	1				1	1	1	1	1													1	1	1
Submaxillary salivary calculus	1						1															1		
Tongue, epithelioma of	1						1															1		
" tubercular ulcer of				1			1															1		
Superior Maxilla—5.																								
Antrum of Highmore, empyema of		1						1															1	
Periostitis of			1						1															1
Sarcoma of		1						1															1	
" " and of abdomen						1						1												1
Tumor of		1						1															1	
Inferior Maxilla—14.																								
Osteomyelitis of	2	3	4	1			2	3	3	1		1										2	3	4
Periostitis of		2						1			1												2	
Sarcoma of	1						1										1					1	1	
Neck—28.																								
Abscess of	3						2												1			3		

Neck—*Continued.*																								
Abscess of, septic infection of glands, general streptococcus sepsis	1						1															1		
" " submaxillary		1						1															1	
Cellulitis of	1						1															1		
Parotitis	1						1															1		
Adenitis, tubercular	1	5	4				1	4	4		1											1	5	4
" suppurative			1						1															1
" submaxillary				1			1															1		
Carbuncle of	2						2															2		
Carcinoma of, supraclavicular, recurrent		1						1															1	
Goitre, hyperplastic	1		1				1		1													1		1
Lipoma of		1						1															1	
Cyst of, pre-thyroid			1						1															1
Sinus of, tubercular	1									1												1		
Contusions of, and head			1						1															1
Pharynx and Larynx—4.																								
Larynx, carcinoma of	1			1						1									1			2		
Pharynx, abscess of, retropharyngeal			1						1															1
Burns of, nitric acid					1			1															1	
Carcinoma of, recurrent	1						1															1		
Shoulder—8.																								
Arthritis of, tubercular	1						1															1		
Furunculosis of, and back	1						1															1		
Lipoma of	1	2					1	2														1	2	
Fracture of clavicle				1			1															1		
Axilla—3.																								
Abscess of	1		1				1		1													1		1
Adenitis of, tubercular			1						1															1
Sarcoma of, recurrent	1									1												1		
Arm—10.																								
Humerus, osteomyelitis of			1						1															1
Dislocation of, subcoracoid	1						1															1		
" " subglenoid					1						1												1	

	Operation.			No operation.			Cured.			Improved.			Unimproved.			No treatment.			Died.			Total.		
	M	W	C	M	W	C	M	W	C	M	W	C	M	W	C	M	W	C	M	W	C	M	W	C
Arm—*Continued.*																								
Humerus.																								
Fracture of, T-shape, lower end						1			1															1
Burns of, and body					1			1															1	
" " " back		1						1															1	
Lipoma of	1	2					1	2														1	2	
Cellulitis of	1						1															1		
Forearm—18.																								
Ulna and radius, fracture of				1						1												1		
Fracture of, badly united			1									1												1
Ununited fracture of			1						1															1
" " " and first metacarpal bone					1			1															1	
Fracture of both radii, right ulna, and first metacarpal bone					1			1															1	
Ulna, paralysis from injury during operation				1						1												1		
Radius, abscess of, subperiosteal			1						1															1
Fracture of				1			1															1		
" " Colles'				1			1															1		
Elbow—5: Ankylosis of			1									1												1
Arthritis of, suppurative	1					1			1													1		1
" " tubercular			1						1															1
Burns of				1					1													1		
Hand—22.																								
Arthritis of phalanges, tubercular	1															1						1		
" " wrist, tubercular					1			1															1	
" " metacarpo-phalangeal articulation	1						1															1		
Cellulitis of	3	4					2	3		1							1					3	4	
" " diabetic		2																		2			2	
Osteomyelitis of metacarpal bones	1						1															1		
Gangrene of fingers	1	1					1	1														1	1	
Gangrene of fingers, thumb, and palmar fascia			1						1															1
Burns of		1						1															1	

Hand—*Continued.*																								
Burns of, and face				1			1															1		
" " " breast					1																		1	
Fracture of metacarpus, compound				1			1															1		
" " phalanx, comminuted				1						1												1		
Lacerated wound of fingers	1						1															1		
Thorax—20.																								
Chest, abscess of, subcutaneous	1		1				1		1													1		1
Abscess of, broncho-pneumonia			1																		1			1
Burns of	1			1			2															2		
Empyema of	3	1					1	1		1									1			3	1	
" " axillary abscess		1						1															1	
" " pyæmia and lobar pneumonia	1	1						1											1			1	1	
" " and subphrenic abscess	1	1					1	1														1	1	
Contusions of					1			1															1	
Dermoid cyst of mediastinum and sepsis	1																		1			1		
Osteomyelitis of sternum, chondritis	1																					1		
" " ribs, osteitis of spine, tubercular		1						1															1	
Tuberculosis of ribs, sternum, and pleura	1							1														1	1	
" " spine, residual psoas abscess		1									1									1			1	
Back—9.																								
Carbuncles of	3	1					2	1											1			3	1	
" " diabetic	3						2												1			3		
Lipoma of	2						2															2		
Lumbo-sacral Region—5.																								
Abscess of																								
Dermoid cyst, sacral region	1			1			1															2		
" " coccygeal region	1			1	1		1			1	1											2	1	
Tumor of spinal cord				1						1												1		

	Operation.			No operation.			Cured.			Improved.			Not improved.			No treatment.			Died.			Totals.		
	M	W	C	M	W	C	M	W	C	M	W	C	M	W	C	M	W	C	M	W	C	M	W	C
Pelvis and Groin—3.																								
Abscess of, dissecting		1						1															1	
" " psoas	1		1				1		1													1		1
Breast—28.																								
Abscess of, multiple		1						1															1	
Abscess of, broncho-pneumonia, tubercular osteomyelitis of ribs		2						2															2	
Mastitis of, suppurative, cardiac failure from chloroform		1																		1			1	
" " acute suppurative	1	4					1	4														1	4	
" " intracanalicular		1						1															1	
" " chronic	1	1					1	1														1	1	
Adenoma of		1						1															1	
Adenofibroma of		2						2															2	
Carcinoma of		9						4						1			2			1			9	
" " recurrent		2						2															2	
" " recurrent, carcinoma pulmonum					1															1			1	
" " Paget's disease, decubitus					1															1			1	
Abdominal Wall—2.																								
Abscess of		1						1															1	
Lipoma of	1						1															1		
Stomach and Œsophagus—9.																								
Carcinoma of œsophagus	2									1									1			2		
" " " and transverse colon	1																		1			1		
" " stomach	1	1												1					1			1	1	
Stricture of œsophagus, inanition			1						1															1
Traumatic œsophagitis				1			1															1		
Ulcer of stomach, perforated, general peritonitis					1															1			1	
" " " thrombosis of splenic vein		1																		1			1	

Liver—11.																								
Abscess of	2			1			1									1						3		
" " necrosis of gall bladder, ischio-rectal abscess, diabetes, cellulitis of hand		1						1															1	
Abscess of, thrombosis of portal vein	1																		1			1		
Carcinoma of liver and peritoneum	1																		1			1		
" " " intestinal obstruction		1																		1			1	
Cirrhosis of		1																		1			1	
Congestion of	1						1															1		
Echinococcus cyst of, hepatic and subphrenic abscess	1																		1			1		
" " " liver	1						1															1		
Gall Bladder—15.																								
Calculus of common bile duct, empyema, pyonephrosis, cardiac asthenia		1																		1			1	
Carcinoma of gall bladder, cholelithiasis, thrombosis of mesenteric artery		1																		1			1	
Cholecystitis purulenta, obstruction of duodenum	1																		1			1		
Cholelithiasis	1	8			2		1	8			1									1		1	10	
" choledochotomy, embolism		1																		1			1	
Spleen—1.																								
Traumatic rupture of, peritonitis			1																					1
Pancreas—1.																								
Acute pancreatitis		1									1												1	
Intestines—7.																								
Adenoma of colon	1						1															1		
Carcinoma of colon	1			1			1			1												2		
Colloid carcinoma of sigmoid flexure and peritoneum, perforation of intestine	1																		1			1		
Intestinal adhesion		1									1												1	
" autointoxication				1			1															1		
Tuberculosis of intestines and suprarenal, tubercular enteritis, multiple perforation of the intestine		1																		1			1	
Intestinal Obstruction—5.																								
Intussusception			1																		1			1

	Operation.			No operation.			Cured.			Improved.			Unimproved.			No treatment.			Died.			Totals.		
	M	W	C	M	W	C	M	W	C	M	W	C	M	W	C	M	W	C	M	W	C	M	W	C
Intestinal Obstruction—*Continued.*																								
Intussusception and gangrene of gut			1																		1			1
Intestinal obstruction, chronic	1																		1			1		
" " idiopathic intestinal paresis	1																		1			1		
" " internal strangulation of ileum into peritoneal fold in posterior cul-de-sac		1						1															1	
General Abdominal Cavity—150.																								
Hæmatoma of omentum	1						1															1		
Lympho-sarcoma of peritoneum, abdominal viscera, and mesenteric glands primary in duodenum			1																		1			1
Sinus, abdominal		1						1															1	
Tuberculosis of mesenteric glands	1									1												1		
Tumor of abdomen, fæcal impaction					1						1												1	
Appendicitis, acute catarrhal	17	18	4				16	18	3							1		1				18	18	5
" " " dermoid ovarian cyst, premature labor		1						1															1	
abscess	28	11	12				28	11	12													28	11	12
" " secondary hemorrhage, gangrene of colon	1																		1			1		
" " secondary, hypostatic congestion of the lungs	1																		1			1		
" " sepsis	1																		1			1		
" " " septic hemorrhage of ileum, intra-intestinal			1																		1			1
" " sepsis, septic hemorrhages of the lungs		1																		1			1	
" adhesions	1						1															1		
" congenital absence of appendix, intestinal adhesions			1						1															1
" empyema of appendix	3	1	1				3		1											1		3	1	1
" gangrenous	1						1															1		
" " sepsis	6																		1			1		
" diffuse peritonitis	1	1	4				4		3										2	1	1	6	1	4

General Abdominal Cavity—*Continued*.																								
Appendicitis, diffuse peritonitis, acute mania	2	2		2	1															1		2	2	
" " " intestinal obstruction	2		1				1		1										1			2		1
" " " subphrenic abscess, empyema	1						1															1		
" " purulent peritonitis	4		2																4		2	4		2
" " " " sepsis			1						1															1
" pericarditis, suppression of urine		1																		1			1	
" diffuse purulent peritonitis, operation, enterostomy, subsequent resection of the gut for fæcal fistula, inanition	1																		1			1		
" perforation, sepsis, septic pneumonia		1																		1			1	
" periproctitis	1						1															1		
" recurrent	1						1															1		
" secondary	1						1															1		
" sinus	2		1	1	1	1	2	1	2				1									3	1	2
" " fæcal fistula	1						1															1		
" sepsis, diffuse peritonitis																								
" tumor of ileum, diffuse peritonitis	1																		1			1		
" ulceration	1						1															1		
Perityphlitic abscess		1						1															1	
Pelvic abscess		1						1															1	
Tubercular peritonitis	1																		1			1		
																						81	39	30
Herniæ—63.																								
Hernia, inguinal—54:																								
" " indirect, reducible	21	2	3				21	2	3							3						24	2	3
" " reducible, double	3						3															3		
" " " congenital	1						1															1		
" " " sapræmia, sepsis	1																		1			1		
" " " with hydrocele	1						1															1		
" " " " varicocele	3						3															3		
" " irreducible	2						2															2		
" " " congenital	1						1															1		
" " " incarcerated				1						1												1		

	Operation.			No operation.			Cured.			Improved.			Unimproved.			No treatment.			Died.			Total.		
	M	W	C	M	W	C	M	W	C	M	W	C	M	W	C	M	W	C	M	W	C	M	W	C
Herniæ—*Continued.*																								
Hernia, inguinal, irreducible, strangulated	7						6												1			7		
Inguinal, indirect, irreducible, strangulated, with gangrene of intestine		2																		2			2	
Inguinal, indirect, irreducible, strangulation of descended ovary, pseudo-hermaphroditism			1						1															1
Inguinal, direct		1						1															1	
" " strangulated		1						1															1	
Hernia, femoral—5:																								
" " strangulated	2	1					2	1														2	1	
" " strangulated sac		2						2															2	
Hernia, umbilical—3:																								
" " single, reducible		1						1															1	
" " abscess		1						1															1	
" " strangulated		1						1															1	
Hernia, lumbar—1: plumbism				1						1												1		
Hernia, internal [see Intestinal Obstruction.]																								
Genito-Urinary Diseases—114.																								
Kidney—25.																								
Acute congestion of		1						1															1	
Cyst of, cystitis	1									1												1		
Sarcoma of		1						1															1	
" " recurrence	1						1															1		
Malignant tumor of		1																		1			1	
Tuberculosis of		1						1															1	
Renal calculus																	1						1	
" " pyelo-nephritis		2						2															2	
" " pyonephrosis		2						1			1												2	
" " sarcoma of kidney, recurrence, general sarcomatosis	1																		1			1		
Pyelitis, sexual neurasthenia				1						1												1		

Genito-Urinary Diseases—*Continued.*[1]																								
Kidney—Continued.																								
Pyelo-nephritis	3	1	1	1	1	1	3	2	..	1	..	1	..	..	..	..	..	..	..	..	..	4	2	2
Pyonephrosis, stricture of ureter, gonorrhœal	1	..	..	..	1	..	1	..	..	..	1	..	..	..	..	..	..	..	..	..	..	1	1	..
Horseshoe kidney	..	1	..	..	..	..	..	1	..	..	..	..	..	..	..	..	..	..	..	..	..	..	1	..
Nephralgia	1	..	..	..	..	..	1	..	..	..	..	..	..	..	..	..	..	..	..	..	..	1	..	..
Bladder—21.																								
Papilloma of	3	..	..	..	..	..	1	..	..	2	..	..	..	..	..	..	..	..	..	..	..	3	..	..
" " vesical calculus	1	..	..	..	..	..	..	..	..	..	..	..	..	..	..	..	..	..	1	..	..	1	..	..
Sarcoma of	1	..	..	..	..	..	..	..	..	..	..	..	..	..	..	..	..	..	1	..	..	1	..	..
Vesical calculi	5	..	..	1	..	..	4	..	..	2	..	..	..	..	..	..	..	..	..	..	..	6	..	..
Cystitis, acute	..	..	..	1	..	..	..	..	..	1	..	..	..	..	..	..	..	..	..	..	..	1	..	..
" " pyelitis	..	..	..	1	..	..	..	..	..	1	..	..	..	..	..	..	..	..	..	..	..	1	..	..
" " false passage in urethra	1	..	..	..	..	..	..	..	..	1	..	..	..	..	..	..	..	..	..	..	..	1	..	..
" chronic	..	..	..	6	..	..	1	..	..	5	..	..	..	..	..	..	..	..	..	..	..	6	..	..
" " tuberculosis, endocarditis	..	..	..	1	..	..	..	..	..	..	..	..	..	..	..	..	..	..	1	..	..	1	..	..
Prostate—17.																								
Abscess of	1	..	..	..	..	..	1	..	..	..	..	..	..	..	..	..	..	..	..	..	..	1	..	..
Calculus of	1	..	..	..	..	..	1	..	..	..	..	..	..	..	..	..	..	..	..	..	..	1	..	..
Hypertrophied	2	..	..	2	..	..	1	..	..	3	..	..	..	..	..	..	..	..	..	..	..	4	..	..
" false passage in urethra, cystitis	..	..	..	1	..	..	..	..	..	1	..	..	..	..	..	..	..	..	..	..	..	1	..	..
" chronic cystitis	..	..	..	9	..	..	1	..	..	8	..	..	..	..	..	..	..	..	..	..	..	9	..	..
" " " diabetes	..	..	..	1	..	..	..	..	..	1	..	..	..	..	..	..	..	..	..	..	..	1	..	..
Seminal Vesicles—1.																								
Seminal vesiculitis, epididymitis	..	..	..	1	..	..	1	..	..	..	..	..	..	..	..	..	..	..	..	..	..	1	..	..
Penis and Urethra—22.																								
Urethritis, gonorrhœal	..	..	..	1	..	..	..	..	..	1	..	..	..	..	..	1	..	..	..	..	..	2	..	..
" " pyelitis	1	..	..	..	..	..	1	..	..	..	..	..	..	..	..	..	..	..	..	..	..	1	..	..
Urethra, stricture of	10	..	..	..	..	..	10	..	..	..	..	..	..	..	..	..	..	..	..	..	..	10	..	..
" " " epididymitis of	1	..	..	..	..	..	1	..	..	..	..	..	..	..	..	..	..	..	..	..	..	1	..	..
" fistula of	..	..	1	..	..	..	..	..	1	..	..	..	..	..	..	..	..	..	..	..	..	..	..	1
" fistula of, perineal	..	..	..	..	..	..	1	..	..	..	..	..	..	..	..	..	..	..	..	..	..	1	..	..
" caruncle of	1	..	..	..	1	..	..	1	..	..	..	..	..	..	..	..	..	..	..	..	..	..	1	..
Periurethral abscess	2	..	..	..	..	..	2	..	..	..	..	..	..	..	..	..	..	..	..	..	..	2	..	..

[1] Here the statistics of the general surgical and of the genito-urinary services were given together.

	Operation.			No operation.			Cured.			Improved.			Unimproved.			Died.			No treatment.			Total.		
	M	W	C	M	W	C	M	W	C	M	W	C	M	W	C	M	W	C	M	W	C	M	W	C
Genito-Urinary Diseases—*Continued.*																								
Penis and Urethra—Continued.																								
Phimosis	1		2				1		2													1		2
Chancroid, inguinal adenitis	1						1															1		
Testicle and Scrotum—27.																								
Abscess of scrotum	1			1			1			1												2		
Epididymitis, acute				4			4															4		
Epididymo-orchitis	1			3			4															4		
" " gonorrhœal, pyelitis	1						1															1		
Hydrocele				1			1															1		
" hypertrophied prostate				1																		1		
" peno-scrotal cicatrix	1						1															1		
" double, tubercular epididymitis			1						1															1
" of cord			1						1									1						2
Orchitis, specific				1			1															1		
Sarcoma of testis	1						1															1		
Varicocele	7		1				7		1													7		1
Rectum and Anus—148.																								
Hæmorrhoids—81	67	14					67	14														67	14	
" strangulated	2						2															2		
" " fissure ani	2						2															2		
Rectum, abscess of			1						1															1
" " " ischio-rectal	17	2	2				17	2	2													17	2	2
" carcinoma of	1																					1		
" stricture of	1						1												1			1		
" carcinoma of, intestinal obstruction	2									2												2		
" polypus of, eczema ani	1						1															1		
" prolapse of				1			1									1						2		
" " " hæmorrhoids	1						1															1		
" ulceration of	1						1															1		
" silk suture in	1						1															1		
Anus, fissure of	1	2					1	2														1	2	
" fistula of	20						18			2												20		
" " " phthisis, enteritis				1									1									1		
" " " hæmorrhoids	6						6															6		
" eczema of				1			1															1		

Lower Extremities—129.

Pelvis—4.																								
Pelvis, sarcoma of	1									1												1		
Ilium, tuberculosis of		1						1															1	
" exostosis of	1						1															1		
" vascular sarcoma of	1															1						1		
Groin—9.																								
Groin, myxosarcoma of		1						1															1	
" abscess of		1									1												1	
" adenitis of	1	2					1	1			1											1	2	
" " suppurative	1		1				1		1													1		1
" " tubercular	1						1															1		
" abscess of, and of leg from puerperal sepsis		1						1															1	
Buttocks—1.																								
Buttocks, abscess of		1						1															1	
Hip—9.																								
Hip, coxitis, tubercular			1	1	1	2					1	2	1		1							1	1	3
" " " and tubercular arthritis of ankle			1									1												1
" " " " Pott's disease of spine	1									1												1		
" traumatism of				1			1															1		
" dorsal-iliac dislocation of femur, cardiac failure from chloroform				1												1						1		
Thigh—32.																								
Thigh, gunshot wound of	2						2															2		
" sinus of			1						1															2
" " " amputation stump		1						1															1	
" abscess of, " "					1			1															1	
" " "			3						3															3
" cellulitis of	2						2															2		
" sebaceous cyst of	1						1															1		
" burns of, third degree				1			1															1		
" fracture of neck					2			1									1						2	
" old fracture of neck				5			4			1												5		
" fracture of shaft				1		2	1		2													1		2
" T-fracture of lower extremity of				1						1												1		

Lower Extremities—*Continued.*	Operation.			No operation.			Cured.			Improved.			Unimproved			Died.			No treatment.			Total.		
	M	W	C	M	W	C	M	W	C	M	W	C	M	W	C	M	W	C	M	W	C	M	W	C
Thigh, fracture of, and clavicle and inferior maxilla, recurrent insanity					1			1															1	
" osteomyelitis of	3	1					3	1														3	1	
" " " chronic	2						1			1												2		
" enchondroma of		1	1					1	1														1	1
Patella—4.																								
Patella, bursitis, suppurative, prepatellar		2						2															2	
" fracture of				1			1															1		
" " " compound, cellulitis of thigh, septicæmia		1						1															1	
Knee—12.																								
Knee, synovitis				2			1			1												2		
" synovitis, traumatic		1						1															1	
" arthritis, tubercular			1		1			1	1														1	1
" " " general tuberculosis	1															1						1		
" " suppurative, pyæmia			1															1						1
" " tubercular, tubercular meningitis			1															1						1
" " gonorrhœal	1						1															1		
" hæmarthrosis	1						1															1		
" tumor of					1						1												1	
" sarcoma of amputation stump		1						1															1	
Leg—28.																								
Leg, genu-extrorsum			1						1															1
" cellulitis of	1	1	1				1	1	1													1	1	1
" gangrene of	1						1															1		
" " diabetic	1															1						1		
" " of, senile		1						1															1	
" ulcer of, specific				2			1			1												2		
" periostitis of tibia, myositis			1						1															1
" osteomyelitis of tibia	2	3	2				2	1			2	1						1				2	3	2
" " " both tibiæ	1						1															1		
" " " " " and fracture			1						1															1
" " multiple, of tibia, varicose ulcers					1						1												1	

Lower Extremities—*Continued.*																								
Leg—Continued.																								
Leg, fracture, compound comminuted, of tibia, osteomyelitis, arthritis of knee, decubitus				1												1						1		
" fibula, fracture of				1			1															1		
" " and tibia, fracture of				1			1															1		
" paralysis from anterior poliomyelitis, arthrodesis, surgical shock			1															1						1
" hæmatoma of calf	1						1															1		
" varicose veins of	1	3					1	3														1	3	
Ankle—9.																								
Ankle, arthritis, tubercular	2			1			2			1												3		
" arthritis, suppurative			1						1															1
" abscess of			1						1															1
" cellulitis of						1			1															1
" external malleolus, fracture					1			1															1	
" sprain of					2			2															2	
Foot—13.																								
Foot, metatarsal bone, fracture				1	1		1	1														1	1	
" tarsus, compound fracture						1			1															1
" os calcis, fracture						1			1															1
" metatarsus, tubercular	1						1															1		
" cellulitis of			2						2															2
" pressure sore of	1						1															1		
" gangrene of, diabetes mellitus, coma				1						1												1		
" gunshot wound of, gangrene, delirium tremens	1						1															1		
" pes planus	1									1												1		
" Reynaud's disease	1						1															1		
" paralysis of	1						1															1		
Toe—8.																								
Toe, hammer toe		1						1															1	
" ingrowing nail of	1						1															1		
" osteomyelitis of		1	1					1	1														1	1
" fracture of, compound			1						1															1
" gangrene, senile dementia				1						1												1		
" contusion of						1			1															1
" ulcer of, specific dactylitis				1			1															1		

	Operation.			No operation.			Cured.			Improved.			Unimproved.			Died.			No treatment.			Total.		
	M	W	C	M	W	C	M	W	C	M	W	C	M	W	C	M	W	C	M	W	C	M	W	C
Skin—11.																								
Dermatitis exfoliativa					1						1												1	
Eczema, chronic, of leg				2	1		2				1											2	1	
" " " foot					1			1															1	
Lupus of face				1												1						1		
" " buttock	2						2															2		
Sycosis barbæ et pudendæ				1						1												1		
Tuberculosis and syphilis of face				1						1												1		
" of hand				1						1												1		
Miscellaneous—20.																								
Anæmia				1						1												1		
Atresia ani vaginalis																					1			1
Chilblains of hands and feet				1						1												1		
Cyst of labium majus		1						1															1	
Enteralgia					1			1															1	
Enteritis				1			1															1		
Fæcal impaction				1			1															1		
Fibrosarcoma of mons veneris																				1			1	
Hydrocele of round ligament			1						1															1
Incipient phthisis				1						1												1		
Lacerated perineum		1						1															1	
Lumbago				1						1												1		
Parovarian abscess, salpingitis		1						1															1	
Pelvic abscess, papilloma of ovary		1																					1	
" tumor				1			1															1		
Pyosalpinx, ovarian abscess		1						1															1	
Pyosalpinx, peritonitis		1						1															1	
Sarcoma of ovary		1						1															1	
Diseased appendages		1						1															1	
Double ovarian cyst		1						1															1	

LIST OF OPERATIONS PERFORMED IN THE DEPARTMENT OF GENERAL SURGERY.

Total—1,052, 72 deaths.

The limits of this publication preclude a thorough analysis of the vast material contained in it. Each one of the more important groups of operations has been tabulated in such a manner as to permit a prompt estimation of the salient facts bearing upon the issue. Main stress was laid upon publishing, first, all of those cases in which death frustrated the surgeons' efforts, or in which a failure of one or another kind rendered the history instructive. Of the successful cases, extracts of those only were given which presented abnormal features, the rest being disposed of in the commentary of each group in a summary manner. Exception was made, however, in this respect in the histories of the operations performed on the kidney, which appear in full.

OPERATIONS ON THE BRAIN AND NERVES—3.

	Total.	Deaths.
Craniotomy, extirpation of Gasserian ganglion	1	
Nerve suture for ulnar paralysis	1	
Resection of inferior dental nerve	1	

1897, ii., page 1331. *Relapsing Trigeminal Neuralgia; Extirpation of Gasserian Ganglion; Recovery.*—Fidelius O., restaurant keeper, had, within the last five years, been operated on five times for a rebellious infra-orbital neuralgia. Carnochan's operation, performed by Dr. Weir, was followed by a pause in the pain lasting two years. Last spring a severe attack occurred, but subsided spontaneously on the arrival of warm weather. On admission, December 9, 1897, he stated that pain had recurred with unusual violence six weeks ago and was excruciating and almost continuous. On the right side of the face a number of scars were visible. Attacks were especially vicious at efforts at deglutition; mastication impossible. Patient presented a well-built frame, somewhat emaciated; internal organs all normal; no ocular disturbances. December 11, 1897: Under Schleich general anæsthesia, the skull was opened according to Hartley-Krause by chisel and mallet, in the right temporal region. The omega-shaped flap being raised, hemorrhage occurred from the injured middle meningeal artery, which was controlled by a suture. Exposure of temporo sphenoidal fossa was easy until the region of the Gasserian ganglion was reached, where the stripping off of the thickened dura was extremely difficult and was followed by profuse venous hemorrhage, easily stopped by pressure exerted with a minute tampon of iodoform gauze applied exactly over the bleeding point. As soon as this tampon became adherent the work could progress near and around it, but the moment it was disturbed hemorrhage compelled its reapplication. Finally the foramen ovale was exposed and the third branch liberated and divided. The second branch, entering the foramen rotundum, was found to be a mere thread and was treated likewise. Isolation of the first branch was not attempted. Now the second and third branches being caught in an artery forceps, the dura over the ganglion was split open and the latter was evulsed, a number of isolated portions being removed separately. Considerable hemorrhage following, this was checked by the application of a slender tampon firmly pressed down by the finger tips over the bleeding point for a couple of minutes. The end of this packing was brought out through the posterior angle of the wound, which was closed by the usual suture. The anæsthesia was excellent throughout, the pulse being firm and quiet, but whenever pressure was brought to bear upon the temporal lobe by the retractor, respiration became noticeably embarrassed and shallow. Operation lasted two hours. Immediate relief from pain followed. Vomited once, some coffee, the same evening; after that retained nourishment. December 12, at 8 P.M., the highest temperature, 101° F., observed. Slight sanguinolent oozing from wound, necessitating change of outer dressings. December 13: Bowels moved by calomel and salts; tongue deviating to the right, pupils looking normal. December 15: Slept well; soft diet; packing removed from bottom of wound and replaced by a short piece of tubing to keep angle patulous. December 16: Temperature normal. December 19: Tube removed. December 22: Picking up rapidly. *Sensibility undiminished along area corresponding to third branch; along that of second branch, abolished.* December 26: Discharged cured. February 15, 1899: Pain in the infraorbital region of moderate intensity, of a week's duration; readmitted for observation. Pain subsiding spontaneously, was discharged February 22.

OPERATIONS ON THE NOSE, ORAL CAVITY, AND FAUCES—6, 1 death.

	Total.	Deaths.
Asch's, for deviated septum	1	
Cheiloplasty, for double harelip	2	1
Enlarging the faucial opening	1	
For empyema of antrum of Highmore, incision and drainage.	1	
Submaxillary salivary calculus, removal of gland for	1	

OPERATIONS ON THE LARYNX AND TRACHEA—3.

Thyroidectomy, partial, by enucleation	2
Tracheotomy for carcinoma of larynx	1

All operations in the oral and nasal cavities, the fauces, larynx, and trachea, with the exception of simple tracheotomy, were done with the aid of Rose's position, the patient's head being dependent over the edge of the operating table. This posture enables the surgeon to proceed with little interruption on account of the fear of asphyxia due to the entrance of blood into the bronchi. The anæsthesia itself was usually a mixed one, that is, a hypodermatic injection of morphia preceding the administration of chloroform.

AMPUTATIONS—15, 1 death.

	Total.	Deaths.		Total.	Deaths.
Hip	1		Foot, Pirogoff	1	
Thigh	5	1	Toe	2	
Leg	3		Finger	3	

Of ten major amputations—nine of which were done for disease, one for an injury—all terminated in recovery. One of the patients, whose thigh was amputated May 28, 1897, died April 1, 1898, of diabetic coma. Of the histories, the following are worthy of note:

1898, vol. i., page 697. *Senile Gangrene of Leg; Amputation of Thigh under Nitrous Oxide Anæsthesia.*—Hannah S., 75 years old. May 28, 1897 (1897, vol. ii., page 143), her left thigh was amputated by Dr. Lilienthal, under nitrous oxide anæsthesia, for the same trouble. She was discharged cured August 1, 1897. Readmitted January 22, 1898, with dry gangrene of right foot and leg. Arteries very calcareous; heart sounds feeble, no murmurs; urine normal; pulse rate normal. January 24: Nitrous oxide by Dr. Goodman. Rapid amputation of thigh in lower third. Patient conversed in a confused manner during the entire operation, but on recovering her senses assured us that she had felt no pain whatever. Open wound treatment; afebrile course of healing; marginal sloughing of moderate extent. Secondary suture March 10, in general anæsthesia, Schleich No. 1. May 7, discharged cured.

1898, vol. ii., page 144. *Tuberculosis of Knee-Joint; Resection; Suppuration; Amputation of Thigh; Sarcomatous Degeneration of Stump; Amputation at Hip-Joint; Recovery.*—Mrs. W. B., 40 years old, admitted June 14, 1897, with typical tuberculosis of knee-joint, for which, June 24, resection was done by Dr. Van Arsdale. The external wound healed kindly, and on June 28 temperature was normal, but by July 6 suppuration became declared. After several ineffectual attempts to control the suppuration, the thigh had to be ablated October 14, 1897, the general condition of the patient requiring a preliminary saline infusion. Necrosis of the edge of the sawn surface followed. In removing, on January 3, 1898, the necrosed bone, it was first noticed that the flabby granulations filling the cavity of the wound had a peculiar grumous consistence. Being examined, they were found to be composed of spindle-celled sarcomatous tissue. On account of the patient's unwillingness, amputation at the hip-joint could not be done sooner than March 1, when, after a preliminary infusion of one quart of normal salt solution, Wyeth's pins were introduced, and a constrictor was applied above them in the well-known manner. When the muscles were divided it was noticed that their stumps disappeared, slipping up behind the constrictor; also, the constrictor was found seriously to interfere with disarticulation, which was accomplished with considerable difficulty. The femoral vessels being secured by ligature, the constrictor was removed, and then considerable hemorrhage took place, apparently from the obturator vessels, which was controlled by two clamps. The patient's condition had become desperately bad by this time, and as there remained a large number of muscular branches untied, it was resolved to expose the external iliac artery and vein and to tie them. This was rapidly accomplished by an incision above Poupart's ligament, and then the wound was packed and dressed, all our attention being directed to the resuscitation of the patient by another saline infusion and hypodermatic stimulation. She rallied slowly. The large wound healed slowly by granulation, the condition of the patient improving marvellously. She was discharged cured on July 23, 1898.

Note.—Several times the Gigli wire saw was used, both in amputations of thigh and leg, but it was discarded on account of the slow manner in which it divided the bone.

REDUCTION OF DISLOCATIONS—2.

	Total.
Subcoracoid—Kocher's	2

DEBRIDEMENT AND DRAINAGE OF COMPOUND FRACTURE—1.

	Total.	Deaths.
Tibia, compound comminuted	1	1

OSTEOTOMIES—15.

	Total.	Deaths.
Of tibia, for genu varum	9	
" ulna and radius, for badly united fracture	1	
Of femur, for enchondroma	1	
" ilium, for exostosis	1	
" inferior maxilla	1	
" tibia, exploratory	1	

OSTEOPLASTY—1.

Femur, ununited fracture of	1

1898, vol. i., page 940.—Annie B., 7 years old, admitted February 3 with ununited fracture of the middle of the shaft of the left femur. Considerable deformity, marked shortening, large callus, abnormal mobility. February 10: Incision on outer side of thigh through vastus. Lower fragment overriding the upper, and both surrounded with large masses of soft callus, which were removed. Line of fracture irregular and oblique; granulation tissue between fragments excised, fragments being dovetailed after proper preparation of surfaces by keyhole saw and chisel. Two fracture clamps were driven in, and were further secured by a circular lashing of stout silver wire; suture, drainage. Considerable reaction, fever, and suppuration followed, necessitating, on March 14, counter-incision. Continued suppuration of mild character until June, when sinuses were healed. April 20: Fragments firmly consolidated. June 30: Discharged cured—clamps and silver wire having healed in—with a shortening of two inches.

FOR OSTEOMYELITIS—80, 2 deaths.

Primary Operations—45

	Total.	Deaths.
Cranium, in xeroderma pigmentosum	1	
Inferior maxilla	11	
Humerus	1	
Metacarpus	1	
Sternum	1	
Sternum and ribs	1	
Sacro-iliac	2	
Femur	3	
Femur, Schede's operation	5	
Tibia	15	1
Tibia, Schede's operation	2	
Tarsus	1	
Phalanx of foot	1	

Secondary Operations—15

	Total.	Deaths.
Ilium	2	1
Femur	4	
Tibia	7	
Ulna	2	

For Osteoperiostitis, suppurative—5

Incision and drainage.

Inferior maxilla	1
Superior maxilla	1
Radius	1
Tibia	2

Incision and curetting for sinuses leading to bones........15

It was the practice, whenever possible, to reserve all cases requiring operation on the skeleton for the Thursday clinic, when the copious material afforded ample opportunity for comparison and study. The principles governing us in dealing with the various forms of osteomyelitis are as follows: In the early acute stages of the disease the principal endeavor was directed toward giving relief from tension and affording ample drainage, which was accomplished by free and often multiple incisions through the soft parts and the exposure of intraosseous foci by means of chisel and mallet. In the later stages of the disorder our object was, freely to expose the seat of the trouble, so as to be able to overlook it in its entire extent. Thus a thorough removal of all morbid matter, as sequestra and granulations, became feasible. After this, the cavity was shaped so as to form a more or less shallow trough, and where the conditions were favorable an attempt was made to have the wound heal aseptically under the blood clot (Schede). Out of seven instances we were successful five times. Twice the blood clot liquefied as late as a fortnight after the operation, and the cavities had to heal by the slow process of granulation. In most of the instances, however, the involvement of the soft parts rendered this plan hopeless, and recourse was had to the various methods of implantation of skin-flaps or a simple treatment by packing. Where healing was retarded by sclerosis and malnutrition of the bony walls of the cavities, the sclerosed portions of the bone were chiselled away until porous and well-vascularized tissue was exposed.

All these operations were done under artificial anæmia by Esmarch's constrictor, which was not removed until the dressings were finished. For rapid and clean work, well selected carpenter's chisels (Buck's) were used.

RESECTIONS IN CONTINUITY—8.

Superior maxilla, for neoplasm..	3
" " partial, for neoplasm.......	1
Inferior maxilla, partial, for sarcoma	1
Inferior maxilla, wiring for non-union	1
First phalanx, tubercular........	1
Metatarsal bone....	1

Thorax, Resection of Ribs—16, 2 deaths.

	Total.	Deaths.
For empyema...... .	11	1
" " Eslander's operation..	1	
" mediastinal dermoid cyst, sepsis,	1	1
For abscess of lung, thoracoplasty..	1	
" tuberculosis of rib	1	
" costal chondritis..	1	

1898, vol. i., page 387. *Anterior Mediastinal Dermoid Cyst; Incision; Drainage; Left Broncho-pneumonia; Sepsis; Death.*—Fanny G., 30 years old. Since ten months noticed a swelling above right breast, corresponding to level of third rib, which had much increased within the last four months. Integument unchanged over the fluctuating mass, the size of an orange, which is adherent to underlying tissues. Extensive dulness corresponding to the site of the swelling, which on puncture yielded a yellow pea soup like liquid loaded with epithelial matter. Other organs normal. January 27 the sac was exposed by separating fibres of the pectoral muscles, and, being incised, yielded large quantities of brown, grumous fluid. The wound being enlarged, a number of lateral pockets occupying the space under the pectoral muscles were successively opened and evacuated; finally it became evident that this extrathoracic extension led through a small aperture between the third and fourth ribs into a voluminous sac located inside of the thoracic wall. Two inches of the third rib having been resected, the interior of the sac could be inspected. It contained the same grumous liquid, interspersed with long tufts of hair and gritty calcareous material. The pleura was accidentally opened in dividing the intercostal muscles, and was closed by a catgut suture. The dermoid débris having been washed out, it became clear that the cyst, holding more than a pint of liquid, occupied the anterior mediastinum, being attached to pericardium, right pleura, and diaphragm. The extrathoracic part of the cyst was cut away, the main cavity being drained and packed. As there was serious doubt whether the pleura had been infected or not at the time of its accidental injury, it was deemed prudent to open the same in the post-axillary line, where, a rib being resected, a drainage tube was inserted. The day following the operation fever was present, with the respirations reaching as high as 44 per minute; temperature 102.8° F., pulse 110. The pleural drainage was copious, sero-sanguinolent; that from the cyst also plentiful. The pulse rate and respirations remained high, with considerable fever, until, on January 31, extensive dulness and bronchial breathing were observed posteriorly, on the side operated upon. It was remarked that ever since the operation the patient's sensorium was seriously beclouded, and frequent twitchings of the facial muscles and an erythematous rash over the outer surfaces of the upper extremities, together with the irregular continuous fever, attested a deep septic intoxication. The rapidly contracting cavity of the cyst was effectually cleansed by a Sprengel air pump arrangement, and it was evident that the sepsis did not depend upon the condition of the sac. On February 2, there being no discharge from the pleural drain, this was withdrawn, and the pleural wound healed rapidly. February 5: Resolution of the pneumonia was noted, the septic state of the patient continuing unchanged. February 11: Area of bronchial breathing and râles much lessened, temperature 100°, but the semi-comatose state continued with little abatement. Stools and urine were passed involuntarily, patient very noisy. February 20: Cheyne-Stokes respiration. Capacity of cyst much diminished. Urine contained albumin. March 17 the emaciated patient died. [For result of autopsy see the report of the Pathologist.]

OPERATIONS ON JOINTS—29, 2 deaths.

Resections—7.	Total.	Deaths
Knee, double arthrodesis for poliomyelitis..	1	1
Knee, tubercular, typical resections.......	2	1
Ankle, tubercular. ..	1	
Shoulder, "	1	
Elbow "	1	
" ankylosis after trauma.....	1	
Aspirations—9.		
Knee	7	

	Total.	Deaths.
Ankle......	1	
Elbow......	1	
Incisions and Drainage—11.		
Knee, for hæmatoma..	3	
" multiple incisions for suppurative arthritis... ...	3	
Knee, Mayo's operation	4	
Ankle, peri-arthritic abscess..	1	
Brisement Forcé—2.		
Knee	2	

1898, vol. i., page 5. *One case of Death following a Double Resection of the Knee to produce Arthrodesis is to be recorded.*—The child, 8 years old, seemed to be sturdy, and both knees were operated upon at one session. Though the hemorrhage was very scant, being perfectly controlled by ligatures and a compressive dressing, deep collapse was noted immediately following the operation, from which, in spite of most energetic and assiduous stimulation, the patient did not recover, dying January 14, on the third day after the operation. In the light of this experience it would have been wiser to do the work on two separate occasions.

1898, vol. i., page 570. *Died of General Miliary Tuberculosis Six Weeks after Resection.*

Mayo's operation, that is, the free and wide transverse incision of the knee-joint, was regularly employed when we have had to deal with an acute suppuration of a phlegmonous character from whatever cause. Whenever œdema of the integument, with reddening and a serious disturbance of the general condition of the patient, points to a virulent kind of infection, the integrity of the limb, if not life, is put in imminent jeopardy. Multiple incisions, as advocated by Andrews, of Chicago, though useful in the sero-purulent forms of gonitis, are inadequate to afford proper drainage in the phlegmonous forms, even if supplemented by permanent irrigation. Ankylosis is a foregone conclusion, even if the limb be saved; hence this factor is frankly accepted by us, and the time of suffering to the patient and uncertainty to the surgeon is markedly shortened by the far more energetic procedure of Mayo. The incision is begun on one side just in front of the hamstrings, extending right across the anterior face of the joint, generally above the patella to give access to the quadriceps bursa, to a corresponding point on the opposite side. In flexing the knee all the recesses of the joint are freely exposed and can be thoroughly cleansed. They are packed with gauze, and the joint is put up in the flexed position under a moist dressing. Even thus fever is usually observed to continue for several days, due undoubtedly to the septic infiltration of the thickened capsule. The dressings are changed daily, generally under brief anæsthesia As soon as the swelling, fever, and suppuration are abated the flexed knee is straightened out and is put up in extension.

OPERATIONS ON THE BURSÆ—3.

Trochanteric, tubercular, excision of	1
Prepatellar, suppurative incision of	2

OPERATIONS ON THE ABDOMINAL CAVITY—224, 38 deaths.

Gall Bladder and Gall Ducts—16 operations on 16 patients, 6 deaths.

	Total.	Deaths.
Cholecystotomy	10	3
Choledochotomy	2	1
Cysticotomy	1	1
Cholecystectomy	2	
Cholecystorrhaphy	1	1

Note.—Cholecystotomy was done also on 3 other patients classified under choledochotomy and cysticotomy, but these operations are here ignored for the sake of simplicity.

Diagnostically, none of the 16 patients operated upon presented unusual difficulties. In most of the cases a characteristic tumor was present at the time of admission, together with a previous history of jaundice or gall-stone colic. In all of them the urine contained more or less coloring matter of bile. Where there was an apparent tumor the incision was placed longitudinally; where, from the indistinctness or an absence of a palpable tumor, technical difficulties were expected, a transverse incision was preferred, as it gave incomparably better access than the former, and, according to our experience, has never led to ventral hernia. Formerly cholecystotomy was preferably done in two times. But operating in one session has come more and more in vogue, and growing familiarity of technique has justified this preference. Whenever the gall bladder was found to be very tense, as soon as it was sufficiently exposed and freed from adhesions, the contents were withdrawn with a stout aspirating needle until its walls became flabby. The puncture hole was now secured by a small clamp, and the gall bladder, cystic and common ducts were examined by external palpation through the peritoneal cavity. Next the surrounding field was carefully protected by packing, the patient rolled on his right side, and the gall bladder freely incised, evacuated, and cleansed by swabbing. Then stones in the duct were removed, by the internal route if possible, or by an incision if necessary; or stones lodged in the common duct were exposed and removed through an incision, which was closed if advisable. Finally the bladder was attached to the external wound, and, all possible points of leakage being protected by gauze drains, the external wound was reduced to a minimal aperture by button sutures.

Of 10 patients upon whom cholecystotomy was done, 3 died: 1 from cholangitis; 1 from septicæmia, peritonitis, and suppression of urine, possibly caused by the overlooking and non removal of a stone lodged at the junction of cystic and common ducts; the third one from a gastric hemorrhage and shock.

1898, vol. i., pages 386 and 716. *Cholelithiasis, Chole-*

cystitis, Cholecystotomy, Cholangitis; Death.—Mary M., 24 years old. History of abdominal cramps for nine weeks; jaundice; vomiting. Tenderness in right hypochondriac region, but no distinct tumor felt. April 12: Vertical incision. Gall bladder found enlarged. Aspirated; one and a half ounces of bile and purulent fluid withdrawn. Thirty small stones removed Gall bladder sewed to parietal peritoneum and drained. After operation patient vomited frequently. Slight fever. After third day profuse bleeding from gall bladder. Hemorrhages, discharge of bile, vomiting, and fever continued despite local and general treatment. May 24, died. Autopsy: All ducts free from stone; cholangitis; kidneys acutely congested.

1898, vol. i., page 532. *Cholelithiasis; Empyema of Gall Bladder; Cholecystotomy; Suppression of Urine; Intestinal Obstruction (?); Death.*—Max W., 20 years old. Two years ago an attack of pain and vomiting. Four days before admission, vomiting and continuous pain in right hypochondrium; no chill or jaundice; temperature 100.6°, pulse 78. Elongated tumor in right hypochondrium. April 18: Vertical incision; much distended gall bladder, extensive omental adhesions. Gall bladder sewed into wound. April 20: Evacuation of muco-pus from gall bladder. No stone found. Drainage. April 23: Copious discharge of bile. Absolute suppression of urine. Suppuration of stitch holes. Two intravenous infusions. April 24: Died. Postmortem revealed congestion of visceral peritoneum. Stone found at junction of cystic and common ducts. Kidneys congested. Diagnosis: Peritonitis and septicæmia.

1898, vol. ii., page 1047. *Cholelithiasis; Cholecystotomy in two times; Septic Hemorrhages from Stomach; Death.*—Sophie B., 50 years old. Since eight days severe abdominal pain, no jaundice, persistent vomiting, constipation; marked resistance on pressure in right hypochondrium; other organs all normal. Pulse 74, temperature 99.8°. November 23: Exposure of distended gall bladder, which was deeply seated and densely adherent to surrounding organs. Puncture and fixation of gall bladder by packings placed under and around it, this being necessary because it could not be brought up to the abdominal wall. Vomiting all night, the pulse becoming very frequent and feeble. The temperature, which was 101° F. right after the operation, fell during the night to 99.4°. November 24: Packings removed, gall bladder incised, pus and a large number of stones evacuated. A coil of small intestine, evidently close to the stomach, was seen distended with blackish-blue fluid. After due protection by gauze pads, a small incision was made into it, evacuating clotted and liquid blood and bloody mucus. Drainage tubes inserted both into gall bladder and intestine in great haste, as patient was seriously collapsed. Intravenous infusion. Death after six hours. Permission could not be secured from the relatives for a full postmortem, hence the organs could only be examined through the wound. The stomach was found to be filled with liquid and clotted blood and bloody mucus. Mucosa covered with hemorrhagic erosions. Small intestine filled with the same material for a considerable distance. Lungs, heart, kidneys, spleen, and liver normal.

The remaining seven patients were all cured, some of them with a slightly discharging sinus, all of which, however, closed within a brief period of time.

Two cases of stone in the common bile duct, one fatal, the other successful, are here reported; also one fatal, in the cystic duct:

1897, vol. ii., pages 333 and 1323. *Cholelithiasis; Empyema of Gall Bladder; Cholecystotomy, evacuation of Pus and four Small Stones; Healing of Wound; Readmission; Choledochotomy, evacuation of Stone; Death.*—Bessie S., 45 years old. Admitted with tumor in hypochondrium, fever and pain. May 3: Cholecystotomy, evacuation of pus and four small stones; many more discharged with mucus and bile. August 4: Discharged with healed wound. Ever since then had frequent chilly attacks of fever with pain. December 13: Readmitted. December 17: Old scar incised; a large number of adhesions had to be severed before common duct was exposed. In a very deep situation, stone of the size of a hazelnut was felt. Duct incised, stone extracted. Suture of duct, drainage. Much vomiting and rising pulse rate with slight fever followed. December 19: Death from exhaustion, probably due to peritonitis. No autopsy was permitted.

1898, vol. i., page 909. *Cholelithiasis; Choledochotomy; Cure.*—Rebecca G., 52 years old. For two months epigastric pain, jaundice, pruritus, clayey stools, vomiting, chills and fever. April 25: Transverse incision. Gall bladder atrophied and adherent to stomach. Gall bladder incised and found empty. In common bile duct large stone felt, which was removed by choledochotomy. Duct then stitched by Lembert suture. Gall bladder drained. Wick of gauze inserted leading to duct wound. Uneventful convalescence. June 30: Discharged cured.

1898, vol. i., page 123. *Cholelithiasis; Empyema of Gall Bladder; Cholecystotomy; Cysticotomy; Death.*—Rosie N., 36 years old. After a blow in right hypochondrium, had vomiting, chills, fever, and pain over site of injury for three weeks up to time of admission on November 25, 1897. Large, globular, fluctuating tumor extending from lower border of liver to level of umbilicus. Chronic diffuse nephritis; mitral insufficiency. November 26: Operation under local anæsthesia (eucaine) by Dr. Lilienthal. Eight ounces of purulent fluid aspirated. Wound packed. Two days later gall bladder opened. Stone felt impacted in cystic duct, but could not be removed. Subsequently stone crushed, but only partially removed. Wound rapidly contracted to a discharging sinus. General condition good. January 18, 1898: Cysticotomy; general anæsthesia (Dr. Gerster). Wound reopened. Dense adhesions about gall bladder divided. Stone felt in cystic duct near neck of gall bladder. Several unsuccessful attempts made to extract stone through gall bladder with assistance of finger over the duct. In one such attempt forceps perforated neck of gall bladder. Through this perforation stone was removed. Patient showing signs of collapse, operation hastily concluded by inserting gauze packing through perforation in duct. Gall bladder and wound drained. Intravenous infusion required. Patient did well for next three days; on fourth day dull and unresponsive. During progress of first change of dressings sudden epileptiform convulsion. Death. No autopsy.

Two successful cases of extirpation of the calculous and shrunken gall bladder will be found interesting:

1898, vol. i., page 541. *Atrophy of Gall Bladder; Cholelithiasis; Extirpation of Gall Bladder; Cure.*—Mrs. Fanny H., 20 years old. Since two years frequent attacks of pain. One year ago jaundice. Pain on deep pressure in right hypochondrium. No tumor to be felt. April 4: Vertical incision. Gall bladder shrunken, adherent to liver, of size and shape of a large appendix; contains several stones. Ligature of cystic duct, excision of gall bladder. One gauze drain. Uninterrupted recovery. Discharged cured May 1.

1898, vol. i., page 560. *Atrophy of Gall Bladder; Cholelithiasis; Extirpation of Gall Bladder; Cure.*—Mrs. Bertha H., 70 years old. Eighteen years ago attack of jaundice. Five years ago left hemiplegia. Since four weeks severe pain in right side, obdurate constipation extending over fourteen days. On admission, March 29, in right hypochondrium painful tumor felt; colon visibly distended, showing peristalsis; suspicion of cancer of gall bladder involving colon. March 31: Vertical incision, exposing transverse colon bound down by adhesions, which being severed, the contracted gall bladder came in sight; it was filled with stones. Being freed from deep adhesions and the liver, the duct was ligatured and tied off. Gauze drainage. Uninterrupted recovery. Discharged cured April 19.

LIVER—9 operations on 7 patients; 3 deaths.

	Total.	Deaths.
Cœliotomy for abscess of liver	2	1
" and partial resection of liver for cancer	1	
By posterior route, combined with resection of one or more ribs.		
For abscess of liver and perforation into bronchus	1	1
" subphrenic abscess following appendicitis [1]	1	
" echinococcus of liver	1	
" " " " suppurating	1	1

1898, vol. i., page 395. *Samuel R.; Abscess of Liver; Incision; Drainage; Cure.*—History of chronic diarrhœa. Tumor of liver, with chill, fever, and local pain. December 30, 1897: Stitching of liver to parietal peritoneum. December 31: Incision and drainage. Uninterrupted recovery. Discharged cured March 20, 1898.

1898, vol. i., page 749. *Abscess of Liver; Cœliotomy and Stitching of Liver to Parietal Peritoneum; Incision and Drainage; Continued Suppuration; Posterior Counter incision through Pleura and Diaphragm; Through Drainage; Death.*—Frederick H., 42 years old, Southerner. Five months ago daily chills and fever at Charles-

[1] See chapter "*Appendicitis,*" page 190, Case 1898, vol. i., page 807.

ton, S. C., followed by deep jaundice, prostration, and hepatic pain. February 15, 1898: Large hepatic tumor; diarrhœa; slight evening fever; emaciation. February 18: Cœliotomy; stitching of liver to parietal peritoneum. February 20: Incision; evacuation of thirty-five ounces of brown, bloody, grumous material; continued breakdown of hepatic tissue, evidenced by sudden fluctuations in the amount of discharge. March 28: To improve drainage the abscess was attacked from behind. Two of the lowermost ribs being resected, the parietal pleura was circularly stitched to diaphragmatic pleura; packing. March 30: Incision through diaphragm. Very free through drainage and frequent irrigation did not influence disintegration of liver, to which patient succumbed May 4. No postmortem allowed.

1898, vol. i., page 754. *Suppurative Portal Thrombosis; Multiple Abscess of Liver; Empyema; Incision; Death.*—Abram A., 36 years old. Six weeks' history of pain in region of liver; fever; night sweats. Since two weeks fetid expectoration. Physical signs both of empyema and liver abscess. May 20: Excision of seventh, eighth, and ninth ribs; incision and evacuation of fetid pus; expiratory escape of air from cavity; continued fever; profuse discharge and emaciation. May 28: Death. Same day autopsy: Suppurative thrombosis of portal vein and branches; multiple abscesses of liver; open communication with right pleura and a bronchus of right lung. (Lilienthal.)

The histories of two cases of echinococcus are as follows:

1898, vol. ii., 789. *Tumor of Liver; Escape of Secondary Cysts by Rectum; Incision by the Pleural Route; Drainage; Cure.*—Adolph E., 30 years old. Had complained of pain in epigastrium for three years. Since August attacks of chills accompanied by fever, and an enlargement of the liver upward and backward. Grape-like, white bodies escaped with the stools. September 30: Aspiration in seventh space, axillary line, yielded clear hydatic fluid. Incision over site of puncture, seventh and eighth ribs being resected. Pleura pushed aside, then incision of diaphragm; also opened sac, discharging fourteen to sixteen ounces of fluid and many daughter cysts; drainage. End of October the detached mother cyst was withdrawn. Rapid closure of sac. November 15: Discharged cured. (Lilienthal.)

1898, vol. ii., page 502. *Large Tumor of Liver with continued Fever and frequent Chills since five weeks; Probatory Cœliotomy and Closure of Wound; Aspiration and Incision in Seventh Space; Drainage; Mediastinal Abscess; Perforation into Bronchus; Death.*—Admitted August 22 with large tumor extending from sixth rib to three fingers below free border. Chill, and temperature of 104°. General condition very bad. August 24: Anterior probatory cœliotomy not yielding any encouragement for attacking the tumor transperitoneally, the incision was immediately closed. Then puncture was made in the axillary line in the seventh space, drawing pus; following this, the eighth rib being resected, the pleura was opened, packed off with gauze, and then the diaphragm was incised, giving exit to a large quantity of thick, brown, foul-smelling pus containing hooklets and (culture) proteus vulgaris; drainage. August 28: Temperature 103° F. Signs of fluid in the right pleura. August 29: Aspiration of pleura yielded several ounces of turbid serum. August 31: Same. September 6: Ninth rib resected; pleura entered, and found communicating with cavity in liver; unabated fever; profuse discharge of pus. September 15: Purulent expectoration commenced. September 26: Sudden attack of dyspnœa and death. *Postmortem through wound:* Right lung carneous, much compressed by a large collection of pus below and to its inner side, occupying the anterior mediastinum, communicating with a bronchus. (Van Arsdale.)

Noteworthy is the following history of excision of a hepatic adenoma:

1898, vol. ii., page 526. *Globular Tumor of Left Lobe of Liver; Excision; Cure.*—Aaron M., 44 years old, admitted July 29 with gastric symptoms of two months' duration. A globular tumor, moving with respiratory excursions, was to be felt in the right epigastric region; not painful. General condition good. Examination of stomach by test meals and washings indicated normal conditions. August 9: Cœliotomy; exposure of tumor of the size of a peach attached by broad pedicle to under surface of the left lobe. A suture line of catgut was carried around the base of the mass; then distally from this line an incision was carried through the liver tissue to the depth of these sutures; then a second row of deeper sutures was inserted from the bottom of this incision, the incision deepened; then a third row of sutures applied, and so on until the mass was severed from its attachment. No hemorrhage. Packings of iodoform gauze. Uneventful recovery. September 23: Discharged cured. The pathologist reported the tumor to be an adenoma of the liver. (Lilienthal.)

SPLEEN—2, 2 deaths.

	Total	Deaths.
Cœliotomy for rupture of spleen	1	1
Cœliotomy for gangrene of spleen and lung, posterior route, resection of two ribs	1	1

1898, vol. i., page 885. *Laceration of Spleen; Peritonitis; Cœliotomy; Death.*—Rosie S., 4 years old, admitted June 23. Forty-eight hours before, had been run over by wagon, wheel passing across hypogastrium. Soon afterward vomited coagulated blood. Continued vomiting and fever; abdomen increasing in size. No urinary symptoms. Bowels had moved normally the night of the injury. Pulse 160, temperature 102.4°, respiration 32. Urine normal. Abdomen much distended, tympanitic except in flanks, where dulness was present. Immediate median incision. Peritoneal cavity found filled with fluid blood; intestines congested and distended; enterotomy of a coil of small intestine relieved meteorism. Along the lower surface of the spleen a transverse rupture nearly bisecting the organ. Abdomen cleared of clots by sponging; rupture was packed; gauze drain; profound collapse; infusion. Patient died ten hours after operation. *Postmortem:* Bloody fluid in both pleuræ. Congestion at base of left lung. Spleen in state of hemorrhagic infiltration, adherent to surrounding viscera, severed nearly in two by a transverse laceration, the gap being filled with some fresh blood clots. Retroperitoneal tissues on right side infiltrated with blood. Excessive general anæmia. (Lilienthal.)

1898, vol. ii., page 12. *Ulcer of Stomach; Thrombosis of Splenic Vein; Necrosis of Spleen and Lung; Subphrenic Abscess; Aspiration; Incision by Pleural Route; Gastric Fistula; Sepsis; Inanition; Death.*—Sarah F., 33 years old, admitted June 23, 1898. Referred to Dr. Gerster by Dr. Strauss. Had been under treatment for gastric ulcer.

Seven weeks before admission, had sudden pain in umbilical region; since then continuous fever; no chills; vomiting of intensely fetid matter. On left side increasing dulness extending from lower border of ribs to sixth space posteriorly, apparently connected with a tumor mass in left hypochondrium. Occasionally after vomiting of fetid matter the dulness was replaced by tympanitic resonance with succussion. Puncture by Dr. Strauss yielded material of the same appearance and odor as vomitus, containing particles of food. June 24: Aspiration in eighth left intercostal space, axillary line, withdrawing brown, decomposing pus. Longitudinal incision along needle; seventh and eighth ribs resected; pleural cavity walled off by gauze packings; diaphragm incised, and a large cavity opened into, situated in retrogastric space, its upper anterior wall formed by a gangrenous part of spleen, its anterior wall formed by posterior surface of stomach, and communicating by an opening through the diaphragm with an abscess cavity in the lung. The cavity was filled with fluid with peculiar methyl alcohol odor. The gangrenous portion of spleen was easily removed. At bottom of cavity was seen a large gastric fistula, which could not be repaired on account of the necrotic condition of the neighboring parts. Cavity evacuated and drained; fistula plugged. June 25: Profuse discharge of material from stomach and necrotic tissues of the wall of the cavity. Posture did not affect gastric discharge. July 1: Death from inanition and sepsis. *Postmortem:* Perforation about six centimetres in diameter in stomach. Along edge of ulcer a branch of splenic vein is thrombosed and occluded. Spleen gangrenous in its upper part; a large infarct at lower edge of gangrenous area. Left lobe of liver contains a large abscess. Left lung gangrenous at its lower part.

STOMACH—8 operations, 8 patients, 3 deaths.

	Total.	Deaths.
Cœliotomy, exploratory, for carcinoma of stomach..........	1	
" " " " " " and colon	1	1
" and gastrostomy, for œsophageal stricture.. ..	3	1
" " gastro-enterostomy (Murphy button)........	3	1

Of the three patients on whom gastrostomy was done, two suffered from cancerous stricture of the œsophagus.

In both of these cases Marwedel's method was employed, and yielded an excellent result in the patient who survived. The other one came upon the operating table in a condition of extreme emaciation, and died on the third day after the operation, of simple exhaustion.

1898, vol. i., page 361. *Cancer of the Œsophagus; Gastrostomy; Death.*—Admitted March 3 in a state of far-gone inanition and absolute inability to swallow even liquids. Stomach tube arrested near cardia, No. 9 French passing with some difficulty; regurgitated fluid alkaline, containing blood. March 8: Gastrostomy, Marwedel. In spite of efforts at stimulation and methodical feeding, the patient steadily lost ground, temperature remaining normal to the end. March 11: Died. *Postmortem:* Extensive ulcerated carcinoma of cardia and œsophagus.

1899, vol. i. *Benign Cicatricial Stricture of Œsophagus; Gastrostomy; Combined Direct and Retrograde Instrumental Dilatation; Spontaneous Closure of Gastric Fistula; Cure.*—Dora Heller, 18 months old, admitted August 2, 1898, with tight stricture of the œsophagus eight inches from the incisors, through which a No. 8 French sound could be passed only with a great deal of difficulty. Solids and cold liquids regurgitate invariably, warm liquids quite often. Child emaciated, evidently losing ground from inanition. August 12: Gastrostomy (Kader) performed by Dr. Van Arsdale. Wound did well, permitting proper feeding through the tube, but patient's condition did not improve much. November 1: Under chloroform anæsthesia French bougie No. 8 was passed from above with considerable coaxing through stricture into stomach, whence its point was withdrawn through the fistula with a dressing forceps. A stout silk thread being tied to the olive point of the bougie, this was withdrawn backward and out of the mouth. To the ends of this silk thread were now tied successively larger and larger bougies up to No. 18 French, each being pulled through the stricture point forward by means of the silk thread. The ends of this thread were tied together and were left *in situ.* Each morning the same process was gone through with until on November 7 No. 24 was passed. Very soon the child began to swallow solids as well as liquids, her general condition improving very much.

November 30: The bougie could be readily passed from above, hence the thread was removed. The fistula healed rapidly. December 18: The child was discharged, with directions to have the regular use of the bougie continued for a long time.

In three cases gastro-enterostomy (retrocolica posterior) was performed for extensive gastric carcinoma, the anastomosis being made with the Murphy button, the operation in each case proving to be rapid and easy. Two of the patients recovered, deriving much relief and benefit from the operation. The one who died succumbed to pneumonia.

1898, vol. i., page 842. *Carcinoma of Stomach and Retroperitoneal Glands; Gastro enterostomy; Pneumonia; Death.*—Max H., 41 years old, admitted June 5 with palpable tumor and dilatation of stomach; history of persistent vomiting after meals; great emaciation. June 10: Transverse incision; piloric carcinoma involving most of stomach; extensive adhesions; many large glands to be felt through Winslow's foramen. Rapid anastomosis. Collapse of patient, overcome by stimulants. Closure of wound. June 11: Temperature slightly elevated (100.2° F.), but pulse very rapid and irregular (136); dyspnœa. Physical examination omitted on account of patient's weakness. June 13: Died. *Post-mortem:* Extensive piloric carcinoma of stomach with extreme stenosis. Wound and vicinity of anastomosis normal. A small quantity of blood clot in pelvis. Pneumonia of left lower lobe of lung.

1898, vol. i., page 126. *Carcinoma of Stomach: Persistent Vomiting: Extreme Emaciation; Gastro-enterostomy; Recovery.*—Mordechai G., 55 years old, admitted November 22. Three months ago, began to complain of pain in epigastrium. First vomited only solid, later also liquid nourishment soon after ingestion. Lost flesh to an alarming extent. Vomited coffee-ground matter. General condition extremely poor, extremities cold. Stomach dilated; in the epigastrium a nodular, movable mass to be felt, not connected with liver. Abdomen drawn in. Temperature 96.8°. No free hydrochloric acid in stomach contents, but lactic and butyric. Constipation relieved by calomel and salts. November 28:

Posterior gastro-enterostomy under chloroform. Rallied well from operation with the aid of a stimulating enema. In the evening persistent singultus, stopped by morphia hypodermatically given. November 29: Singultus again; morphia. Vomited eight ounces of dark brown fluid. Nutrition by mouth with small quantities of peptonized milk. November 30: Vomited brown fluid; stool by calomel. December 3: Stitches removed. December 6: Edges of normal looking wound parted for lack of adhesion; resutured. December 10: Retained food in growing quantities since three days. Condition markedly improved. Urination, formerly scanty, now copious. December 14: Wound healed. Patient visibly gaining flesh, eating and digesting solid food. Complaining of pain in tumor. Had gained twelve pounds of flesh. January 21, 1899, discharged improved. Button has not been passed.

1899, vol. i., page 114. *Carcinoma of Stomach; Vomiting of Food; Emaciation; Gastro-enterostomy; Bronchopneumonia; Recovery.*—Isaac S., 61 years old, suffered for many years from indigestion and constipation. Since five weeks began to vomit two or three hours after each meal. Great thirst and obstinate constipation. Lost much flesh and became very weak. Admitted November 5, 1898, to medical service, where stomach contents were repeatedly examined. Absence of free hydrochloric, presence of lactic and butyric acids. November 24: Transferred to surgical service. Great emaciation. In the epigastrium a hard nodular movable tumor, moving with the respiratory excursions, and changing its position downward on inflation of the stomach. Pulse and temperature normal. November 25: Posterior gastro enterostomy. The pyloric half of the stomach formed a large cancerous mass. Retroperitoneal glands much involved. November 26: Feeding by mouth with peptonized milk commenced. November 27: Vomited a small quantity of green fluid; stool by calomel. November 28: Dyspnœa; dulness at bases of both lungs, with crepitant râles and sharpened breathing. Temperature 102.4° Fah. November 30: Temperature 103.8°, but physical signs of pnemonia diminishing. December 8: Sutures renewed Had retained all nourishment; temperature 100.2°. December 9: Great improvement; coughs much less. December 22: Leaves bed. December 25: Gaining flesh, but complaining of pain in epigastrium (button?). No nausea, stools regular. January 3, 1899: Had gained seven pounds in weight. January 16: Appetite good; is eating all kinds of food with relish, but complains of pain in the region of the stomach. January 20: Button was not passed. Discharged improved.

APPENDICITIS—158 operations, 149 patients, 27 deaths.

I *Cœliotomy, excision of appendix, closure of wound*—48 patients, no deaths.

	Total.	Deaths.
Cœliotomy for acute or subacute non-perforative appendicitis	35	
Cœliotomy for acute non-perforative appendicitis, ovarian cyst and pregnancy	1	
Cœliotomy for chronic non-perforative appendicitis, secondary operation, following incision and drainage	6	
Cœliotomy for empyema of appendix	6	

II. *Cœliotomy, acute perforative appendicitis, circumscribed or diffuse peritonitis*—57 patients, 22 deaths.

	Total.	Deaths.
Appendix removed, no adhesions:		
For acute appendicitis, perforation, circumscribed abscess	22	2
" gangrenous appendicitis, circumscribed abscess	5	2
" ruptured abscess, diffuse peritonitis, enterotomy and peritoneal drainage	7	3
Appendix not removed:		
In ruptured abscess, diffuse peritonitis, peritoneal drainage,	18	12
In ruptured abscess, diffuse peritonitis, enterotomy and peritoneal drainage	2	
In ruptured abscess, diffuse peritonitis, entero-paralysis, irrigation of peritoneum	2	2
In intramural abscess of cæcum, perforation, peritoneal drainage	1	1

III. *Cœliotomy, circumscribed appendicular abscess, well-defined tumor, appendix not removed*—53 operations on 44 patients, 5 deaths.

	Total.	Deaths.
Ileo-inguinal route.		
Parker's operation, incision and drainage	39	3
Secondary abscess, " " "	5	1
Lumbar route.		
Abscess, gangrene of colon, secondary fatal hemorrhage	1	1
Counter-incision for improving drainage	4	
Rectal route.		
Incision and drainage	4	

The exceedingly rich and instructing array of facts contained in the preceding tabulation is based upon the histories of 149 patients, of whom there were 80 men, 39 women, and 30 children, operatively treated during the year ending December 1, 1898. Of these 149 patients

27 died, making a total death rate of a trifle more than 18.6 per cent.

But by excluding Group 1, which does not contain a single fatal case, and charging the mortality to Groups 2 and 3 where it belongs, we shall see that in the 101 cases (with 110 operations) tabulated in these latter columns the rate of mortality rises to 26.8 per cent.

The significance of these relations, however, will be fully understood only by a detailed study of the items, arranged mainly on the basis of the pathological condition found at the time of the operation. Thus it will be perceived at once to what extent the morbid condition to be dealt with will influence the surgeon's procedure, but still more to what decisive extent the same morbid condition will determine the final issue.

We observe, then, the material arranged in three groups, according to pathological conditions found.

GROUP I.—Group 1 contains only cases either mild and chronic in character, or, if acute and violent, dealt with at a time *when the infectious process was still strictly confined within the appendix itself, its peritoneal coating being intact.* We must except 6 cases in which, an abscess having been incised and drained, there remained behind either a fistula or a tumor, or both, which indicated the secondary removal of the appendix. All of these were difficult and tedious operations. This group contains also a fair proportion of chronic relapsing cases, operated upon during the so called interval between two attacks.

We see that these early operations are not only prophylactic or curative in the true sense of the word, but also that they are remarkably safe, entailing very slight risk indeed. Examination of the appendices almost invariably revealed morbid changes of a pronounced character, such as ulceration of the mucosa, stenosis due to swelling of the mucosa, to stricture or flexion, and fæcal concretions—conditions that were certain to cause further trouble. Comparing the gratifying and lasting results achieved in this group with the appalling mortality that belongs to the two subsequent groups, the conclusion seems fully to be justified that the removal of the appendix is urgently indicated whenever it becomes clear that it is diseased.

Furthermore, it is to be added that operation at this stage insures great freedom from ventral hernia, as the closure of the abdominal incision by a methodical suture of all the components of the abdominal wall, layer by layer in the anatomical order, is permissible, and is usually followed by primary union.

In most of these cases the abdominal incision was laid vertically over the outer half and parallel with the edge of the right rectus muscle, dividing the aponeurosis of the external oblique and the anterior wall of the sheath of the rectus. This muscle being somewhat displaced toward the median line, one or two branches of the epigastric vessels and their accompanying nerves were divided; then the inner lamella of the sheath of the rectus, the transversalis fascia and peritoneum were divided, and thus the iliac fossa was exposed. Then the appendix was found—occasionally a difficult problem—and its mesenteriolum and the base of the appendix being ligatured, both were cut off and the stumps thoroughly charred by the actual cautery and dropped. Finally the wound was closed by three layers of buried continuous chromicized catgut sutures and by the skin suture, all of these enforced by a number of silkworm-gut button sutures that had first been passed through all the components of the abdominal wall. In a few cases McBurney's incision was employed, consisting in the main in the blunt separation of the fibres of the several layers of the abdominal wall. The result in these cases as to the freedom from subsequent ventral hernia was excellent. The aperture was adequate, in simple cases free from adhesions; but where these were encountered and extensive, the work was much cramped on account of lack of space.

Only in a few of the cases thus treated did suppuration of the stitch holes occur, and that exclusively in the skin, sometimes as late as a fortnight after the operation. But where the union was faultless the patients were permitted to leave the bed in a fortnight or in three weeks. The wearing of a belly band was discouraged as tending to weaken the abdominal muscles.

Diagnostic Errors.—The key to the successful treatment of appendicitis is an early diagnosis. Though we have learned to recognize the trouble in its early phases, still errors will occasionally occur. Two instances are here reported:

1897, December 3, page 1173a. *Pregnancy at the End of the Eighth Month; History of Many Mild Attacks of "Appendicitis" followed by a Violent Attack; Laparotomy; Removal of Small Dermoid Cyst of Right Side (Twisted Pedicle) and of an Adherent Appendix inflamed through Juxtaposition; Premature Labor; Safe Delivery; Recovery without Ventral Hernia.*—Mrs. C. K., æt. 23, primipara, had, during and before her pregnancy, suffered from attacks of violent pain in the right iliac fossa at frequent intervals, which were looked upon as due to appendicular colic or a mild appendicitis. On admission it was stated that since two days the old pain has recurred with greater intensity than ever, accompanied by severe and frequent vomiting and great dejection. The abdomen was occupied by the enlarged uterus of a proper size; per rectum and per vaginam palpation yielded, on account of the presenting head, negative results, the only local symptom of significance being the rigidity of the abdominal walls over the right iliac region, and an exquisite pain on pressure corresponding to the abdomen adjoining the anterior upper rim of the pelvis. The pulse had been rapidly rising and was up to 136 per minute, though the temperature was only 100.4 F. The constant vomiting, the growing pulse rate, and ominous facial expression determined an immediate operation, in the presence of the gynæcologist of the Hospital, Dr. Mundé, on December 3, 1897, at 11 P.M. The incision along the outer edge of the right rectus gave exit to a large quantity of bloody serum. As soon as the pregnant womb was drawn aside a small, flattened, blue black tumor was seen occupying the deeper parts of the iliac fossa, proving to be a dermoid cyst twisted on its long pedicle. Closely adherent to it and much congested was found the appendix, which was removed together with the cyst. It was sharply bent upon itself, atresic near the base, and much distended by turbid fluid. As the ligature securing the cystic pedicle lay close to the cornu of the pregnant uterus, it was justly expected that uterine contraction and expulsion of the fœtus might soon follow, hence the closure of the abdominal wound was attended to with the greatest care as to durability of the sutures under the muscular efforts of delivery. A close row of double-gutted silkworm button sutures, reinforced by a separate suture of each layer of the abdominal walls, was applied, and the usual adhesive plaster strips and a snugly fitting binder were added. Following the operation, vomiting continued for another day, undoubtedly on account of the local peritonitis; but the pulse rate began to fall, especially after flatulence was relieved by a high enema. December 5, at 3:20 A.M., labor commenced and was carried to a successful termination by Dr. Morrison, the house surgeon The sutures held admirably, and the patient made an uneventful recovery, being discharged cured December 17, her child also doing well.

The coincidence of a twisted pedicle, of a very small ovarian cyst, and of an appendicitis, together with the impossibility of a satisfactory palpation, rendered an exhaustive diagnosis impossible in this case.

1898, vol. i., page 212. *Colitis simulating Appendicitis; Cœliotomy; Congenital Absence of Appendix; Cure.*—Gustave M., 13 years old, admitted January 23. Two years ago abdominal pain in right iliac region, on account of which he was confined to bed for eight months. His physician declared the case to be one of inflammation of the bowels. Four months ago a similar but milder attack, lasting four weeks. Nine days ago persistent pain in right iliac region of a colicky character; vomited once; bowels moved without aid every day. Since two days began to improve. At present pulse and temperature normal. Internal organs appear to be normal. In the right iliac region some tenderness on pressure, no distension, and an elongated, indistinct mass can be felt. It was assumed that we had to deal with a case of relapsing non-perforative appendicitis, and that the removal of the organ was justified. January 25: Cœliotomy. The iliac fossa being exposed by the usual incision, a portion of the colon presented, firmly adherent to the anterior abdominal wall, to adjoining small intestine, and to the omentum, from which it had to be laboriously dissected away. As soon as the adhesions were severed, search for the appendix was made, and that ineffectually for a long time. Finally it was decided to make a systematic investigation. It was ascertained that the ascending and transverse colon were fastened by an extremely long mesentery, the colon itself being inordinately long. Where the ileum was seen to pass into the colon the mesentery was also very long, permitting the displacement of cæcum, ileum, and colon to the left side of the abdominal cavity, so as to empty the right iliac fossa of all its contents, the lateral and posterior parietal peritoneum being everywhere exposed. There was no trace of an appendix present. The first four inches of the ascending colon appeared to be appreciably thickened, rigid, and somewhat congested, this portion corresponding to the site of the adhesions severed at the beginning of the operation. Wound closed. Uneventful recovery. Discharged February 8.

Remarks.—Evidently we had to deal here with a case of absence of the appendix. Attacks of colitis, occurring in an abnormally elongated and very lax colon, had simulated appendicitis and had caused the formation of adhesions.

Group II.—In examining the facts contained in the several items of this group, the irresistible conclusion must be drawn that by a perforation, or the extension in contiguity of the infection to the peritoneum, the aspect of things is immediately changed, and that the danger caused by these factors is in direct proportion to the extent of the area of the invasion. We see that of 22 patients suffering from perforation with a circumscribed abscess, only 2 died ; where the abscess had ruptured, out of 7 patients 3 died. Where the appendix was gangrenous *in toto*, out of 5 patients, 2 died, both of an acute septicæmia not complicated with exudative peritonitis.

Under the following four headings we meet with the highest death rate, 65.2 per centum—primarily determined by the lesser or greater extent of the diffuse infection of the peritoneum; probably, though to a lesser extent, also by the virulence of the character of the infectious agent, by the power of resistance of the individual, and also by the manner of the treatment.

Considering the extent of the infection and the severity of the local and general symptoms, it is gratifying and noteworthy that even so many as 8 patients, out of a total of 23, recovered. Not many years ago surgeons used to decline to operate in cases of the character contained under these headings. As some of the most desperately sick patients have unexpectedly recovered, we now follow the rule—as in cases of strangulated hernia —never to decline to operate, unless the patient is actually dying.

Most of these patients were admitted during the late afternoon or in the night, and consequently were operated upon by the adjunct visiting surgeon on duty, or occasionally by the house surgeon. To both Drs. Van Arsdale and Lilienthal fell the seemingly thankless task of dealing with most of these desperate cases, and to their enterprise and energy belongs the honor of success. Extensive and multiple incisions, ferreting out of the extent of the infection and of hidden recesses and abscesses; where the meteorism was excessive, one or multiple enterotomies, affording exit to pent-up gas and fæces; finally, a comprehensive scheme of drainage by tubing and packings, constituted the essence of their procedures. Twice the entire intestine was eventrated and the peritoneal cavity washed out by large quantities of normal salt solution, but in both cases without any good effect, both patients dying. A more detailed publication concerning this interesting field of surgery will appear from the pen of Dr. Lilienthal, to which those seeking further information are referred.

The contrast in the nature of the after-treatment of the cases contained in Group 1 and Group 2 is also noteworthy. Where, in the former, the surgeon's work is practically finished on the operating table, in the latter the critical general condition of the patient, the management of the multiform exigencies of the wound, call forth unflagging watchfulness and continuous exertion, extending over days and weeks, until the matter is settled either by death or recovery. The necessity for keeping the wound wide open results quite often in the formation of ventral hernia, though we have learned to combat this tendency by the employment of secondary suturing of the severed abdominal wall, performed as soon as the deeper recesses and pockets have been obliterated by granulations Fæcal fistulæ have also been observed in a small fraction of the cases, most of which, however, closed spontaneously. In those cases where the intestine had been incised for giving vent to fæces and gas, the aperture in the gut was usually closed by a few Lembert sutures as soon as the peritonitis appeared to be warded off.

1898, vol. i., page 807. *Appendicitis, Diffuse Peritonitis, Excision of Appendix, Drainage; Subphrenic Abscess, Incision, Drainage; Empyema of Right Side, Incision, Drainage, Collapse, Saline Infusion; Recovery.*—Charles K., 28 years old. Had had two years ago an attack of abdominal pain. Five days ago was seized with abdominal pain, fever, chills, vomiting, and constipation. The emaciated, anxious patient was admitted March 19, 1898. A large mass occupied the right iliac region, which could also be felt by rectum, extending to the small pelvis. Immediate operation. A large quantity of extremely fetid pus was evacuated by an iliac incision, together with fæcal concrements, and then it was found that an open communication existed between the abscess and the pelvis, from which a large quantity of brown, odorless serum was sponged out. The appendix was perforated and disintegrated, so as to tear on manipulation. It was tied off and removed; cavity swabbed with peroxide of hydrogen and drained. Cultures yielded bacillus coli communis. Fever continued until April 5, when a chill and a rise to 104.8° occurred. The next day a dulness was found extending on the right side from the angle of the scapula downward, with distant breathing and voice. On puncturing the ninth space pus was found. Immediately the tenth rib was resected; then, following the guidance of the aspirating needle, the pleura, diaphragm, and liver were successively severed, the first of which was found obliterated at this place. To gain additional space the ninth rib was also resected, and then the abscess situated above the liver was opened and drained. The fever lessened gradually after this, but never disappeared entirely. The purulent discharge was tinged with bile for a while. On April 17 coughing set in and fetid matter was expectorated. The dulness over the base of right lung, after diminishing, again increased in size, and the aspirating needle withdrew pus. The patient's condition was becoming worse and worse, and incision and drainage of the evident empyema on May 2 was followed by a deep collapse, necessitating a saline infusion. In the meantime the abdominal wound was closing rapidly. After this the patient's condition began to improve immediately, and he was discharged cured on June 12.

GROUP III.—In this group we find those cases that, having been treated on the expectant plan outside of the Hospital, did not develop a diffuse peritonitis, but were admitted with a more or less well-defined tumor and indications of suppuration. On 44 patients 53 operations were done to give exit to pus and sloughing material. Of these 5 died: 3 from septicæmia, 1 from sepsis and intestinal hemorrhage due to an extensive gangrene of the colon (1898, vol. i., page 207), and the last one of diffuse peritonitis, caused evidently by an infection of the peritoneum. This occurred while a secondary operation was being done during convalescence for the reduction of the size of the large wound (1898, vol. i., page 181). There was present a fæcal fistula, and probably one of the silkworm-gut sutures used, having been soiled by fæces, penetrated the peritoneum. At the autopsy general fibrinous peritonitis was found; the appendix had evidently sloughed away, as it could not be detected.

This last fact explains the observation made by many surgeons, that in a large number of cases presenting an abscess containing sloughing matter no recurrence of suppuration takes place, though no steps were taken to remove the appendix. It also justifies the position of those who deprecate a persistent search for the appendix in an extensive fetid abscess. Breaking down of protective adhesions and an accidental infection of the sound peritoneum would be risked to no purpose whatever in the search for a non-existent appendix. It is much safer to permit the abscess cavity to contract or to heal, and, if there be further trouble, to operate a second time later on, when the infectiousness of the field will have been eliminated by proper drainage.

Subjoined history is given in extract on account of the important and interesting findings in the condition of the colon, indicating the way in which the walls of the appendix and colon become infected through the follicles of the mucosa. Necrosis and suppuration extending to the serous coat lead ultimately to perforation and to the infection of the adjoining peritoneum.

1898, vol. ii., page 494. *Gangrenous Typhlitis; Submucous Abscess of Cæcum; Diffuse Septic Peritonitis; Cœliotomy; Death.*—Mrs. Aschne H., 40 years old, admitted September 26. First attack of two weeks' standing, with colic, vomiting, diarrhœa, fever, but no chill. Within the last four days the pain became localized in the right iliac fossa. She had not passed urine for twenty-four hours, but three ounces were drawn by catheter on admission. She had had ten foul watery stools in the last twenty-four hours. Pulse 128, temperature 102.4°, respiration 28. Faint icterus of sclerotic. Symptoms of bronchial trouble on both sides. Liver and spleen normal. Right rectus abdominis tense. General abdominal gaseous distension. A tender mass extending from ileum inward to the umbilicus. Immediate operation. Right iliac fossa opened by the usual incision. Immediately fetid pus welled up between the colon and parietal peritoneum. Surrounding intestines fixed by adhesions. The colon appearing much distended, congested, and thickened, the free peritoneal cavity was protected by suitable packings and the former organ was investigated. Its serous coat was œdematous, thickened, and in spots gangrenous. On incising the serous coat, pus was seen to escape from a cavity evidently situated within the wall of the colon, the probe not entering the lumen of the gut. But on account of the far-gone destruction it was impossible exactly to determine whether this pus was contained between serous and muscular or between muscular and mucous coats. It was not deemed prudent to make a search for the appendix. The intramural abscess and the iliac fossa were drained by gauze wicks. The external wound was left open. September 27: Patient vomited; temperature rose to 103°, and, the distension becoming more marked, the colon was incised, permitting gas and fæces to escape. Condition grew rapidly worse. September 28: Fæcal vomiting. Evident peritonitis. Died. (Van Arsdale.)

INTESTINAL OPERATIONS—17, on 16 patients, 10 deaths.

	Total.	Deaths.
Cœliotomy, exploratory, for carcinoma of sigmoid flexure (general carcinomatosis)	1	
Cœliotomy and resection of ascending and transverse colon for adenoma, Murphy button [1]	1	
Cœliotomy and resection of carcinoma of descending colon, Murphy button	1	
Cœliotomy and resection for gangrenous inguinal hernia, Murphy button	1	1
Cœliotomy and resection for fæcal fistula, Murphy button	1	1
Cœliotomy and resection for intussusception, Murphy button	1	1
Cœliotomy and colotomy for reduction of intussusception	1	1
Cœliotomy and enterostomy for intestinal obstruction	1	1
Cœliotomy for intestinal obstruction due to internal hernia	1	
Cœliotomy and enterorrhaphy for typhoid perforation [2] (Van Arsdale)	1	1
Cœliotomy and colostomy, median, for intestinal paresis	1	1
Cœliotomy and right inguinal colostomy	2	2
Cœliotomy and left inguinal colostomy	4	1

The large percentage of mortality is due to the wretched general condition of those patients that succumbed. See histories.

[1] See report by Dr. Lilienthal in succeeding pages of this volume.
[2] Patient's history preserved in the records of the Children's Ward.

1898, vol. ii., page 239. *Carcinoma of Sigmoid Flexure; Resection; Murphy Button; Fœcal Fistula; Cure.*—Joseph H., 64 years old, had suffered for a long time from obstinate and increasing constipation and tympanites. Admitted June 16. Since four days no movement of bowels; great distension relieved by enema, after which tumor could be felt in left groin. June 23: Typical resection of six inches of gut. Accidental escape of liquid fæces while proximal button was being inserted. Toilet. Drainage. Moderate reaction and fever. June 24: Liquid diet; bowels moved spontaneously. June 27: Profuse fæcal discharge from wound. July 17: Button passed. July 19: Wound closing rapidly, very little discharge. August 7: Discharged cured. (Lilienthal.)

1898, vol. i., page 766. *Strangulated Gangrenous Inguinal Hernia; Herniotomy; Resection of Gut; Murphy Button.*—Emma O., 42 years old. Reducible hernia of five years' standing. Admitted June 8. Five days ago hernia became irreducible, with pain and vomiting. Small red tumor in right groin. Pulse 114, temperature 100.4°. Fæcal vomiting. Immediate herniotomy. Knuckle of small intestine found gangrenous. Wound enlarged. Difficult resection of eight inches of gut, on account of tearing of the friable tissues. Soiling of field of operation. Murphy button. Wound packed and left open. Stomach relieved of much fæcal matter by lavage. Profound collapse, from which the patient did not recover; died the same night.

1898, vol. ii., page 868. *Diffuse Purulent Peritonitis of unknown origin; Enterotomy; Fœcal Fistula; Resection of Gut; End to-end Anastomosis; Death.*—Samuel S., 23 years old, admitted September 27 with enormously distended abdomen, fæcal vomiting. Temperature 101.6°, pulse 104, respiration 28, general condition very bad. Immediate median cœliotomy done by Dr. Van Arsdale. Much diffuse pus found in peritoneal cavity. Washing out by saline solution and incision of a much-distended coil of small intestine to relieve distension. Intestinal wound left open. Patient recovered from peritonitis, so that, beginning October 3, several ineffectual attempts were made to close the fæcal fistula, each attempt being followed by vomiting, which persisted until the gut reopened spontaneously or was reopened. On account of the strongly acrid fæcal discharge a florid eczema developed around the wound. This did not yield to ordinary local treatment until by the proper choice of the diet and by the administration of alkalies the reaction of the fæces was converted from acid to neutral or alkaline. November 21: The patient evidently getting weaker from inanition, a more energetic attempt was made to close the fistula. It was evident that below the fistula, in the distal part of the gut, some obstruction was present, which had to be eliminated before the gut was closed. The fæcal fistula, being cleansed and packed, was tightly sewed up with silk sutures passed through the adjoining skin. Then the peritoneal cavity was opened parallel to and near the old scar, and, the afferent and efferent parts of the leaky coil being found, freeing of the extensively adherent gut was begun. This proved to be a very tedious and difficult undertaking, during which a part of the serous coat of the gut was torn and stripped off for a distance and had to be sutured back in place. Resection of four inches of gut, followed by circular silk suture, and a comprehensive packing placed to protect the line of suture. The patient was much exhausted, and repeatedly collapsed, requiring the next day, November 22, an intravenous infusion. Vomiting set in soon after the operation, and, though the bowels moved freely after the administration of calomel on November 24, continued to sap the patient's strength. The temperature did not rise above 100.6°, but the pulse remained thready and the facial expression anxious. The stomach was washed out repeatedly, the packings were renewed, and the union of the suture was found perfect. In spite of rectal nutrition and stimulation of every known kind, the patient died on November 29. *Postmortem* examination of the wound revealed injection of the peritoneum wherever packing had been placed. Suture of the gut was found tight, the entire intestine collapsed and empty. No general autopsy was permitted by the relatives.

1898, vol i., page 203. *Acute Ileo-colic Intussusception; Gangrene of Intestine; Resection; Murphy Button; Death.*—Samuel R., 6 months old, admitted February 2. Obstruction, distension, vomiting, passage of bloody mucus of four days' standing. Presentation of a dark mass at anus. February 3: Median cœliotomy. Ileocolic intussusception. Close adhesion between intussusceptum and intussuscipiens at ileo-colic valve. In attempting reduction the colon gave way, and a gangrenous ring was found on the reduced ileum nine centimetres from the ileo-cæcal valve. Resection of seventeen centimetres of ileum and eighteen centimetres of colon. Murphy button. Collapse during the greater part of the operation. Died one and a half hours after.

1898, vol. ii., page 464. *Acute Ileo-colic Intussusception; Cœliotomy; Reduction; Death.*—Isaac G., 7 months old, admitted September 15 with the usual symptoms of two days' standing. Tumor in right iliac fossa; lateral incision. The mass proved to be the ileum invaginated in the ascending colon. Reduction by manipulation being impossible, the region of the ileo-cæcal valve was opened by a longitudinal incision, after which reduction was effected with some difficulty. The much-distended small gut was also incised and a large quantity of liquid fæces evacuated. Suture of both intestinal incisions; gauze drainage. The collapsed child died soon after the operation. (Lilienthal.)

1898, vol. ii., page 878. *Internal Strangulated Hernia in a Preformed Sac in Douglas' Pouch; Cœliotomy; Reduction; Cure.*—Rosie S., 40 years old, admitted October 27. Has had prolapse of uterus to the ostium vaginæ for a long time. For six days previous to admission symptoms of chronic obstruction. No fever; occasional vomiting; no movement of bowels could be caused by laxatives or enemata. Abdomen distended; visible peristalsis. By rectum a painful, hard, elastic mass could be felt occupying Douglas' pouch, relations of which were not influenced by the replacement of the uterus. October 30: Median cœliotomy. Among distended intestines a collapsed coil of small gut being found, it was followed down to Douglas' pouch. In Trendelenburg's position it was ascertained that a circular aperture one inch in diameter was formed by a fold of the peritoneum, on the floor of the pelvis, behind the uterus, leading into a cavity having a capacity of about a pint. A coil of small intestine of about two feet passed through this aperture into the sac, and was tightly compressed by the falciform fibrous edges of the aperture. This having been laterally nicked in several places, the gut could easily be withdrawn, and was found to be viable at the site of incarceration. The aperture being closed by a catgut suture, the abdominal wound was also closed. Uninterrupted recovery. Discharged cured November 20.

1898, vol. i., page 872. *Intestinal Paresis simulating Chronic Intestinal Obstruction; Colostomy; Death.*—Frank S., 60 years old, admitted June 21. For a long time bowels moved once in five or six days. For six days before admission no stool; considerable nausea; some vomiting. Examination per rectum gave negative result. Abdomen much distended; no localized area of tenderness; general condition bad: pulse weak, rapid; temperature normal. June 21: Median colostomy; evacuation of fluid fæces; anæsthesia very badly borne. Patient collapsed at the end of the operation; did not rally; died June 22. Postmortem failed to establish the cause of the distension.

1898, vol. i., page 235. *Carcinoma of the Liver involving Transverse Colon; Obstruction; Right Inguinal Colostomy; Death from Carcinomatosis.*—Theresa S., admitted and operated upon Jan. 24. Died Feb. 9.

1898, vol. i., page 641. *Intestinal Obstruction of unknown origin; Fæcal Vomiting; Excessive Distension; No Fever; Right Inguinal Colostomy; Death.*—Mendel B., 60 years old, admitted May 20. Had always suffered from constipation. Four days ago severe abdominal pain; bowels had not been moved since then. Fæcal vomiting, distension, deterioration of general state. Rectum collapsed and empty. Distension most marked in right side of abdomen; no tumor could be felt; immediate right inguinal colostomy. A number of bands of adhesions compressing the ascending colon were divided, but without visible effect upon distension. Ascending colon being incised, a large quantity of fluid fæces came away. The gut being closed, another ineffectual search was made for the cause of the obstruction; then the gut was reopened and stitched to the external wound. The next day a profuse escape of fæces was noted. Temperature 101°; general condition somewhat improved. May 22: Temperature normal; patient gradually went into collapse, and died May 23. (Lilienthal.)

On four patients inguinal colostomy on the left side was performed in two sittings, once for syphilitic stricture of rectum, twice for carcinoma of the rectum, and once for general tubercular peritonitis. The first three recovered, the last one died. A spur was formed by suturing, and the gut was divided transversely to prevent the entrance of fæces into the distal portion. As far as could be ascertained, no prolapse followed.

1898, vol. ii., page 249. *Intestinal Chronic Obstruction from General Tubercular Peritonitis; Colostomy; Death.*—Armin S., 31 years old, admitted August 6. General abdominal distension; free exudate in both flanks; anxious expression; obstinate constipation; slight fever. Immediate colostomy; breaking up of a number of fibrinous adhesions; evacuation of ascitic fluid. August 7: Gut incised; pulse 126, temperature 99.8; vomiting of green fluid. August 9: Death. (Van Arsdale.)

MISCELLANEOUS ABDOMINAL OPERATIONS—14, 1 death.

	Total.	Deaths.
Cœliotomy for acute pancreatitis and fat necrosis [1]	1	
" " omental thrombosis from strangulation	1	
" " pyosalpinx	1	
" " ruptured pyosalpinx	1	
" " ovarian cyst	2	
" " " abscess	1	1
" " " sarcoma	1	
" exploratory	3	
" for retroperitoneal lympho-sarcoma	1	
" " osteo-sarcoma of ilium	1	
Cœliotomy for peritoneal tuberculosis and retroperitoneal lymphadenitis	1	
Cœliotomy for colitis simulating appendicitis [2]	1	

Note.—Another cœliotomy performed for ligaturing the internal iliac artery will be found under the heading "Operations on Blood Vessels," page 219.

Diagnostic Errors.—In disposing of this column occasion is taken to call attention to two cases, interesting mainly because they gave occasion to errors in diagnosis. Two more cases, belonging here, are reported under "Appendicitis" on page 194.

1898, vol. ii., page 1001.—Mrs. Anna W., 34 years old, admitted November 16, 1898, with a history of acute, never-ceasing, but in intensity paroxysmal pain located in right iliac region; fever, and acceleration of pulse with continuous nausea were present. Abdominal walls over the right iliac fossa were extremely rigid, and exquisite pain was complained of even on gentle palpation. Examination was further made unsatisfactory both by free liquid in the abdomen and a considerable distension of the bowels. Yet a hard, seemingly immovable mass

[1] Communicated by Dr. M. Manges on page 69.
[2] History found on page 187 in the chapter on "Appendicitis."

could be felt filling the right iliac fossa and extending nearly to the median line. Per vaginam the genitals presented nothing remarkable. A large quantity of sanguinolent serum escaped through a lateral incision, and soon it became evident that we had to deal with a congested ovarian cyst thrice twisted on its pedicle from the right to the left. Pedicle tied off and incision closed in the usual manner. December 4: Discharged cured.

1898, vol. i., page 889. *Inguinal Hernia of Right Side said to have been Cured Twenty Years ago with a Truss; Pain in Iliac Fossa; Nausea; Constipation; Tumor of Right Iliac Fossa; Cœliotomy; Ablation of Mesentery showing Thrombosed Blood Vessels; Cure.*—Isaac C., 36 years old, admitted April 15, 1898, stating that he was taken suddenly with pain located in the right groin two days ago. On admission the temperature was 103.6°, pulse 92, tongue dry and furred. Signs of emphysema and bronchitis; apparently no hernia. Marked persistent tenderness in right iliac region, where a large mass could be felt, most of which, however, disappeared on withdrawing by catheter forty ounces of urine. A small, rather movable, and very painful mass could be still felt in the iliac fossa; hence, on account of the fever, it was suspected that we had to deal with an appendicitis of the meso-cœliac type. April 18: The abdomen being opened in the usual place, a bluish, pear-shaped tumor, evidently a portion of the omentum, came into view, overlying a normal cæcum, appendix, and iliac fossa. It was about the size of a hen's egg, showing a neck-like attenuation at the base, its veins all thrombosed and the fatty tissue in a state of sanguinolent infiltration. It was then ascertained that we had to deal with a case in which the omentum had slipped into an old hernia but was reduced spontaneously. Yet the changes wrought in the strangulated omentum were severe enough to cause peritoneal irritation with fever. In the absence of a correct explanation, appendicitis was suspected. The mass was tied off in sections, the pedicle dropped, and the outer wound was closed. Suppuration of the stitch holes compelled reopening of the outer wound, which healed by granulation. Discharged cured June 26.

Finally we have to report a case in which, while removing an ovarian abscess, the surgeon injured accidentally the bladder near the insertion of the left ureter. The patient died.

1898, vol. i., page 759. *Ovarian Abscess; Cœliotomy; Accidental Injury of Ureter and Bladder; Peritonitis; Death.*—Mrs. R. S., 38 years old, admitted May 28. Cœliotomy May 30. Left ovary distended by an abscess holding about two ounces of thick pus. Dissection and removal of left ovary and tube. Abscess ruptured, but soiling of peritoneum was warded off by a wall of packings. The fornix of the vagina had been preliminarily incised for the establishment of drainage, which would enable the surgeon to close the abdominal wound again. In establishing this counter-opening the bladder was injured, but the fact was not noticed. Vaginal gauze drainage; closure of abdominal wound after the operation. The patient soon began to complain of severe colicky pains, and spent a restless night, vomiting considerably. She passed four and one-half ounces of bloody urine during the night. In the morning it was immediately seen that the abdomen contained free fluid. The wound being reopened, it was seen that the peritoneal cavity was filled with urinous, bloody liquid. This was removed by sponging; the bladder was drained downward by the insertion of a tube; then the peritoneal cavity was copiously irrigated with normal saline solution, and suprapubic gauze drainage was also employed. The septic symptoms, however, continued unabated until the patient's death, which occurred on June 1.

HERNIOTOMIES—73, 68 patients.

Primary Union, 60; *Suppuration*, 6; *Open Treatment*, 4; *Deaths*, 3.

	Totals.	Primary Union.	Suppuration.	Open Treatment.	Death.
Inguinal, reducible, Bassini's operation.	48	42	6	..	..
" irreducible, enormous in size, Bassini's operation.......	2	..	..	1	1
" irreducible	4	4	..	..	..
" strangulated...............	10	7	..	1	2
Femoral, "	5	3	..	2	..
Umbilical, "	1	1	..	..	..
" irreducible	1	1	..	.	..
Ventral, "	1	1	..	..	..
" reducible.......	1	1	..	..	..

In surveying this table, it will be seen that the radical operation of reducible inguinal hernia is a very safe operation. Five times double herniotomy was done at one sitting. In three cases primary union followed on both sides ; in two cases suppuration took place on one side, the other healing by first intention. Altogether, out of 48 operations, primary union was observed 42 times, suppuration of a more or less extensive character 6 times ; all patients recovered. Bassini's method was employed exclusively, Kocher's and MacEwen's having been finally abandoned since two years. As primary union is here the most essential requisite of success, the greatest care was employed in the preparation of patient and operative apparatus, this including the surgeon and his assistants. All hands were covered with sterilized cotton gloves, which were changed whenever a suspicion of unclean contact arose. Formerly fine silk was used for the deep buried sutures with entire satisfaction. But a number of late suppurations having been observed to occur, this material was replaced by chromicized catgut, which was exclusively in use during the past year. By examining the complete table we see that primary union was aimed at and hoped for in 67 operations. Sixty times this hope was fulfilled. In 7 cases it was disappointed, viz., in 6 cases of Bassini's operation done for reducible inguinal hernia, and in 1 case of an enormously large, irreducible scrotal hernia, which contained almost all the intestines and the greatest part of the omentum. This is the only case in which death followed Bassini's operation done for a non-strangulated hernia. Diligent search for the causes of infection in our unsuccessful cases resulted in the conviction that it was conveyed to the wounds through infected hands. In two cases death followed herniotomy performed for strangulated hernia: in one instance by pneumonia, in the other by peritonitis. Altogether, out of 16 patients operated upon for various forms of strangulated hernia, 2 died. Four times the open treatment of the external wound was adopted, either because the gut was suspected to be or was actually damaged, or because in very fat patients the closure of the external wound seemed to be too risky. These 4 were the only cases in which any form of drainage was employed.

1897, vol. ii., page 1157*a*. *Irreducible Inguinal Hernia of Enormous Size; Bassini; Infection of Wound; Septicæmia; Death.*—Henry F., 42 years old, admitted December 13, 1897. Excessively obese man of large stature. Since nine years right inguinal hernia, irreducible for past year. Hernia measured on admission 21 inches longitudinally, 25 inches in circumference. December 20: Operation. Hernial sac contained almost all small intestines, part of colon and omentum; numerous and extensive adhesions were divided and omentum resected. To replace the intestines the abdominal wall had to be incised upward six inches beyond external ring. Radical operation according to Bassini was performed. Drainage by scrotal opening, with gauze and tube. December 21: Patient vomited considerably after operation; bowels moved only very slightly in spite of all efforts; temperature 102°, pulse 120. December 24: General condition was bad, expression anxious; temperature 102°, pulse 140. On December 25 the wound was opened; tissues, especially the subcutaneous fat, were found extensively necrosed and fetid; liquid fat in the wound. General condition became rapidly worse, patient dying of sepsis the same day.

Remarks.—A great deal of difficulty was encountered in replacing the intestine and massive omental stump, and unavoidably much rather energetic manipulation had to be employed. Though surgeon and assistants had their hands protected with cotton gloves, a very virulent infection must have occurred, causing little local swelling, though extensive necrosis, especially of the subcutaneous fat and the fasciæ. Had the wound been opened to its full extent immediately after operation, the patient's life might have possibly been saved.

1898, vol. i., page 505. *Irreducible Inguinal Hernia of*

very large Size; Bassini; Open Treatment of Skin Wound; Secondary Suture; Cure.—Moses W., 54 years old, admitted February 7. Very stout, large man. Right inguinal hernia of very large size, extending almost to the knee. February 15: Bassini's operation. The sac contained most of the small intestine and the hypertrophied omentum, both more or less adherent to the sac. Abdominal wall was immediately slit up five inches above the ring, the omentum resected, and the hernial contents replaced with some difficulty. Suture of abdominal wound, supplemented by Bassini suture of inguinal end of hiatus. External wound down to the aponeurosis of the external oblique was left open and packed. Slight febrile movement followed. February 16: Bowels moved with calomel. Slight suppuration in the stitch holes of the abdominal suture. March 25: Secondary suture. Discharged cured April 27.

1898, vol. ii., page 397. *Strangulated Inguinal Hernia; Herniotomy; Bassini; Œdema of Lungs; Death.*—Abraham I., 55 years old, admitted September 2 with strangulation of twenty-four hours' standing. Systolic murmur at apex. Immediate operation under chloroform and Schleich. Gut found viable. Typical Bassini. Anæsthesia very bad, marked by embarrassed respiration and stertorous breathing. Within a few hours after the operation, chill with temperature 102.4°, pulse 144, respiration 50. Died three hours after the operation with symptoms of œdema of the lungs. No postmortem permitted. (Brickner.)

1898, vol. i., page 37. *Strangulated Inguinal Hernia; Gangrene of Gut; Herniotomy; Wound left Open and Packed; Peritonitis; Sepsis; Death.*—Deborah C., 44 years old, admitted January 12. Old hernia, strangulated thirty-six hours. General condition very poor, pulse very feeble, 120, temperature 100.4°; fæcal vomiting. January 13, 8:30 A.M.: Herniotomy under eucaine local anæsthesia, patient's condition not warranting general anæsthesia. Gangrenous small intestine found, strangulation relieved, wound packed. Continued fæcal vomiting, temperature remaining high, up to 104.6°. Growing rapidly worse. January 15: Died with temperature 105.2°. No postmortem permitted.

OPERATIONS ON THE KIDNEY—22, on 17 patients, 1 death.

	Total.	Death.
Nephrorrhaphy for floating kidney	1	
Nephrotomy, exploratory	2	
" for pyelonephritis	2	
" " pyonephrosis	7	1
Nephrectomy for pyonephrosis	5	
" " sarcoma of kidney	1	
" " pyelonephritis and stricture of ureter	1	
Perinephritic abscess, incision and drainage	2	
Ureteroplasty for stricture of ureter	1	

Ureteral catheterization, both by Casper's and by Kelly's methods, was practised in the general surgical service nine times.

Seventeen patients were treated for various disorders of the kidney, upon whom 22 operations were performed. The only death recorded occurred in a case of old hydronephrosis of very large size, in which the sac had suppurated. Incision and drainage of this sac was sufficient to sap the vitality of the patient, who died of shock shortly after the operation. Out of 7 nephrectomies primary removal of the diseased organ was done only twice, once for neoplasm and once for pyonephrosis. Ordinarily it was preferred to incise and drain first, thus to allow the tumor to shrink and to bring about defervescence of the existing fever. As a rule a marked improvement of the patient's condition followed this measure. The dangers of subsequent nephrectomy were thus materially reduced. The patient became more fit to withstand the shock often accompanying nephrectomy, and the shrinkage of the mass reduced the technical difficulties of the operation considerably, both as regards the extent of dissection and the hemorrhage. Finally, the interval elapsing between nephrotomy and nephrectomy offered good opportunities to form an opinion regarding the function of the other kidney. This experience does not militate against the principle that where the organ is totally useless, the fellow-kidney competent, and the state of the patient warrants it, the primary removal of the offending part is preferable.

The result of the ureteroplasty included in the table was a failure, principally on account of the ulcerative process existing in the pelvis of the kidney, and also because the atrophy of the ureter created nearly insurmountable technical drawbacks. As the secreting tissue of the kidney proved to be sclerosed and atrophic, ablation of the useless organ did not represent a real loss. For details of the technique the reader is referred to the subjoined histories.*

1898, vol. ii., pages 81 and 749. *Renal Calculus; Pyonephrosis; Nephrotomy; Extraction of Large Uratic Calculus; Nephrectomy; Cure.*—Amalia Z., 28 years old, admitted July 1. Had suffered from difficulty of urination since childhood. Since three years urine became very turbid and offensive. She was married about a year ago, and was recently delivered of a child. In May she began to feel acute pain in left loin, having periodical attacks of fever, and became extremely anæmic and thin. On examination the urine was found loaded with thick, consistent masses of sticky pus; its reaction acid; odor fetid; no sugar; slight amount of albumin; no casts. In the left loin a smooth, movable, painful, and nonfluctuating mass could be felt, extending to the level of the umbilicus, evidently the kidney. The right kidney could also be palpated, though it was not as large as the other, nor was it painful. Other organs normal. July 2: Nephrotomy; a large quantity of fetid pus was evacuated from a free incision of the kidney, carried through parenchyma into the pelvis, from which a uratic stone, two and a half inches long, three-quarters of an inch thick, bifurcated at one end and tapering at the other, was extracted. Drainage. Though it was found that hardly any of the renal parenchyma was left, extirpation of the organ was refrained from. First, it was expected that the patient's general condition would improve after establishment of drainage; and secondly, a later nephrectomy, done on a collapsed and contracted organ, would be easier and less shocking. There was some febrile reaction following the operation, apparently due to the contamination of the wound by the fetid discharge. Urine became nearly clear, containing much less pus, averaging twenty-five ounces per day. She was sent home to recuperate July 14. Readmitted October 25 in a remarkably improved condition, having gained over thirty pounds in weight. Sinus discharging fetid pus only. Urine: acid, clear, no albumin, microscopical quantities of pus. Nephrotomized kidney still forming a large mass; the other kidney palpable, but not painful. October 25: *Cystoscopy* by Nitze's instrument. The right ureteral opening found normal, puckering with each discharge of a jet of urine. The right, presumably healthy, kidney was then punctured several times with a negative result. Then the removal of the left kidney was proceeded with. The separation of the kidney from the surrounding fat was easy, and the vessels of the pedicle could be isolated and separately ligatured with catgut. Very slight reaction followed. October 26: Passed eight and a half ounces of extremely fetid and turbid urine in twenty-four hours. Temperature 101.8°; general condition excellent; patient cheerful; pulse good, 98 to 108 per minute—the only alarming feature being the scantiness of the urine and some nausea. October 27: Vomited considerably. Retained eleven pints of saline solution administered since yesterday per rectum. Amount of urine, thirty-four ounces. October 28: Passed seventy-four ounces of very clear urine. Wound dressed, found in excellent condition. November 6: Urine normal microscopically and chemically. Discharged with healing wound, to be taken care of by her family physician. December 6: Presented herself with healed wound, feeling perfectly well.

1898, vol. i., page 551. *Renal Calculus in Right Kidney; Pyonephrosis; Nephrotomy.* 1898, vol. ii., page 260. *Nephrectomy; Cure.*—Pauline B., 25 years old, admitted December 25, 1897, with a history of fever and chills, with abdominal pain of a week's duration. Urination was not painful. Urine normal. Tenderness, resistance, and a tumor in right loin. General condition very poor on account of marked anæmia. Temperature 102.2°. December 28, 1897: Nephrotomy; evacuation of much thick pus; drainage. Patient bore the operation badly, needing much stimulation. December 29: Urine, hitherto normal, became loaded with pus; acid; no tubercle bacilli; slight reaction. The wound gradually closed, urine continuing to contain pus. January 24, 1898: Probe reveals calculus in kidney. Cystoscopy: Right ureteral orifice congested, discharging a plug of thick pus on massage of kidney and ureter; left ureteral orifice appears normal, discharging jets of clear urine; no catheterism. February 22: Attempt at extraction of stone. Patient collapsed at the very beginning of the operation, so that it had to be abandoned. April 23: Sent home to recuperate. Readmitted July 4, 1898. General condition much improved; considerable serous discharge from the old sinus; urine contained pus. July 11, 1898: Nephrectomy. Vessels of pedicle secured *en masse* with elastic ligature; external wound packed. Patient was infused intravenously during the operation to ward off collapse. Operation was well borne. July 12: Patient had reacted well; pulse of good quality; total urine passed, about thirty-five ounces, acid, clear, 1028; only a trace of albumin. The wound gradually closed by granulations. The general condition became very good; urine normal. Discharged cured August 11.

1898, vol. i., pages 171 and 679. *Pyelonephritis of old standing; Calculus of Kidney; Pyonephrosis; Nephrotomy; Calculi were felt; Improved.*—Johanna L., 26 years old, admitted January 5. History of pyelitis and cystitis of five years' standing. Left kidney forming a large, painful tumor extending to the level of umbilicus. Right kidney palpable, not painful. Urine: acid, loaded with pus, containing albumin, no casts. Slight febrile movement every evening. Wretched general condition. Cystoscopy by Kelly's method unsuccessful. By Leiter's cystoscope the right ureteral orifice appeared normal; from the left ureter vermicular masses of pus were seen to escape on massage of the kidney. A tapeworm having been found, this was expelled by the administration of an anthelmintic, which weakened the patient very much. Hence she was sent home to recuperate. February 21: Nephrotomy; three large abscesses located in the parenchyma were evacuated. A stone was felt in the pelvis, but could not be extracted, as the patient went into a state of collapse. Intravenous infusion. Condition continued to be precarious, developing uræmic symptoms, especially a deep coma, which lasted until March 2. There was a copious urinous discharge from the incised kidney, the quantity of urine voided by the urethra being scanty—from four to eight ounces per twenty-four hours until February 28, when it became more copious—eighteen ounces—and the uræmic symptoms subsided, her mind becoming clear. She complained of pain in the right kidney, and the quality of the urine voided from the bladder made it clear that the right kidney also was seriously compromised. Her condition gradually improved, and she was discharged May 18 with a renal fistula.

1898, vol. ii., page 269. *Renal Calculus; Pyonephrosis; Nephrectomy; Cured.*—Blanche W., admitted July 16. Had since five months severe pain in right side of abdomen. Lost flesh and strength. Urine contained small amount of albumin and pus, no casts. On right side of abdomen was a large, hard, painful, movable mass. It could not be positively determined whether it originated from liver or right kidney. Left kidney could not be palpated. July 18: Exploratory cœliotomy at edge of right rectus muscle; mass found to be the kidney. Abdominal incision closed and nephrectomy performed. The kidney was with considerable difficulty separated from the surrounding structures, to which it was densely adherent. The pedicle was secured by an elastic ligature, the outer wound closed with drainage. Kidney, on section, was found to contain a large abscess, and in the pelvis a branching calculus. July 19: Slight febrile movement, some vomiting, but general condition was good. Passed twenty-one ounces of urine. Patient continued to pass fair amount of urine—about twenty-five ounces. She gained rapidly in her general condition, and was discharged August 13 cured. (Lilienthal.)

1898, vol. i., page 711. *Acute Congestion of Left Kidney; Bisecting Nephrotomy; Recovery.*—Mary C., 26 years old, admitted from medical department April 1. Had been having a continuous fever for two weeks, with local pain in the left loin and much scalding at urination. Urine contained albumin and white blood cells. Pressure on kidney painful. Spleen much enlarged, but no roseola nor diarrhœa present. Same day nephrotomy. Enlarged and congested kidney freed and withdrawn from wound. While assistant compressed renal vessels the organ was bisected. Cortex was considerably thickened, looking waxy pale. A wedge-shaped segment of cortex excised for examination. Pelvis and calices normal; no calculus found. Divided halves of kidney were brought together and sutured with six catgut stitches passed through the entire thickness of the parenchyma. Slight hemorrhage. External wound closed; gauze drainage. Urine became markedly bloody, and remained so for a few days. Febrile temperature continued for two weeks. April 8: Temperature 103.4°, but the local pain much diminished. General condition considerably improved. Primary union of wound. May 22: Discharged cured with normal urine. Examination of the excised portion of kidney showed acute parenchymatous inflammation and congestion.

1898, vol. ii., page 640. *Symptoms of Renal Calculus; Exploratory Nephrotomy; Recovery.*—Heyman C., 36 years old, admitted August 26 with rational symptoms of vesical calculus. For four years had had attacks of lumbar pain in the left side, accompanied by vomiting and pain radiating to the head of the penis. Urination was frequent and scalding. Passed a small stone three months ago. Urine was acid, contained crystals of oxalate of lime and microscopical quantities of pus. Cystoscopy yielded a negative result. August 27, directly after the cystoscopy, patient passed a small, hard calculus. The painful symptoms continuing, an exploratory operation was done on September 13. First a catheter was passed up the left ureter by means of Albarran's instrument; then, the left kidney being exposed, a small cyst was found occupying the region of its upper pole. This was incised and packed. Then the kidney was developed and brought out of the wound. Palpation and multiple puncture did not reveal a stone. The catheter was felt lying in the pelvis. The kidney being returned, the wound was closed, drained, and sutured. October 13: Vague bladder symptoms still present. Discharged improved. (Lilienthal.)

1898, vol. i., page 101. *Hydronephrosis; Pyelonephritis with Degeneration of Left Kidney; Nephrotomy; Death.*—Annie G., 43 years old, admitted January 4. Since three weeks had pain in the left side of the abdomen; fever; no urinary symptoms. On left side of abdomen a fluctuating mass of the shape of a kidney, extending above to the cardiac area, in front to the umbilicus, and backward to the loin, having no respiratory movements. The colon could not be felt. Aspiration of the mass yielded a whitish, serous fluid containing pus cells, no urinary components. General condition very poor, pulse weak and intermittent. Temperature 100.8°. January 7: Exploratory cœliotomy in left lumbar region, bisecting the axillary line. Mass found to be the kidney. Wound closed and nephrotomy done. About two quarts of pus evacuated; pelvis of kidney enormously dilated. Kidney drained, outer wound packed. Patient was collapsed at end of operation, the pulse very weak and rapid. She failed to rally in spite of all stimulation, and died ten hours later. January 8, *Postmortem*: Left side, only a fragment of degenerated kidney tissue was present, attached to an enormous sac, which was adherent to the surrounding structures. The right kidney was the seat of hemorrhagic infarction.

1898, vol. i., pages 604 and 608; vol. ii., page 211. *Chronic Ascending Pyelitis; Acute Hydronephrosis from Stricture of Renal Orifice of Ureter; Nephrotomy; Ureteroplasty; Renal Fistula; Nephrectomy; Cure.*—Harry G., 29 years old, admitted November 18, 1897, and operated upon by Bassini's method for a congenital inguinal hernia of the left side. December 12: Transferred, cured, to Eye Ward, where he was again operated upon successfully for a milky cataract. While convalescing there he was seized by an attack of violent renal colic of the left side, the temperature rising to 105° several times. He admitted having suffered repeatedly from gonorrhœa, cystitis, and had had before this several similar attacks, though none as violent as this. Retransferred January 6, 1898. Urine showed a deposit of pus, urates, no casts; specific gravity 1024. There was a very tender tumor in the left loin. The rigors and high temperatures recurring, nephrotomy was done on January 7. Kidney very much distended and congested, and, being freely incised through the convexity, voided a large quantity of ammoniacal sero-purulent fluid. Drainage. The local and general disturbances were promptly relieved, but the large quantity of urine escaping from the sinus justified the assumption that the left ureter was completely blocked. He passed on an average forty ounces of urine by urethra in twenty-four hours, this urine being acid, its specific gravity 1024, containing no pus, blood, or other formed elements. March 18: Ureteroplasty. Capacity of pelvis, four ounces. The much-adherent kidney was developed and the ureter found where it entered the pelvis. The latter was now incised, exposing within the pelvis the orifice of the ureter, which was located in the centre of a granulating patch and completely occluded. A fine silver probe finally entered the ureter with some difficulty, then a No. 8 French bougie was passed down to the bladder. Now the ureter was severed from the pelvis close to its emergence and distally from the stricture, and proximal end of the ureter was inverted and closed by a running Lembert suture. Then a small incision was made in the most dependent part of the distended sac, and the ureter, having been twice slit longitudinally, was drawn through this incision and secured internally and externally by a suitable number of catgut sutures. The pelvis was then closed by a catgut suture, the kidney returned, and, the outer wound being drained by several gauze packings, a drainage tube was slipped into the pelvis through the sinus remaining after nephrotomy. Open treatment. Methylene blue solution injected into the pelvis appeared in the bladder. Some fever followed, the cause of which was found to be the retention of pus in the upper angle of the wound. March 23: Considerable abdominal pain, no distension. Pulse 120, temperature 102.6°. Bowels moved freely by calomel. March 25: Defervescence. Passed thirty five ounces of urine by urethra. April 23: Considerable urinous discharge from sinus leading to left kidney. Methylene blue test negative, showing that the left ureter was impervious. June 2: The kidney was again exposed by an incision carried through cicatrix. The ureter, embedded in dense cicatricial tissue, was found with some difficulty. It appeared almost thread-like, and, being slit open to identify it, its lumen was found again obliterated by cicatricial deposits near the renal orifice. The cortex of the kidney appeared much thinner than at the time of the first plastic operation. Evidently an interstitial nephritis had caused the shrinkage. A small silver catheter—No. 6 French—was passed in through the nephrotomy wound and was forced through the stricture and placed within the ureter. The wound in the ureter was left patulous on account of the impossibility of suturing the atrophied organ. Wound packed. The silver catheter was fastened to remain *in situ*. June 20: Silver catheter removed. In its place an elastic catheter was slipped, which remained in for two days. June 24: An aniline pencil was placed in the pelvis of the kidney to dissolve there, but coloring matter failed to tinge the urine passed by urethra. July 1: The hope to restore the function of the ureter was abandoned. In addition to this it became manifest that the kidney itself had become degenerated. Hence nephrectomy was done. The operation was easy on account of the small size of the kidney. Pedicle secured *en masse* by elastic ligature. The parenchyma of the kidney appeared to be much atrophied. Uneventful recovery followed, the other kidney performing its work excellently. Discharged cured August 2.

1898, vol. ii., page 368. *Pyonephrosis; Bisecting Nephrotomy; Drainage; Improvement.*—Moses H., 42 years old, admitted June 9. Two years ago had an attack of renal trouble. Since four days developed severe abdominal cramps in left side, with vomiting, chills, fever, and sweating. A very tender nodular mass the size of a lemon to be felt in left loin, bimanually easily palpable, not influenced by respiration. Temperature 101.2°, pulse 80. Urine acid, contained albumin, pus, and epithelial cells, together with a few granular casts, no tubercle bacilli. Puncture yielded pus. June 13: Bisection of kidney through a large oblique incision, made necessary by the large size of the kidney. Bisection exposed several small abscesses in the cortex near the lower pole and half ounce of thick pus in the pelvis. Evacuation; drainage by two wicks of gauze passed into the pelvis, then catgut suture of bisected kidney. Open treatment. A segment removed from the vicinity of one of the abscesses was preserved for examination. June 14: Passed twenty-six ounces of bloody urine containing pus, hyaline and granular casts. Temperature 101.6°. The subsequent course of the history was uneventful. The wound healed; the urine became clear, containing only microscopic quantities of pus. The patient's condition improved very much, and the size of the kidney receded, but the organ could still be felt. Discharged much improved August 29. Pathologist's report on specimen: Pyelonephritis.

1898, vol. ii., page 198. *Pyonephrosis of old standing; Nephrotomy; Nephrectomy; Cure.*—Jenny L., 20 years old, admitted March 9. She stated that she had never been ill before, and that eleven days ago she began to have severe pains in the left side with chills and fever. On admission, internal organs, except left kidney, normal; in the left loin a hard, painful, rounded, somewhat movable mass, not influenced by respiration, and extending to the level of the umbilicus. Urine was acid, specific gravity 1023; contained albumin, no sugar, many pus and red blood cells, and hyaline casts; quantity, thirty-four and one-half ounces for twenty-four hours. Temperature 103.2°, pulse 88–100. March 14: Puncture yielding thick pus, nephrotomy was immediately done. The kidney represented a much-distended, disorganized pus sac, the secreting tissue being all destroyed. On account of the large size of the tumor nephrectomy was deferred for a later time. Drainage. There was no calculus present. The general disturbances subsided. The discharge from the left kidney showed no traces of urine, consisting only of thick pus. The urine passed by urethra was copious and normal. March 28: A rapid and easy nephrectomy was done, owing to the small size of the shrunken organ, which contained only traces of renal tissue. Uneventful recovery. Discharged cured June 27.

1898, vol. ii., page 889. *Pyonephrosis of old standing; Nephrotomy; Improvement; Subsequent Nephrectomy and Cure*, January, 1899.—Tillie L., 35 years old, admitted October 27 with a history of repeated attacks of renal colic, with rigors extending over the past five years. A growing tumor, that varied in size, with corresponding fluctuations in the amount of urine passed, and continuous turbidity of the urine, were observed. On admission there was in the right loin a large, round, smooth mass extending forward almost to median line, movable with respiration. Urine acid, specific gravity 1014, containing a large amount of albumin and a thick sediment of pus. October 31: Nephrotomy; evacuation of two large cortical abscesses and of pus from the pelvis of the kidney, which did not contain calculi. Drainage. December 4: Discharged much improved as to general condition, wearing tube in kidney, from which pus was discharging freely. Urine had cleared up. She was directed to return in January. In January, 1899, nephrectomy was done and patient was cured.

1898, vol. i., page 518. *Ascending Pyelonephritis; Perinephritic Abscess; Incision and Drainage; Nephrectomy; Cure.*—William B., 30 years old, admitted November 22, 1897. Had gonorrhœa five years ago, followed by urethral stricture and cystitis. Since five weeks he has had periodic attacks of chills and fever, and since the past two weeks has had severe pain in right loin. On admission his temperature was 103.2°. In the right lumbar region a large, globular, tender, and fluctuating mass was to be felt. The soft parts of the loin much indurated. November 27, 1897: Aspiration of the indurated tissues yielding pus, a large perinephritic abscess, holding a pint of pus, was incised, evacuated, and drained. The abscess was found to lead down into the right kidney. December 24: The general constitutional symptoms having abated, and the right kidney being still enlarged and extremely tender, a cystoscopic examination was made. The right ureteral orifice was found congested, and pus could be seen to squirt through it when the right kidney was massaged. January 4, 1898: Exploration of kidney followed by nephrectomy. The organ was with difficulty withdrawn from the wound on account of dense adhesions. On its being bisected it was found to be much shrunken, containing a number of small abscess cavities, and its secreting tissue had disappeared. Nephrectomy done at once; pedicle secured *en masse* by an elastic ligature. Open treatment of the wound. January 6: Patient passed sufficient quantity of urine, which still contained albumin and pus. Slight febrile movement. The patient continued to pass abundant urine, which soon contained only microscopic pus. March 25: While dressing the wound the patient showed signs of collapse. Temperature rose to 105°, and then spontaneously fell three degrees in an hour. Pulse 100–120. Some vomiting. March 28: Temperature 100°–102°. Considerable difficulty in breathing. He gradually improved, and was discharged cured April 16.

1898, vol. ii., page 158. *Acute Degeneration; Horseshoe Kidney; Splitting of Capsule; Cure.*—Rosie S., 41 years old, admitted May 5, 1898, with a history of repeated attacks of renal colic on the right side, with rigors. No kidney to be felt in either loin. Urine contained albumin and much pus. Temperature 99.8°. May 22: Exploratory operation. It was noticed at once that the right kidney did not occupy its usual position. Well over toward the median line was to be seen a dark, bluish-red mass which felt like the kidney. With much difficulty this mass was brought out into the wound, and proved to be a horseshoe kidney. It was divided by a longitudinal sulcus into an upper and lower half, each one of which had a separate ureter. No stones could be detected in either portion of the organ, and aspiration yielded negative results. As the kidney was very much congested, its capsule was split, a segment of the upper half was cut out for examination, the organ replaced, and the wound packed and drained. Slight febrile reaction followed, the urine gradually became normal in character, the wound slowly healed, and patient was discharged, July 23, cured. Pathologist's report on specimen: Acute degeneration.

1898, vol. ii., page 945. *Sarcoma of Kidney: Nephrectomy: Cure.*—Max R., 48 years old, admitted September 29, 1898. During the past three months patient had noticed a gradually increasing growth in left lumbar region, painful at times. General condition on admission was poor. In left lumbar region a large, hard, smooth, movable tumor, extending downward to the iliac crest, divided by a transverse ridge into an upper and lower half, movable with respirations, and the colon to its inner side. No fluctuation. Urine alkaline, 1018, no albumin or formed elements. Slight febrile movement (99° to 100°). October 3: Exploratory cœliotomy at outer edge of left rectus muscle. Tumor found to be the left kidney. Peritoneum closed, and then, together with the colon, was peeled away from the lateral abdominal wall. The enlarged kidney was with difficulty brought into the wound, its pedicle ligated, and then the organ removed. Wound drained and closed. October 4: Patient passed seventeen and a half ounces of urine, which contained albumin, red blood cells, leucocytes, and hyaline casts. General condition fair. October 5: Passed forty ounces of urine. October 10: General condition good; passes sufficient quantity of urine; urine acid, no albumin or casts. Patient made an uneventful recovery, and was discharged October 20 cured. The kidney on section showed very little cortical substance remaining, and was represented by hard, sarcomatous tissue, which had degenerated in places. (Van Arsdale.)

OPERATIONS ON THE RECTUM AND ANUS—177.

	Operations.	Deaths.
Carcinoma of rectum. Kraske's operation	1	1
Dilatation of sphincter ani for fissure	13	
Fistula in ano, opened and packed	31	
" " " dissected out	1	
" " " ligature operation	1	
Hemorrhoids, clamp and cautery operation	91	
" ligature operation	8	
" Whitehead's operation	1	
Ischio-rectal abscess, incised and drained	23	
" " urethral fistula, dissection	1	
Periproctitis, incised and drained	1	
Plastic on sphincter ani	1	
Rectum, prolapse of, cauterization for	1	
" removing suture from	1	
" stricture of, specific, incision and dilatation	1	
Stricture of sphincter ani, incised and dilated	1	

Large experience gathered from our great material has led to the conclusion that, among the various operations advocated for the cure of hemorrhoids, their radical treatment by the clamp and cautery deserves the preference over the ligature and Whitehead's method of excision. It is simple, safe, and gives excellent and permanent results. The average duration of the after-treatment was ten days, the patients being discharged with rapidly contracting wounds, after having been taught how to cleanse and dress them. Usually only one dose of an anodyne was given, and that immediately after the operation. As we lay great stress upon the proper cleansing of the bowels by calomel and salts before operation, the first defecation after the operation has no terrors or suffering for the patient. As the sphincter has been thoroughly stretched, a tampon tube is well borne, and serves not only to permit the escape of flatus, but also for the administration of the oil enema regularly given three times twenty-four hours after the operation, followed by a large soap and water injection. Preceding this, on the morning of the third day, a saline laxative is administered. When the patient feels the approach of the peristaltic wave to the rectum, the oil and then the soap enemata are applied, whereupon tampon tube, fæces, and packings—should they be in use—are all expelled without pain or hemorrhage. From this time on the patient receives solid food and is permitted to leave the bed. Mild laxatives and cleansing enemata are continued until the patient is discharged. Whitehead's and the ligature operation were only done occasionally for purposes of demonstration.

1898, vol. ii., page 29. *Carcinoma of Rectum; Preliminary Colostomy; Resection of Rectum (Kraske); Death.*—Fred'k K., 84 years old, admitted June 15. For one year past has had increasing difficulty in moving his bowels; during the last three months stools have been involuntary and contained considerable quantity of blood. On admission there was an extensive carcinoma of anus, involving the entire lower segment of the rectum. No glandular enlargement. Patient insisted upon a radical operation, which, in view of his excellent general condition, was granted to him. June 20: Preliminary colostomy; the rectum was thoroughly cleansed preparatory to its resection. June 27: Resection of lower four inches of rectum together with the anus. The carcinomatous tissue was found to involve the prostate and posterior urethra, and during the difficult dissection the urethra was injured; it was at once sutured with fine silk, and a permanent catheter was inserted into the bladder. Wound packed. Patient bore the operation very well, but the next day his pulse became very irregular and intermittent; temperature 100.6° F. In spite of stimulation his heart's action became weaker, and he died of sepsis and exhaustion July 4.

PLASTIC OPERATIONS—24.

	Operations.
Rhinoplasty—4.	
For ulcer	3
" " by forehead flap	1
On abdomen	1
" back	1
" foot for ulcer	3
Skin Grafts—20.	
Of palm, transplantation in flap from back	1
" palm, transplantation in flap from abdomen	1
" foot, frog-skin graft	1
" face, Reverdin	1
Thiersch method, various regions	16

TUMORS, REMOVAL OF—22.

	Total.	Deaths.
Cyst, dermoid, subcutaneous, of chest	1	
" " of coccygeal region	5	
" " " scalp	2	
" " " thigh	1	
" of labium majus	1	
" prethyroid, mucous	1	
Epithelioma of lip, excision	1	
Lipoma of epigastrium	1	
" arborescens, supraclavicular	1	
" of thigh	1	
" " shoulder	5	
Sarcoma of axilla	1	
" " groin	1	

1898, vol. i., page 424. *Dermoid Cyst of Labium Majus; Excision; Cure.*—Mary M., 46 years old, admitted March 7. For past eighteen years had a soft, movable swelling in the right labium majus, which gradually increased in size. A week ago it became very painful and much larger. On admission there was in the right labium majus a large, smooth, fluctuating, tender swelling, yielding on aspiration brown fluid. March 10: Swelling found to be a dermoid cyst, which was completely excised. Smooth recovery. Discharged cured March 23, 1898.

1898, vol. i., page 489. *Arborescent Lipoma of Neck; Excision; Cure.*—Mathilda B., 43 years old, admitted March 21 with a lipoma occupying the right supraclavicular fossa, and about the size of an orange. March 22: Excision of the tumor; the growth was found to be an arborescent lipoma, its branches extending into the upper anterior mediastinum and between the fascial planes of the neck. After difficult and tedious dissection it was completely excised, the wound closed and drained. During a coughing fit occurring on the fourth day after excision, a copious venous hemorrhage took place, filling the wound with a massive and solid blood clot, which continued to yield blood serum for nearly two weeks afterward, remaining, however, sweet and undecomposed. Patient was discharged from Hospital on April 3, the wound healing definitely two weeks later. The discharge gradually lost its sanguinolent character, becoming limpid toward the end.

INCISION AND DRAINAGE—74.

	Operations.	Died.
For phlegmon—35.		
of neck	2	
" " angina Ludovici	3	1
" face	2	
" finger	2	
" hand	9	
" " and forearm	5	
of hand and forearm, diabetic	2	2
of thumb	1	
" forearm	1	
" groin	1	
" thigh	2	
" leg	1	
" ankle	2	
" foot	2	
For abscess—20.		
of neck	2	
of neck, streptococcus, sepsis	1	1
of axilla	3	
" arm	2	
" chest	1	
intramural, abdominal	2	
of groin	5	
of pelvis and groin, dissecting	1	
of psoas	2	
" amputation, stump	1	
(*See also operations on Glands.*)		
For carbuncle—6.		
of lip	1	
" neck	1	
" back	1	
" " diabetic	3	1
For hæmatoma—2.		
of hand	1	
" calf	1	
For gunshot wounds—3.		
of thigh	2	
of thigh, extraction of bullet	1	
Of sinuses, curetting—8.		
(*See also Bone and Miscellaneous Operations.*)		
of abdomen	2	
" groin	1	
" lumbar region	1	
tubercular	3	

OPERATIONS ON GLANDS—52.

	Operations.	Died.
Mammary—26.		
Adenoma of, excision	3	
Cyst-adenoma of, excision	1	
Carcinoma, amputation for	12	
Carcinoma, recurrent, excision of	2	
Mastitis, acute suppurative, incised and drained	5	
Mastitis, acute suppurative, tubercular, incised	2	
Sarcoma, amputation for	1	
Cervical—17.		
Carcinomatous, removal of	4	
Tubercular, removal of	11	
Suppurating, removal of	2	
Face—3.		
Parotitis, suppurating, incised	3	
Axillary—1.		
Tubercular, removal of	1	
Inguinal—5.		
Suppurating, chancroidal bubo, removal of	1	
Suppurating, tubercular, removal of	1	
Suppurating, syphilitic, removal of	1	
Suppurating, incision and drainage of	2	

OPERATIONS ON BLOOD VESSELS—7, 1 death.

	Operations.	Died.
Ligations of arteries—2.		
of internal iliac, for suspected aneurism (vascular sarcoma of ilium)	1	1
of radial, for hemorrhage	1	
Varicose veins—5.		
of leg, excision of	5	

(See also Intravenous Infusions under Miscellaneous Operations.)

1898, vol. i., page 272. *Vascular Perithelial Sarcoma of Ilium; Ligation of Internal Iliac Artery; Death*— Abraham L., 65 years old, admitted February 12. For past nine months had severe constant pain at right side of sacrum above the tuberosity of ischium; pain was increased by walking, relieved by lying on the left side; no pain along the sciatic nerve. No urinary symptoms. Over right sacro-sciatic notch was a swelling, pulsating synchronously with the heart beat, and over it was to be heard a distinct bruit. There was also an old endocarditis and general arteritis. The diagnosis rested between an aneurism of the gluteal artery and a vascular sarcoma of the ilium. As the patient insisted upon something being done to relieve his intense pain, it was decided to ligate the internal iliac artery. February 14: Internal iliac artery ligated transperitoneally. Pulsation of tumor ceased after the ligation of the internal iliac artery. After the operation the patient's general condition began to fail. There were no signs of peritonitis, but heart failure supervened, and he died of exhaustion. February 18: *Autopsy* showed a sarcoma of ilium at the upper rim of the great sciatic notch, with extensive erosion of ilium and sacrum. Pathologist's report of the sarcoma: Perithelial sarcoma.

MISCELLANEOUS OPERATIONS—94.

	Total.	Deaths
Cauterization of ulcer of foot	1	
Controlling secondary hemorrhage	9	
Empyema of mastoid	1	
Excision of scar tissue, resuturing	1	
Forcible correction for pes planus	2	
Hydrocele of round ligament, extirpation of.	1	
Ingrowing toenail, Anger's operation for	3	
Intravenous saline infusion	43	
Perineorrhaphy	1	
Removing of wire suture from jaw	2	
Relieving of constriction of cord after herniotomy	2	
Secondary suture	11	
" " abdominal	1	
" " " after appendicitis	12	
Shaving lupus of buttocks	2	
Vaginal section, pelvic abscess	1	
Venesection	1	

Intravenous Infusions.

During the past year forty-three intravenous infusions were performed. Of these most were done to combat the effects of hemorrhage, several were pre-operative procedures employed as a prophylactic against shock, one was indicated for the relief of suppression of urine, while a few were done for diabetic coma or other toxic conditions.

Standing always ready in the house surgeon's room is a suitable box containing the armamentarium for infusion. This box is divided into one large and three small compartments.

In the large division are kept, all sterilized and rolled in two layers of sterilized gauze, the following instruments: one scalpel, wrapped in sterilized cotton; one pair straight scissors; one pair curved scissors; one anatomical forceps; one mousetooth forceps; one pair small, sharp retractors; two artery forceps; one metal infusion canula, with rubber tube and glass attachment tip; one needle-holder; two surgical needles.

The three small compartments contain the following articles respectively: a small jar holding a reel of medium-sized catgut in alcohol; several small pieces of iodoformized gauze, wrapped in sterile gauze; a sterilized two-inch bandage, also protected by gauze.

Pasted inside of the cover of the box is a list of the above-mentioned contents, with directions to the nurse for their resterilization, replacement, and replenishment.

When an intravenous infusion is ordered or anticipated this box is sent for by the head nurse while she and her assistants are preparing the other essentials. These consist in a rubber sheet to protect the bed; several sterilized towels; several cotton sponges; sublimate solution, and soap, brush, water, and ether for the cleansing of the field of operation. While these articles are being placed in readiness, the deci-normal salt solution is being heated and filtered into the irrigating bottle. Each ward is provided with one of these graduated five-pint-infusion (irrigating) bottles, which, with its rubber tubing attached, is held strictly reserved to this single use, and is always aseptic.

While the operator is disinfecting his hands his assistant is doing the same to the field of operation. The arm is almost invariably chosen, only one infusion having been performed in the lower extremity (saphenous vein).

Usually no anæsthetic (local or general) is used. After the customary towels are spread, as in any operation, a few turns of the sterilized bandage are wound about the arm tightly enough to constrict the veins. An incision is then made over the most prominent vein in the cubital fossa (usually the median basilic). The vein, when not collapsed from extreme anæmia, is dissected out easily for a distance of half to one inch. Double catgut ligatures are then passed under the vein. The distal ligature is tied tightly. At this juncture the infusion canula is attached to the rubber tube leading from the infusion bottle, and the solution allowed to escape, the operator thus assuring himself that it is of a temperature of about 120° F., free from air bubbles and cotton threads. The vein is then nicked obliquely with the curved scissors, and the canula tip thrust into the vein through this wound. The proximal ligature is tied in a single knot, preventing reflux of fluid.

In cases of shock, one to one and a half pints of salt solution are employed, occasionally two pints. Where the solution is injected to supply loss of blood, the quantity employed is regulated in a measure by the severity of the hemorrhage.

As the canula is being withdrawn from the vein the proximal ligature is tied firmly about the latter. The vein is then divided between the two ligatures. The external wound may be closed by a few catgut sutures. An iodoformized gauze pledget is then applied, is covered with a roll of gauze, and these held in place with the partly-used bandage.

With expeditious assistants, the preparation for, and performance of, the infusion can be accomplished within fifteen minutes.

In about one case in seven a chill followed by an evanescent rise of temperature (sometimes as high as 106°) has been observed after intravenous infusion; but no fatality or permanent damage could be traced to this operation.

ACCIDENT SERVICE—TOTAL, 426.

Note.—The following report does not include mention of those cases referred from the accident room to the general service.

SCALP.

Contusion of	11
Hæmatoma of	1
Incised wound of	18
Lacerated wound of	28
Punctured wound of	3
Incised wound of forehead	7
Lacerated wound of forehead	6
	74

EYES AND EYELIDS.

Eyelids:	
Cellulitis of	1
Contusion of	7
Incised wound of	6
Hæmatoma of	2
Eye:	
Foreign body in cornea	5
" " " eye	9
Contused wound of eyebrow	1
Lacerated " " "	10
	41

EAR.

Incised wound of	1
Lacerated wound of	1
	2

NOSE.

Fracture of	1
Contusion of	8
Epistaxis	3
Foreign body in nose	1
Incised wound of nose	1
	14

NECK

Incised wound of	2

SHOULDER.

Stab wound of	1
Contusion of	2
Dislocation of	1
Fracture of clavicle	1
	5

ARM AND FOREARM.

Contusion of elbow	4
Dislocation of humerus	2
Fracture of humerus	3
" " radius	1
" " " and ulna	2
Incised wound of arm	2
Punctured wound of forearm	1
Sprain of forearm	1
Furuncle of forearm	1
Burns "	1
Colles' fracture	12
	30

WRIST.

Abscess of	1
Burns of	3
Contusion of	3
Dislocation of	2
Incised wound of	1
Lacerated " "	3
Sprain of	5
Lacerated wound of wrist	3
Division of tendons, tenorrhaphy	2
	23

FACE AND THROAT.

Abscess of tonsil	2
Abscess of gums	1
Cellulitis of face	3
Contusion " "	7
" " lips	1
Incised wound of face	2
" " of cheek	2
Infected " " "	1
Incised " " chin	1
Lacerated " " lip	10
Foreign body in larynx	1
Elongated uvula, uvulotomy	1
	32

HAND AND FINGER.

Abscess of hand	2
Gangrene of finger, amputation	1
Burn of hand	6
Cellulitis of hand	4
" " finger	7
Contusion " "	7
" " hand	7
Dog-bite " "	2
Hæmatoma of finger nail	1
" " hand	1
Fracture of metacarpal bones	4
" " phalanx	3
Foreign body in hand	3
" " " finger	8
Incised wound of hand	6
" " " finger	13
Lacerated " " hand	19
" " " finger	40
Punctured wound of hand	2
" " " finger	5
Sprain of finger	2
	143

THORAX AND BACK.

Burn of chest	2
Contusion of chest	1
Stab wound of chest	2
	5

THIGH AND ABDOMEN.

Burn of thigh	1
Dog-bite of thigh	2
Punctured wound of thigh	1
	4

LEG.

Burn of leg	1
Contusion of calf of leg	3
" " knee	3
Dog-bite of leg	1
Hæmatoma of calf	3
Incised wound of leg	3
Infected " " "	1
Lacerated " " "	2
" " " knee (opening of prepatellar bursa)	1
	16

ANKLE.

Punctured wound of ankle	1
Sprain of ankle	5
	6

FOOT AND TOE.

Contusion of foot	3
Cellulitis " "	4
Foreign body in foot	2
Fracture of toe	3
Infected wound of foot	1
Lacerated " " "	2
	15

MISCELLANEOUS.

Alcoholism	3
Abrasion of skin	1
Gastritis	1
Hydrochloric acid poisoning (?)	1
Ischio-rectal abscess	1
Powder burns	6
Pleurisy	1
	14

Total, 426

CAUSES OF DEATH.

General Surgical Service—96.

	Operation.			No operation.		
	M	F	C	M	F	C
Abscess of breast	..	1	..	..	..	..
" " liver	1	..	..	1	..	..
" " " portal thrombosis	1	..	..	..	..	..
" " neck, septicæmia	1	..	..	..	..	..
Appendicitis, abscess, secondary hemorrhage, gangrene of intestines	1	..	..	..	..	..
" abscess, secondary, beginning pneumonia	1	..	..	..	..	..
" " sepsis	1	..	1	..	..	..
" " " septic hemorrhages in lungs	..	1	..	..	..	..
" abdominal tumor	1	..	..	..	..	..
" gangrenous	1	..	..	..	..	..
" general peritonitis	6	2	3	..	..	..
" " " intestinal obstruction	1	..	..	.	..	..
" " " perforation	..	..	1	..	..	..
" " " typhlitic abscess	..	1	.	..	..	..
" " purulent peritonitis	1	..	1	..	..	..
" " " " perforation of intestine	1	..	..	.	..	..
" intestinal obstruction	1	..	..	..	..	..
" perforation, sepsis, septic pneumonia	..	1	..	..	..	..
" septicæmia, pericarditis, suppression of urine	..	1	..	..	..	..
" empyema of appendix	..	1	.	..	..	..
Angina Ludovici, sepsis	1	..	..	..	..	..
Arthrodesis for anterior poliomyelitis, surgical shock	..	..	1	..	..	..
Carbuncle of back, diabetic coma	1	.	..	..	..	..
Carcinoma of abdominal viscera	..	1	..	..	..	..
" " breast	..	1	..	.	..	..
" " larynx	..	..	..	1	..	..
" " liver, intestinal obstruction	..	1	..	..	..	..
" " " and peritoneum	1	..	..	..	..	..
" mammæ, recurrent, carcinoma pulmonum	..	..	..	..	1	..
" of rectum	1	..	..		..	..
" " stomach	..	1	..	..	..	..
" " " and transverse colon	1	..	..	..	..	..
" " sigmoid flexure and peritoneum	1	..	..	..	..	..
Calculus of common bile duct, pulmonary tuberculosis, pneumothorax	1	..	..	..	..	..
Cirrhosis of liver	..	1	.	..	..	..
Cholelithiasis	..	2	..	..		.
" carcinoma of gall bladder (?), thrombosis of mesenteric artery	..	1	..	..	..	..
Compound comminuted fracture of tibia, osteomyelitis of tibia, arthritis of knee, decubitus, inanition	..	..	..	1	..	..
Diabetes, gangrene of leg	1	..	..	..	..	..
Diabetic gangrene of toe, diabetic coma, arterio-sclerosis	..	..	..	1	..	..
Dorso-iliac dislocation of the hip, endocarditis, cardiac failure from chloroform	..	..	..	1	..	..
Empyema	1	..	..	..	..	..

	Operation.			No operation.		
	M	F	C	M	F	C
Empyema of gall bladder, suppression of urine	1	..	..	..	..	..
" " " pyæmia, lobar pneumonia	1	..	..	..	..	..
Facial erysipelas following injury	..	..	..	..	..	1
Fracture of neck of femur	..	..	..	..	1	..
General purulent peritonitis (cause unknown)	2	..	..	..	..	..
" " " enterostomy, resection of intestine for fæcal fistula, inanition	1	..	..	..	..	..
" peritonitis, tubercular	1	..	..	..	..	..
Hernia, inguinal, sapræmia, sepsis	1	..	..	..	..	..
Harelip, cleft palate, inanition	..	..	1	..	..	..
Hydropyonephrosis	..	..	..	..	1	..
Intestinal obstruction	1	..	..	..	..	..
Idiopathic intestinal paresis	1	..	..	..	..	..
Intrathoracic dermoid cyst, sepsis	..	1	..	..	..	..
Intussusception	..	..	1	..	..	..
" gangrene of intestine	..	..	1	..	..	..
Lympho-sarcoma of mesenteric glands, gall bladder, kidney, spleen, lung, primary, in duodenum	1	..	..	..	..	..
Miliary tuberculosis, acute, tubercular enteritis with perforations, osteomyelitis of tibia, septicæmia	1	..	..	..	..	..
Paget's disease of the nipple with carcinomatous degeneration, decubitus, senility	..	..	..	..	1	..
Perforated ulcer of the stomach, general peritonitis	..	..	..	..	1	..
Phlegmon of hand, diabetes, coma	..	2	..	..	..	..
Pulmonary tuberculosis, fistula in ano, tubercular enteritis	..	..	..	1	..	..
Pyonephrosis	..	..	..	1	..	..
Renal calculus, sarcoma of kidney, recurrence, syphilitic dementia	1	..	..	..	..	..
Retroperitoneal sarcoma, general sarcomatosis	1	..	..	..	..	..
Rupture of spleen, peritonitis	..	..	1	..	..	..
Strangulated hernia, gangrene of intestine	..	1	..	..	..	..
" inguinal hernia	1	1	..	..	..	..
Stricture of œsophagus, inanition	1	..	..	..	..	..
Subphrenic (hepatic?) echinococcus abscess, mediastinal abscess ruptured into bronchus	1	..	..	..	..	..
Suppurative arthritis, traumatic, pyæmia	..	..	1	..	..	..
Tubercular arthritis of knee, tubercular meningitis	..	..	1	..	..	..
" " " " general tuberculosis	..	..	1	..	..	..
" ulcer of face, pulmonary tuberculosis, pneumothorax	1	..	..	..	..	..
Tuberculosis of sternum, ribs, and pleura	1	..	..	..	..	..
Ulcer of stomach, thrombosis of splenic vein, necrosis of spleen and lung, gastric fistula, sepsis, inanition	1	..	..	..	..	..
Vascular tumor of ilium (sarcoma)	1	..	..	..	..	..
Totals	47	21	15	7	5	1

Thanks are due to Dr. A. A. Berg and Dr. W. M. Brickner for valuable help rendered in extracting histories and arranging the material included in this report.

XV.

CONSTRICTING ADENOMA OF THE HEPATIC FLEXURE. RECOVERY AFTER EXTENSIVE RESECTION OF THE COLON.

By HOWARD LILIENTHAL, M.D.,
ADJUNCT ATTENDING SURGEON.

The following case is remarkable on account of the great length of the piece of large intestine resected, and the recovery of the patient in spite of so severe an operation in a desperately cachectic individual.

Dr. M. Levy, of New Orleans, brought his patient, Mr. A. E. M., to New York for surgical advice after two years of wasting illness. The trouble began with an attack of severe general abdominal pain and tenderness, with fever and great prostration. The attack resembled one of appendicitis from the fact that in addition to the symptoms mentioned there was an especially tender point in the right iliac region. Three months later there was another similar attack, with pain, fever, vomiting, and other signs of the presence of dangerous abdominal disease. This, like the first one, passed off, leaving little if any trace, but a few months later a third attack occurred, and then others in more or less rapid succession. The later ones were less and less like appendicitis, however, since the fever and the other signs of inflammation were absent, though the pain and prostration, if anything, increased. The trouble usually came on a few hours after eating, and the symptoms were generally relieved by purging or vomiting. Within the past year the attacks had become very frequent, and the patient had lost much weight and strength, while his anæmia became profound. For some time a tumor had been noted in the right half of the abdomen, situated in the region of the hepatic flexure. Because of this tumor the case had been diagnosed as disease of the gall bladder or of the pylorus by most of the physicians who examined the patient. Hematemesis, however, had never been noted.

On September 6, 1898, the man first came under the writer's observation. At that time he was so weak and so yellow with anæmia that I was unwilling to advise even an exploratory operation, but expressed myself as being willing to undertake it with the understanding that I should not be blamed for a possibly fatal issue.

The physical examination made at this time yielded practically the same observations as those made in the Hospital, so I will quote from the Mount Sinai notes:

A. E. M., aged 36, by occupation a broker, was admitted as a private patient on September 7, 1898.

Physical Examination.—General condition poor. Great anæmia and apparent cachexia. Pulse weak and thready. Heart: apex systolic murmur transmitted to the left. Lungs and spleen negative. Liver: seventh space to two finger-breadths below the free costal border. Stomach: tympany extends down to the umbilicus. To the right and above the navel, extending toward the hepatic and right renal regions, is a somewhat nodular, insensitive mass as large as a small orange. This mass is somewhat movable, and strongly suggests by its feel neoplasm about the pylorus. The lymph nodes, especially in the groins and in the left axilla, are somewhat enlarged. Examination of the rectum is negative.

Pulse rate 100, respirations 28°, temperature 99.6° F. Urine acid, specific gravity 1.008; no abnormal chemical constituents found. By the microscope a few pus cells were seen, but no casts or other renal elements.

Examination of the stomach-contents after a test meal gave the following observations: Reaction, acid; color, yellowish; sediment fairly well digested; butyric acid odor; free hydrochloric acid, 14; hydrochloric acid in combination, 15; acid salts and butyric acid, 21; total acidity, 50; no lactic acid present, and but a slight butyric acid reaction.

Examination by the inflation of the stomach, then of the colon, yielded no result worthy of mention. This was partly because the patient was so sensitive that he would not stand the presence of the stomach tube.

The writer's diagnosis was very much in doubt, but the presence of the tumor in the characteristic locality, together with the cachexia and the history of vomiting, made the theory of pyloric neoplasm plausible even in the presence of the comparatively normal gastric contents as shown by the analysis. Accordingly the patient was prepared for operation, with the idea that a gastro-enterostomy for palliation would probably be performed. I certainly had no thought of the possibility of anything radical.

Operation on September 9. Anæsthesia, induced by nitrous oxide gas followed by ether, was carefully managed by the house surgeon, Dr. W. M. Brickner. A crescentic incision five or six inches long was made through the right rectus, the navel being between the horns of the crescent. The blood of the patient was noticeably thin and watery in appearance. Great care was taken with the hemostasis, even the non-spurting vessels being secured by ligature. On entering the abdominal cavity the liver was the first organ to be inspected; it was enlarged, but perfectly smooth. The gall bladder was normal. The stomach was rather small and normal in appearance. The transverse and the ascending colon were bound together at the hepatic flexure, the tip of the vermiform appendix being adherent to the mass. The whole ascending colon was more or less drawn out of place, but the involvement of the transverse colon extended only for about one-fourth of its length. The tumor was very hard and bound the various parts of the intestine together very firmly. A dimple-like depression could be felt through the uninvolved wall of the transverse colon, showing where the lumen of the gut was probably situated. The entire mass could be moved about with some freedom, although it was not possible to bring it actually out of the abdominal cavity. No enlarged lymph nodes were discovered, so I determined at once to make an attempt to remove the entire neoplasm, and I was all the more tempted to do this because of the very satisfactory manner in which the patient took the anæsthetic.

A considerable piece of omentum had to be first removed beyond numerous catgut ligatures, for this membrane was firmly adherent to the general mass. Then, using gauze fillets to constrict the intestine so that no fæces should escape, section was made through the transverse colon at a point more than one third of the distance from the hepatic to the splenic flexure. Into this end of the intestine the male half of a large Murphy button was sutured, and, after similarly ligating the cæcal end of the colon, section was made here also; but it was found that this section ran so close to the ileo-cæcal valve that it would be unsafe, on account of the danger of mechanical obstruction by the large button, to make the anastomosis in this manner. I therefore cut the ileum through just in front of the valve and inserted the female half of the next size smaller button, having assured myself previously that the two halves of dissimilar size would fit into each other properly. The mixed button was then firmly coupled, and the anastomosis was found to be perfect. I then proceeded to remove the tumor-bearing coil of gut, so that all that portion of large intestine between the end of the ileum and the end of the first third of the transverse colon was actually excised. The work was rather slow, because of the great care necessary with the hemostatic ligatures in the mesocolon. The patient now showed signs of weakness, so that closure of the slit in the mesocolon could not be very perfectly accomplished. The peritoneum was closed with a running suture of fine catgut, with the exception of openings for drainage which were left at each end. The muscles and fasciæ were similarly approximated by five stout chromic catgut sutures, but the skin wound was not sutured at all. Small gauze drains were put in at each end of the wound and the usual drèssing applied. The operation had lasted two and a half hours, and, as the patient's pulse had become extremely weak, the infusion of a pint and a half of saline solution was practised; but the improvement in the pulse was not great and full stimulation by drugs was also kept up.

After the operation the temperature rose to 103° while the pulse was 134 and the respirations 42. Morphine in large doses was now administered and the condition gradually improved. There was absolutely no vomiting. No movement of the bowels was permitted until four days after the operation, when, after the first dressing with removal of the gauze drains, an enema of peppermint water was ordered and this was followed by a copious evacuation. Gas had been frequently expelled from a few hours after the operation. On the fifteenth day the button was passed spontaneously and without difficulty. Seventeen days after the operation an abrupt rise of temperature from the neighborhood of 100° to 102° caused me to make a careful examination of the wound, and by aspirating at a point of tenderness in the upper angle, pus was found. The cavity, not a large one, was evacuated under cocaine and a small drainage tube inserted. This little mishap did not, however, seem to retard the patient's recovery. His appetite was now excellent and he rapidly took on flesh and gained in strength. On October 6 Dr. Levy took his patient South, practically well. There was still a small sinus requiring a tiny dressing, but I have since heard that this also has closed. Our pathologists reported that the tumor was a pure adenoma, so the chance of a permanent recovery is good.

Gross examination of the specimen showed that there was a tortuous channel no larger in calibre than a goose quill. It seems remarkable that with such severe constriction there should have been any periods of comparative freedom from pain. It is also worthy of mention that our efforts to obtain an empty alimentary canal before the operation were completely successful in spite of so great an anatomical difficulty.

June 12, 1899: The patient reports himself perfectly well. He has gained fifty pounds in weight.

XVI.

GENITO-URINARY DEPARTMENT.

By WILLIAM F. FLUHRER, M.D.,
ATTENDING SURGEON.

GENITO-URINARY OPERATIONS—107.

	Operations.
Circumcision for phimosis	4
Cystoscopy	22
Cystotomy, suprapubic, exploratory, with ureteral catheterization	2
" " for papilloma of bladder	2
" " " vesical calculi	8
Endoscopy	2
Epididymis, resection of	1
Epididymitis, tubercular	1
Epididymo-orchitis, incised and drained	1
Hydrocele, Volkmann's operation	4
Incision and drainage of abscess of scrotum	1
" " " " prostatic abscess	1
" " " " periurethral abscess	3
Meatotomy	5
Orchidectomy, for sarcoma	1
" " tubercular orchitis	1
Perineal section, for foreign body in bladder	1
" " " urethral fistula	4
Plastic operation on penis	1
Prostatectomy, perineal incision (Nicoll's operation)	1
Prostatotomy, perineal incision	1
" suprapubic incision	1
Ureteral catheterization (Casper)	9
Urethroplasty for fistula of urethra	3
Urethrotomy, external	1
" internal	5
" combined	9
" " with suprapubic cystotomy for stricture	1
Varicocele, ligature operation	11

DEATHS—5.

	Operation.	No operation.
Cystitis chronica, endocarditis, asthenia	..	1
" " " tuberculosis	..	1
" pyelitis, perineal fistula	1	..
Papilloma of bladder, vesical calculus, inanition	1	..
Tumor " " cachexia, cardiac failure	..	1
Total	2	3

XVII.

GENITO-URINARY SERVICE.

THREE CASES OF PROSTATECTOMY.

By WILLIAM F. FLUHRER, M.D.,
ATTENDING SURGEON.

In the genito-urinary service there have been performed three prostatectomies, which have sufficient interest to merit brief mention.

CASE I.—J. L., aged 63 years, was admitted into the Hospital February 13, 1896, suffering from the usual symptoms consequent upon an enlargement of the prostate. He was greatly troubled with frequent and painful urination, passing with much straining only about an ounce of urine at each effort. The bladder was relieved by catheter of the retained foul urine at regular intervals. Antiseptic washings of the bladder and internal medication had been thoroughly tried without benefit.

Rectal examination showed the prostate much enlarged. The presence of stone was excluded.

Operation February 15: Under the local anæsthesia of cocaine both vasa deferentia were cut and ligated. No improvement resulted from the operation.

Operation March 7: Under ether anæsthesia both testicles were removed. No benefit followed the operation. On the contrary, the patient declined in general health and the local conditions became worse. It was necessary to use opiates freely. Rectal examination showed no decrease in the size of the prostate. It was more difficult to introduce the searcher.

Operation May 6: Under ether a suprapubic cystotomy was performed. The incision opened a diverticulum of a capacity of about three ounces, communicating with the bladder through an opening scarcely an inch in diameter.

The mucous membrane was intensely injected. The

evenly enlarged prostate, projecting into the cavity of the bladder, felt about the size of the body of a normal uterus. A grit of crystals mixed with mucus was removed from behind the prostate, but no stone was found. It was impracticable to remove the prostate operating within the bladder. Siphon drainage was afforded by a tube passed through the wound.

For a few days after the cystotomy the urine remained clear, but soon became decomposed again. The patient's general health declined and he was comfortable only under opiates. Under the existing conditions a fatal outcome was only too apparent.

Operation June 25: Under chloroform the prostate was uncovered through a crescentic incision in the perineum. The perineum was very vascular, and by the time the prostate was exposed the patient was so feeble that the operation was stopped, the wound packed with iodoform gauze and its edges held together by a few stitches.

Operation June 29: Under chloroform the iodoform packing was removed and the prostatectomy was proceeded with. With the aid of the left index finger working through the bladder wound the right forefinger removed the left lobe of the prostate and the posterior isthmus. Inspection of the bladder then showed the mucous membrane lying flat and normally around left side of the internal meatus. At this stage of the operation the patient became alarmingly weak. The wound was packed and he was removed from the table. The portions of prostate removed weighed forty-eight grammes.

July 2: The dressings were removed. The wound was not septic.

July 3: The patient was very weak, with an irregular pulse, and delirious. After that date he began to improve.

August 29: He has been about the Hospital grounds. The urine, although passed with more than normal frequency, is no longer decomposed. There is about an ounce of residual urine, sometimes less.

December 1: The patient writes from the country that till November 1 his urine was as clear as "spring water" and that he passed it naturally. About this time, for some unknown reason, sounds were passed into the patient's bladder and then the urine became foul again. He usually found two ounces of residual urine.

December 24, 1898: The patient writes that he now urinates about seven times a day and three times at night. The stream of urine is larger than a year ago. The interval of urination is sometimes four hours. He never strains to urinate. There is still some cystitis. His general health is good, with the exception of the ailments incident to advancing years.

The prostatectomy in this patient was handicapped by the operations preceding it, which seriously weakened the patient. His enfeebled power of resistance determined the choice of Nicoll's procedure in preference to that of Alexander, for it was considered important that the deep perineal wound should be saved from contact with the foul urine. A small opening was made by a retractor into the deep urethra while operating, but there was no exit of urine into the wound. A reference, however, to the two succeeding cases will show that had the prostate been completely removed it is probable the prostatic urethra would have been torn, and therefore the consideration that influenced the choice of procedure would have been without force.

Case II.—S. G., aged 62 years, was admitted into the Hospital June 20, 1897. He was suffering from frequent and difficult urination, due to enlargement of the prostate. There were, on an average, five ounces of residual urine, which was acid and contained pus but no casts. There was some difficulty in introducing a catheter.

June 20: The prostate was exposed by a similar procedure to that described in the case of patient No. 1. To identify the urethra, and therefore reduce the chances of its being torn, a soft bougie was passed into the bladder. The lateral and posterior portions of the prostate were removed. In peeling out the left lateral portion, in spite of every care, a rent was made in the floor of the prostatic urethra. In addition to the usual bladder drainage by a tube through the suprapubic wound, a tube was introduced through the perineal wound. The prostatic growths removed weighed forty-six grammes. The wounds healed without untoward event.

August 3: The residual urine was found to be from one ounce to an ounce and a half. The use of the catheter was discontinued.

August 17: There was no residual urine, and the patient was discharged from the Hospital.

January 12, 1899: The patient writes that he urinates once or twice at night and about six times a day. He passes a large stream of clear urine, without straining, and never has occasion to use a catheter. He is in good health, and declares himself free from any urinary trouble whatever.

Case III.—M. L., aged 56 years, was admitted into the Hospital November 30, 1897, suffering from an attack of retention of urine. There were the usual symptoms of enlargement of the prostate. The residual urine, which was decomposed, varied from five to seven ounces. Through the rectum the prostate was felt, evenly and considerably enlarged

Operation January 3: Under ether a suprapubic cystotomy was done, and then the prostate was exposed to view by a perineal dissection as described above. As in the preceding case, a soft bougie was passed through the urethra into the bladder. While removing the prostate especial care was taken to save the urethra from being torn. In separating the growths from the overlying mucous membrane near the median line, it was impossible with the most considerate and gentle handling to avert lacerating the membrane. Rents an inch long in the mucous membrane were made on each side of the floor of the prostatic urethra. Some of the thin mucous membrane, that would otherwise have been sacrificed, was only saved by seizing the growth and dissecting it cleanly away with the knife. Considerable hemorrhage followed the operation. Suprapubic and perineal drainage were provided for as in the preceding case. The prostatic growths removed weighed 44.3 grammes. The wounds healed satisfactorily, the only event being an epididymitis which appeared at the end of a week and resulted in an empyema of the sac.

February 9: No residual urine was found, and catheterization was stopped. There still remained some cystitis.

January 1, 1899: The patient urinates four to six times daily, without pain or straining, in fact normally. The urine is in every respect normal. A full-sized catheter passes without obstruction into the bladder, and no residual urine is found. The patient is in the best of health.

XVIII.

GYNECOLOGICAL SERVICE.

By PAUL F. MUNDÉ, M.D., LL.D.,
ATTENDING GYNECOLOGIST.

(With six illustrations.)

Cases admitted	480
Operations	572
Cured	385
Improved	39
Died	13
Unimproved and not treated	43

In a detailed report of the gynecological service for the twelve years from January, 1883, to January, 1895 (published in the *American Journal of Obstetrics* for October, November, and December, 1895, and in book form), covering 4,211 patients, with 3,960 different diseases, on whom 1,767 operations were performed, I have given a description of the service, of the most prominent diseases and of the methods employed by me for their treatment, and of the results obtained. I shall therefore refer for a consideration of these topics to that report, which can be found in the library of the Hospital, and shall merely briefly touch upon such points in this article as seem to me worthy of special notice.

In a gynecological service, more than in one devoted to general medicine or surgery, the range of diseased conditions is comparatively limited in accordance with the restricted area of the body occupied by the organs under consideration; and the number of patients must necessarily be smaller, since of the three classes of human beings—men, women, and children—only one-third falls to the share of the gynecologist. Hence repetition of diseases and therapeutical measures is naturally unavoidable, and an often tedious uniformity and monotony are but too frequent. It is to avoid repetition that I abstain from entering into many details which have been thoroughly discussed in the above-mentioned recent report.

I will, however, for the sake of rapid comprehension, append a synopsis of the most prominent diseases treated and of the operations, using these as a basis for such remarks as they may seem to call for.[1]

The number of patients treated during the year is about equal to the average during the past four years. Before 1893, with the same number of free beds (20), the annual number of patients was below 300; since then it has averaged 500—an increase which would seem to denote a rising popularity of the Hospital and the service rather than a greater frequency of gynecological diseases. Possibly the growth of the population of the city may have also been a factor in the increase of applications for admission.

During my usual summer vacation the service was in charge of the adjunct gynecologist, Dr. Joseph Brettauer.

The increase in the activity and, if I may so term it, popularity of the gynecological service is shown by the fact that in the four years from January 1, 1895, to January 1, 1899, there were admitted 1,955 patients to that service, as against 4,211 admitted during the twelve years from 1883 to 1895; but still more is that activity demonstrated by the number of operations performed in these respective periods, there having been 1,767 from 1883 to

[1] Only such diseases are mentioned as seemed to me desirable; hence the figures are not complete and do not agree with the total.

The 13 cases of Intravenous Saline Infusion are not included in the 572 gynecological operations.

My practice and experience with anesthesia, being substantially the same, have been included in the report on this subject furnished the Department on General Surgery by the house surgeon.

The gynecological diseases mentioned in the report of the Department of General Surgery occurred either in private patients of the surgeon in charge, or were admitted under an erroneous diagnosis, the true nature of the disease not being discovered until the operation.

1895, and 1,958, or 191 more operations, from 1895 to 1899. Of these operations there were 663 abdominal sections: 464 during 1883-95, 169 during 1895-99.

Gynecological patients, 1883-95	4,211
" " 1895-99	1,955
Total	6,166
Gynecological operations, 1883-95	1,767
" " 1895-99	1,958
Total	3,725
Abdominal sections, 1883-95	464
" " 1895-99	169
Total	633

SYNOPSIS OF DISEASES.

Vulva—6 cases.

Kraurosis	1
Congenital imperforate hymen	2
Bartholinian cyst	1

Urethra and Bladder—17 cases.

Urethrocele	1
Caruncle	2
Vesico-utero-vaginal fistula	1
Chronic cystitis	13

Perineum—9 cases.

Laceration, complete	5
" incomplete	2
" recto-vaginal fistula	1

Vagina—48 cases.

Cystocele	29	More or less coexisting.
Rectocele	19	
Lacerated cervix	15	
" perineum	9	
Retroversion	17	
Endometritis	23	

Uterus—204 cases.

Endometritis, chronic	45
" gonorrheal	1
" post-abortive	14
Abortion, incomplete	46
Pregnancy	12
Fibroids	33
Carcinoma	6
Congenital absence of uterus, ovaries, and vagina	2
Anteflexion and stenosis	29
Retroversion and retroflexion	25
Prolapsus, complete	10
Lacerated cervix	84
Erosion of virginal external os	3
Hypertrophy of cervix	2

Ovaries—33 cases.

Cyst (dermoid, 2)	23
Abscess	5
Hematoma	1
Double carcinoma	1

Tubes—58 cases.

Double salpingo-oöphoritis, chronic (purulent salpingitis)	49
Hydrosalpinx	1
Pyosalpinx	3
Ectopic, { Unruptured, 1; Ruptured, 4 }	5

Pelvic Peritoneum and Cellular Tissue—49 cases.

Peritonitis with exudate	12
Cellulitis " " (puerperal)	8
Hematoma and hematocele	11
Abscess, extra- and intraperit. { ante-ut. . 2; retro-ut. . 14 }	16

Miscellaneous—10 cases.

Septic general peritonitis	1
Aneurism of uterine artery	1
General carcinosis of abdominal viscera	1
Sinus after celiotomy, abdom.	3
" " " vaginal	1

SYNOPSIS OF OPERATIONS (572).

VULVA—4 cases.

Plastic for kraurosis	1
Excision of labium majus	1
Bartholinian abscess	1
Incision of hymen for hematocolpos	1

URETHRA AND BLADDER—3 cases.

Excision of caruncle	1
Vesico-utero-vaginal fistula	1
Intraperitoneal fissure of bladder, celiotomy	1

VAGINA—79 cases.

Congenital atresia	2
Anterior colporrhaphy (Stoltz'),	27
Posterior " (Hegar's),	49
" " (Emmet's),	1

PERINEUM—17 cases.

Laceration, incomplete } (flap-splitting)	12
" complete.. }	5

COCCYX AND RECTUM—2 cases.

Excision of coccyx for dislocation,	1
Resection of rectum for prolapse,	1

UTERUS—263 cases.

Cervix—108 cases.

Laceration (trachelorrhaphy)	75
Erosion "	2
Curetting for carcinoma	2
Amputation for hypertrophy and laceration	7
Discission and dilatation for stenosis	22

Body—255 cases.

Curetting for endometritis, menorrhagia, and retained secundines	208
Shortening of round ligaments (Alexander's)	24
Excision of polypus	2
Accouchement forcé for placenta previa	1
Induced labor for nephritis; high forceps	1
Vaginal hysterectomy for carcinoma	3
Morcellement for fibroids	1
Abdom. hysterect. for fibroid	10
" " " fibro-cyst.	1
" " for fibro-sarcoma	1
" " " diseased appendages,	3

OVARIES AND TUBES—72 cases.

Celiotomy, Abdominal—33 cases.

For ovarian cyst		16
Single	10	
Double	1	
Intralig	3	
Dermoid	2	
For ovarian abscess		2
" chronic salpingo oöphoritis,		11
" ectopic pregnancy		4

Celiotomy, Vaginal—39 cases.

For ovarian cyst	4
" " abscess	28
" intraligamentous ovarian cyst	1
Exploratory	2
Ectopic pregnancy	2
Salpingo-oöphoritis	2

PELVIC CELLULAR TISSUE AND PERITONEUM—13.

Abscess	6
Hematoma	4
Hematocele	2
Abdom. sinus	1

Miscellaneous—3 cases.

Explor. celiotomy for general carcinosis of abdominal organs	1
Celiotomy for ligation of int. iliac artery	1
Median enterostomy through abdominal wound	1
Saline intravenous infusion	13

Kraurosis Vulvæ, that rather rare and curious form of degeneration of the skin covering the vulva, first described by Breisky, was observed only once, under the care of Dr. Brettauer, who effected a cure by dissecting off the affected skin and uniting the edges of the wound by catgut sutures.

This disease may at first sight, and in its early stage, be mistaken for eczema, and indeed I have heard it called such by so well known a dermatologist as the late Dr. Charles Heitzmann. But a closer study of its features at once reveals its individuality. The white, shiny, parchment-like appearance of the affected portions of the skin, here and there broken by fissures and red, eroded patches, the quite defined limits of the disease, the absence of moisture and of acute inflammatory redness as seen in eczema, are characteristic of kraurosis and readily mark the difference between it and eczema. Besides, the pain complained of in kraurosis is different, more acute, darting, severe, not itching and burning like that of eczema. Only prolonged scratching in eczema might possibly obscure the diagnosis and produce a slight resemblance to kraurosis. A further characteristic of kraurosis is the shrinking and contraction of the parts affected; the labia shrivel up, as it were, the vaginal orifice, whether in virgin, nullipara, or pluripara, contracts, and may become almost obliterated. Nothing like this occurs in eczema. Typically the two diseases are entirely distinct. I have seen about half a dozen cases of kraurosis. The disease attacks more or less of the vulva, the clitoris, vestibule, labia minora, posterior commissure, and perineum being usually most affected, but at times also the labia majora and the introitus vaginæ. The suffering is intense. So far as its treatment is concerned, I have found the measure usually recommended—namely, the application of a saturated solution of salicylic acid in alcohol to soften the indurated skin, which is then at once scraped away with a sharp curette until the surface bleeds, this procedure being repeated every few days—to be not only ineffectual but also very painful. After several weeks of this treatment, in spite of temporary apparent improvement, the disease reappears in the spots which appeared to have regained their healthy character, and both patient and physician abandon the futile attempts to effect a cure. Narcotic and anesthetic applications give only temporary relief. Hence the method, I believe first employed by Schroeder, of dissecting away all the diseased skin, and bringing together the healthy edges with sutures, seems to me the quickest and most certain means of cure. Fortunately the redundancy of the cutaneous covering of the vulva permits an easy coaptation of the edges of the large wound thus formed. Only on the vestibule is this more difficult; and the whole clitoris may even have to be sacrificed.

In one of the cases of *Imperforate Hymen* the retained menstrual blood had been evacuated through a small incision by a physician who allowed the opening to close. The exposed genital tract had become infected, and a hemato-pyo-colpos existed when the case was admitted. An excision of a portion of the hymeneal membrane and thorough antisepsis effected a speedy and permanent cure.

Two cases of *Congenital Atresia of the Vagina, with apparent complete absence (rudimentary) uterus, ovaries, and tubes*, were admitted.

One was a girl, 24 years of age, well formed in every respect, with perfectly developed external genital organs, large breasts, stocky build, apparently normal female pelvic development; absolutely no vagina, and not even a trace of uterus or ovaries. She had never seen a sign of menstruation. She was engaged to be married, confessed to amorous feelings when with her lover, and positively insisted on having a vagina constructed on being told that nothing else could be done for her. Yielding to her entreaties, I agreed to do so, and succeeded in making a vagina three inches deep and one and a half inches wide, which was kept at those dimensions by the constant wearing of a vaginal plug until her marriage three months later. Whether I was justified in constructing a vagina for a girl simply to permit her to carry out her matrimonial engagement, without informing the prospective husband of the nature of the case, was a question which occurred to me. But I did not feel at liberty to enter into the sentimental merits of the case, nor could

I reveal a professional secret for the purpose of averting a possibly unhappy marriage. Of course I advised the girl to inform her lover of the condition of affairs, but this she positively refused to do.

FIG. 1.—Single, 24 years old. Absence of uterus, ovaries, tubes, and vagina. Vulva normal. Never menstruated. Artificial vagina constructed.

The second case was that of a woman 26 years of age who had been married three years. She claimed to have had a slight bloody discharge on two occasions in her twentieth year, but whence was not obvious, since she had only a shallow pocket between her urethra and rectum, undoubtedly made by persistent efforts at coitus.

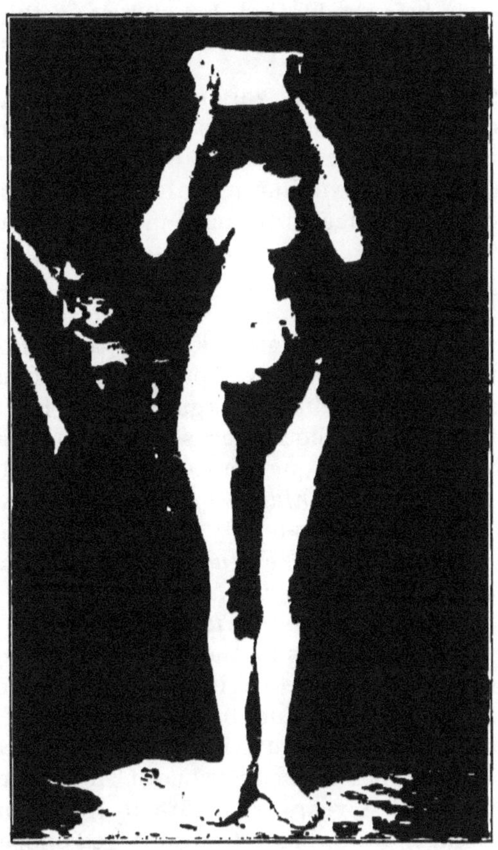

FIG. 2.—Married; 26 years old; rudimentary uterus and ovaries (?); absence of vagina. Menstruated (?) twice. Artificial vagina constructed.

The external genitals were normal, but there was only a crescentic transverse fold to be felt in the pelvis with the finger in the rectum, and on the left side a sensitive nodule as large as a small bean, pressure on which, she said, caused amorous sensations such as she claimed to feel during attempts at coition. Her general configuration was distinctly feminine, except perhaps some diminution in the width of the pelvis. She hoped that something could be done to induce menstruation, but on being told that I could do nothing more than deepen her vagina, requested this to be done.

In both these cases the vagina was made as deep as seemed safe, that is, until the peritoneum was reached, a point which could easily be distinguished by touch and eye. Such artificial vaginæ will always contract unless kept patulous by plugs worn more or less constantly, or by regular coition. Even when lined with skin, introduced by grafts, as practised by Abbe, contraction occurs.

The two photographs were taken for the sole purpose of showing the feminine development of a woman lacking the essential reproductive organs of the female, and to prove that even without uterus and ovaries a person may be to all external appearances a perfect woman.

Of the *Diseases and Injuries of the Urethra and Bladder* I will describe in detail only one, a *Complicated Case of Vesico-Utero-Vaginal Fistula: Accidental Intraperitoneal Rent of the Bladder; Celiotomy; Vesico-Uterine Suture; Closure of Vaginal Fistula; Recovery.*

Of recent years, thanks to the improved management of obstetric cases, vesico-vaginal fistula is a comparatively rare accident. I find but eleven cases of vesico-vaginal and two of vesico-uterine fistula recorded in my Report of the Gynecological Service of Mount Sinai Hospital for the twelve years from 1883 to 1895 (ten cured, one improved, one unimproved—discharged unoperated—and one death from rupture of an unsuspected ovarian abscess). I may have seen a few in private practice, but I doubt if I have met with more than twenty cases in the last twenty years, all told. One of the worst cases was one in which the whole vesico vaginal septum, together with the anterior lip of the cervix, was destroyed, only the urethra being left. Here I was obliged to stitch the posterior lip of the cervix to the urethra in order to secure sufficient material to close the rent. Perfect union and control were obtained by two operations. The external os, to be sure, was turned into the bladder and the woman menstruated through that organ; but this caused her no particular inconvenience, any more than the necessarily resulting sterility.

However, my desire to effect a cure in the present case without resorting to this always disagreeable alternative is to blame, in a measure, for one of the complications attending the case, as the report will show.

Mrs. L. H., aged 34 years, mother of seven children, four born alive, three dead, consulted me at my office on September 27, 1898, with the history that she was confined four months previously, the delivery being instrumental, but of what character she could not say, as she was under anesthesia. Since then there has been absolute incontinence of urine. I found the bladder torn from within less than an inch of the meatus to the internal os uteri, together with the anterior lip of the cervix, which had partly sloughed away. The bladder mucosa protruded into the vagina. (See Fig. 3.) The uterus was retroflexed, and a sound passed into it had to grope for the opening of the uterine canal through the bladder. The true conjugate diameter of the pelvis measured four inches, which accounted for the difficult deliveries and the three dead children. It was strange, however, that the woman had six children before the injury to the bladder occurred.

I sent the woman to Mount Sinai Hospital and operated on her a few days later. In order to be able to close the rent in the anterior wall of the cervix, I attempted to peel the bladder from the uterus with my finger, after making a transverse incision across the cervix. To my surprise my left index finger suddenly burst through the thin adherent peritoneum, tearing also the attached wall of the bladder. I at once repaired these rents with catgut sutures and closed the tear in the cervix, also with catgut, deferring the remainder of the operation to a future time. Ten days later I made a second attempt to close the fistula and readily brought its edges together with numerous silver-wire sutures. In order to make sure that the external os remained in the vagina, I had an assistant keep a sound in it, which accidentally

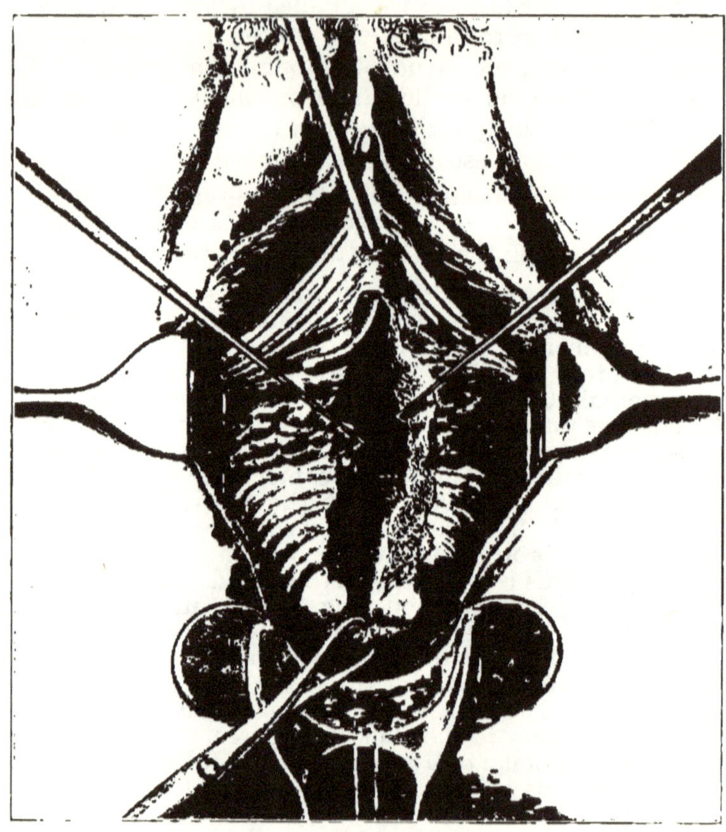

FIG. 3.

slipped out, and on my replacing it I chanced to miss the uterine canal and the sound passed into the bladder, and, to my amazement, through its posterior wall. As no force was used, it was evident that a rent existed in the bladder wall, probably the old tear which had not healed, although the absence of symptoms had led me to assume so. (The head of the bed had been kept raised all this time to facilitate the escape of urine through the fistula; hence no urine remained in the bladder and

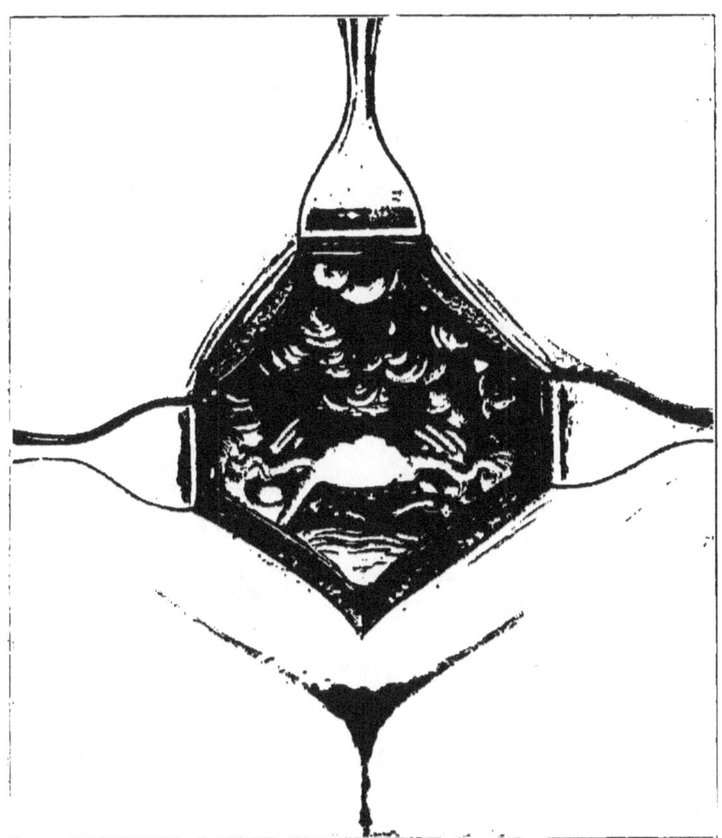

FIG. 4.
(The tip of a sound is shown passed through the fissure in the bladder.)

none escaped into the peritoneal cavity, fortunately, for a septic peritonitis from decomposed urine might otherwise easily have resulted.) I could freely move the sound in the rent, hence it must be of some size. Obviously it could not be left open. I therefore rapidly closed the fistula, moved the patient into Trendelenburg's position, opened the abdomen, and exposed the rent. It extended for fully aninch and a half transversely from about the middle of the bladder toward the left, and was situated at the bottom of the vesico-uterine pouch. It is well shown in the illustration (Fig. 4). I at once proceeded to close the rent with fine interrupted silk sutures, and thought I had successfully accomplished the task when I discovered that some of the stitches had torn through the exceedingly thin bladder

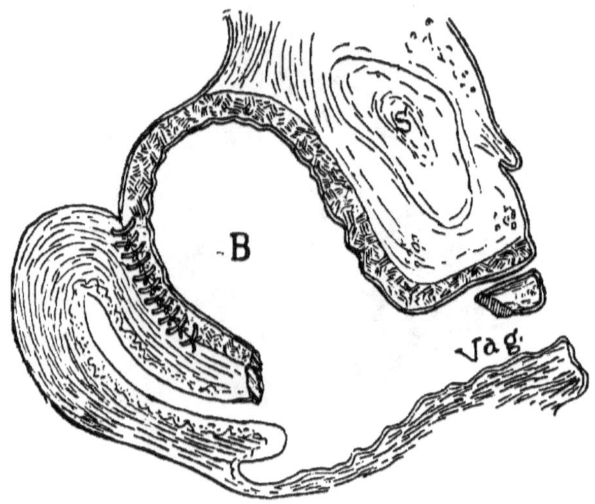

FIG. 5.

wall and that several leakages were visible. Nothing remained then for me to do but to endeavor to close the opening by stitching the body of the uterus and the broad ligament to the bladder, which was accomplished successfully, the whole vesico-uterine pouch being thus obliterated. The line of sutures extended from the bottom of the peritoneal fold (Fig. 5), joining broad ligament and bladder on the left side almost to a corresponding point on the right. The bladder was then distended with a solution of methylene blue and found to be absolutely tight. The usual deep silkworm-gut sutures were used to close the abdominal incision, and the operation, which had lasted over two hours, was happily finished. A soft permanent catheter was placed in the bladder, and the head of the patient's bed elevated to facilitate urinary drainage. Recovery was uninterrupted so far as the abdominal operation was concerned; but the vaginal fistula part was a failure, as I had feared from its necessarily hurried performance. Urine had infiltrated the wound and absolutely no union resulted, not even of the uterine rent. One month later, when there seemed to be no danger of a reopening of the peritoneal fissure, a third attempt was made to close the fistula. Yielding to the necessity, I no longer attempted to restore the normal utero-vaginal communication, but closed the vagina transversely from the posterior vaginal vault to the meatus with a double tier of thin silver-wire sutures, making a wide denudation. As the neck of the bladder was destroyed, I cut out the remnant of the urethra and built up a longer canal by denuding and uniting the nymphæ nearly to the clitoris. A permanent soft catheter was kept in the bladder for fourteen days and the patient directed to lie constantly on the side. There was no leakage; the sutures were removed on the twelfth day and union was found to be perfect. After the removal of the catheter the patient was allowed to sit up and directed to urinate at least every two hours. I had feared that the newly formed urethra might not have regained its retentive power, but fortunately this fear proved groundless. The patient was not only able at once to hold her urine, but could pass it at will. A vagina of sufficient depth for copulation remains. I regret that it did not occur to me, at the time the abdomen was opened, to shorten the round ligaments by doubling them on themselves. and to remove the ovaries: the former operation would have kept the retroflexed uterus more closely in apposition to the bladder, although this did not seem essential to a thorough union of the two organs; and the latter would have removed the persistence of menstruation (a useless function in this case, as also ovulation) and spared the bladder the possible irritation of that discharge.

The closure of an intraperitoneal injury of the female bladder through an abdominal incision is, I believe, a rather unusual operation; at least, I have found only one reference to it in recent literature—namely, in a letter by Dr. A. Lapthorn Smith, of Montreal, describing a visit made by him to the clinics of a number of prominent European gynecologists during the past summer.[1] Smith speaks of having seen Professor Zweifel, of Leipzig, accidentally cut into the peritoneal cavity while operating on a large vesico-vaginal fistula left after a vaginal hysterectomy by another operator. He at once opened the abdomen above the pubes, without changing the patient's position or rising from his own sitting posture between her thighs, and closed the rent with interrupted sutures. The result is not mentioned.

The excellent illustrations are by Dr. W. H. Luckett, of this city, former house-surgeon to this Hospital.

Laceration of the Perineum was so often associated with prolapse of the posterior vaginal wall, or *Rectocele*, that its repair was in those cases performed as a part of the operation on the vagina, by the method known as that of Hegar, which consists in making a triangular denudation on the posterior vaginal wall of a length and width to correspond with the narrowing required, the apex of the triangle being in the vagina, the two lower angles on each labium majus. The vaginal wound was closed by a continuous underlooped catgut suture until the cutaneous margin of the perineum was reached, when deep silkworm-gut sutures caught up the separated fibres of the levator ani muscle and closed the perineal wound. In this way the posterior vaginal wall is not only narrowed in proportion to the size of the rectocele, but it is also lifted up to a desired height indicated by the location of the denudation on the labia. In my opinion this is the best operation for rectocele with or without an incomplete laceration of the perineum. Only once did I perform Emmet's latest operation for rectocele and lacerated perineum, which consists in an

[1] American Gynecological and Obstetrical Journal, October, 1898.

elliptical lateral denudation on each side, that is, the denudation of each lateral vaginal furrow, which is at once closed by interrupted sutures, the posterior or perineal denudation being sutured with deep transverse stitches, the topmost of which includes the projecting tongue of the rectocele. This operation of Emmet is anatomically and logically the ideal one, as it makes lateral linear cicatrices and preserves the natural shape of the vaginal tube; but I have not found it so efficient in relieving the bearing-down sensations and the vulvar gaping which mainly constitute the annoying symptoms of rectocele.

When there is no rectocele, but only an incomplete laceration of the perineum, neither Hegar's nor Emmet's operation is indicated. For both forms of lacerated perineum, incomplete and complete, I have for over ten years preferred the so-called "flap splitting" operation, commonly called Tait's because it was reintroduced by him. It is quick, easy to perform, and for the incomplete laceration always successful. Unfortunately as much cannot be said for it in the complete laceration, where occasionally it fails to secure a perfect union of the sphincter ani, as was still more the case with the older method. Out of the five cases operated there was one failure, which I am inclined to attribute to a miscarriage two weeks before, which had left the genital tissues in a subinvoluted condition unfavorable to primary union. My desire to save the patient a prolonged sojourn in the hospital led me to break my rule never to perform a secondary plastic operation on the genital organs sooner than three months after parturition.[1]

I think I shall in future attempt another method, namely, to separate the rectal from the vaginal wall up to a short distance above the rent, pare the edges of each side of the rent and unite them with underlooped

[1] A second operation performed several months later, in the early part of 1899, resulted in a perfect success.

running suture of catgut or with interrupted sutures of fine silk—in the latter case tying them in the rectum and vagina respectively, cutting them short and allowing them to cut out by themselves. The edges of the rectal wall are to be approximated so as to be turned out slightly, in order to secure a broad surface for union; those of the vaginal wall may be closely coaptated. The rectal and vaginal walls should be kept together by sutures of chromicized catgut passed from the vagina into, but not through, the rectal wall and tied in the vagina. When these sutures have all been tied the recto-vaginal rent must be entirely and securely closed, and it now remains to unite the separated ends of the sphincter ani and restore the perineum, which is done by dissecting out the sphincter ani fibres on either side and bringing them together with fine chromicized catgut or silk sutures, and attaching the sphincter to the recto-vaginal septum also by fine sutures; then two lateral denudations are made up on the labia to the point to which it is desired to restore the perineum, and the wound thus formed is closed by deep silkworm-gut sutures passed through the posterior vaginal wall, as in the flap splitting operation for incomplete laceration of the perineum. In order to make a solid perineum, a certain strip of the posterior vaginal wall has of course been denuded before the buried catgut suture was inserted, and this part is included in these last stitches. I hope in this way to secure more certain union of the sphincter ani, and prevent the all too common occurrence of a minute recto-vaginal fistula just within the posterior commissure.[1]

Cystocele, or prolapse of the anterior vaginal wall, was operated by the method of Prof. Stoltz, of Nancy, in

[1] I have had one successful result with this method, during the early part of 1899. The operation resembles that described by Howard Kelly at the last meeting of the American Gynecological Society, May 24th, 1899, so far at least as relates to dissecting out and uniting the separated ends of the torn sphincter ani.

which a disc is denuded corresponding in size to the cystocele, and a purse-string suture is passed around the denuded area by means of which the latter is puckered into the bladder. The stellate cicatrix thus formed resists the natural efforts at stretching better than the longitudinal scar of elliptical or triangular denudations.

Trachelorrhaphy, or the classical operation of Emmet for puerperal laceration of the cervix, was performed 75 times; twice practically the same operation was done for erosion of the lips of the external os in nulliparæ, this method having been recommended by me for that condition as long as nineteen years ago,[1] in preference to the uncertain and tedious curetting and cauterization usually employed for catarrhal erosions of the cervix.

When there was a decided hypertrophic elongation of the cervix in addition to, and probably produced by, the laceration, I adopted either the method of Schroeder of excision of the hypertrophic tissue of the everted lips, which latter were then turned in and stitched to the healthy endocervical surface, thus forming a vaginal lining of the cervical cavity (not, in my opinion, an ideal method); or I stripped up the vaginal covering of the cervix as high up as I thought suitable, then amputated the whole cervix, and stitched the vaginal wall all around to the border of the endocervical mucosa, thus covering the stump with vaginal tissue. If the stump was very thick I excised a circular wedge-shaped piece before covering it with the vaginal flap, after the method of Gustav Simon (*Kegel-mantel-förmige Amputation des Cervix*). The former method was employed mostly in cases of prolapsus uteri with deeply torn and transversely hypertrophied cervix; the latter, when there was considerable supra- or infravaginal hypertrophy of the cervix in addition to more or less prolapsus.

Shortening of the Round Ligaments was performed in

[1] American Journal of Obstetrics, January, 1879, "The Indications for the Operation for Laceration of the Cervix Uteri."

24 cases, always by the cutaneous method of Alexander, which I have performed on about 200 patients, with so much success, both immediate and subsequent, as to lead me to rest content with it, to the exclusion of the other methods, both intra-abdominal and vaginal, of accomplishing the same object. While occasionally an inguinal hernia has been reported to me, and while in a few instances there has been a return of the retro-displacement of the uterus, especially when there was prolapsus of both uterus and vagina, these cases have been so rare that I have felt justified in continuing to perform the operation, especially as there has been no mortality from it and no worse accident than an occasional stitch-hole abscess. So far as finding the ligaments is concerned, I can safely say that there never is now any difficulty in doing so at once, if ordinary care is exercised in following the landmarks (pubic spine and inguinal ring) laid down originally by Alexander. I make a short incision, not longer than an inch and a half, and prefer to follow up the ligament from the pubic spine rather than to fish for it in its sheath.

The most frequent condition calling for Alexander's operation is marked retroversion or retroflexion, with more or less descensus uteri; usually there is also a laceration of the cervix and more or less rectocele and laceration of the perineum. In addition, cystocele is not uncommon. In such cases I have been in the habit of performing the following "symposium" of operations at the same sitting: 1. Curetting; 2. Trachelorrhaphy; 3. Alexander's; 4. Anterior Colporrhaphy, if indicated; 5. Posterior Colporrhaphy and Perineorrhaphy (usually by Hegar's method). With careful denudation and suturing, thorough asepsis, and rest in bed for three to four weeks, the result of these combined plastics has usually been excellent. If the cervix could easily be drawn to the vulva the wound was sewed with catgut sutures; otherwise with silver wire, which was removed after six or eight weeks when the new perineum could bear the strain of the speculum, during which interval, of course, the patient was at home and about her duties as usual.

Chronic Endometritis was treated by thorough curetting of the endometrium, dull curette above, sharp curette below, internal os (although in aggravated cases the sharp curette was used for the whole uterine cavity), followed by intrauterine irrigation with 1 : 2000 bichloride solution, and, the cavity having been dried, with chlor. zinc 25 per cent solution applied on a swab, or in milder cases iodized phenol, equal parts, the cavity being kept patulous by an iodoform gauze drain. In every case of trachelorrhaphy the endometrium was curetted and irrigated, and a thin strip of iodoform gauze passed through the internal os as a drain, to be removed in forty-eight hours and not renewed.

After trachelorrhaphy only, patients were allowed to leave the bed at the end of a week, and discharged about the fourteenth day, to return in four weeks to have the wire stitches removed. Ordinary curetting cases, whether done for chronic endometritis or retained secundines after abortion, were usually discharged in from ten to fourteen days.

The removal of retained secundines after abortion was accomplished by my large dull curettes, the empty asepticized uterus not being packed with gauze, unless the bleeding continued.

Stenosis of the Uterine Canal came under observation wholly for dysmenorrhea and sterility, usually with marked anteflexion. I have long since discarded office dilatation or treatment for such cases, believing that only thorough dilatation under anesthesia, discission of internal and external os, excision of the flaps formed by the crucial incision at the external os, curetting and gauze packing, followed by the introduction of a large (Peaslee) sound once a week for six or eight weeks, would produce a permanent cure. The patient need be kept in bed only a week at first, the gauze packing being changed every forty-eight hours. I can give no figures as to the results of this treatment for the cure of sterility, but I hear of so many cases where conception has soon followed that I am sure it must be quite frequent. Of course, if the appendages are diseased, this treatment for stenosis is not indicated.

Impaction of Gravid Uterus; Sloughing Cystitis; General Sepsis; Double Pneumonia; Death.

This was a very sad and really inexcusable case. The patient was admitted with the history of a four months' pregnancy and almost total suppression of urine for ten days before admission. The urine was found to be slowly dribbling away (flowing over) and when drawn was intensely fetid. The retroflexed uterus was found impacted in the pelvic cavity; general septic symptoms. The impaction was relieved by protracted manual efforts after the bladder had been emptied; the bladder was thoroughly washed out with dilute peroxide of hydrogen and every effort made by frequent irrigation to improve its condition. The contents of the uterus proving decomposed, the latter was emptied immediately after the reposition of the uterus and carefully disinfected. In spite of every care the general sepsis continued; it had been too deep to yield to local or general remedies; double pneumonia set in and the patient died five weeks after admission.

This case was one of sheer ignorance and culpable neglect, the recollection of which should be a lasting disgrace to the guilty person, whose name or sex (whether physician or midwife) I carefully refrained from ascertaining. The patient stated that she had had medical attendance, but not being relieved had been sent to the Hospital. How any person with the slightest medical knowledge or even with common sense could allow retention of urine to exist for ten days without attempting to relieve it or ascertain and remove its cause, passes all understanding.

Vaginal Hysterectomy for Carcinoma was performed three times by Dr. Brettauer. I have not done this operation for that indication for several years, having lost all faith in its efficacy as a cure for carcinoma of the cervix; for out of the fifty-odd cases in which I have performed it, while only three patients died from the operation itself, in not one was more than a temporary improvement achieved. The longest immunity was nine months. I have since performed it once more for an apparently limited epithelioma of the cervix, the woman being septic from the results of putrid retained secundines. She died of sepsis two weeks after the operation, and metastatic carcinoma of lungs and liver was discovered at the autopsy. In cancer of the body of the uterus I think the operation, vaginal or preferably abdominal, perfectly proper, and the only course to pursue, provided the parametrium is not involved. Once I removed a myomatous uterus per vaginam successfully; and in another case the prolapsed uterus in a woman 60 years of age, a previous operation according to Freund's method of permanent circular wire sutures having failed through cutting out of the wires. The result also was successful.

In all the other cases of complete prolapsus of the uterus and vagina the combined Alexander's, cervical and vaginal plastic operations mentioned above proved satisfactory so long as the patients refrained from hard work or parturition. I know of no operation which will stand the same strain and resist the same factors which brought about the prolapsus.

Of the 23 cases of *Ovarian Cysts*, 16 were operated on by the abdominal (3 intraligamentous, recovery) and 4 by the vaginal route (3 small, free cysts, 1 intraligamentous, recovery).

In the 2 cases of *Ovarian Abscess* the sac of the abscess was enucleated and removed through the abdominal incision; gauze packing; recovery. Of the 33 abdominal sections, for ovarian cysts (16), ovarian abscess (2), chronic salpingo-oöphoritis (11), and ectopic pregnancy (4), 3 died, 2 of septic peritonitis, and 1 of exhaustion after pelvic abscess and prolonged vomiting.

Abdominal Hysterectomy was performed 11 times for fibroid tumor (11 recoveries), once for fibro-sarcoma (recovered), and three times for inflamed and universally adherent appendages (3 recoveries). Supravaginal amputation with covering of stump by peritoneum was the method always employed; drainage, only when there were extensive adhesions, or the tumor was intraligamentous; and then, by gauze per vaginam, through the cervical canal or Douglas' pouch.

The case of abdominal hysterectomy for fibro-sarcoma presented a number of interesting features:

P. G., 40 years, married, multipara. Abdominal tumor had developed during last nine weeks. When admitted, hard, irregular-shaped tumor from right hypochondrium to pelvic brim. Operation September 28, supravaginal amputation, stump covered with peritoneum, no drainage. Recovery fairly smooth, but more or less steady slight elevation of temperature, without appreciable cause. Out of bed in three weeks; then relapse with pain in right side and fever. On November 9, fluctuating mass on right side protruding into vagina; aspirator shows pus. Hard, brawny mass on left side. November 10, evacuation of large quantity of pus through vaginal incision; counter-opening in right flank; drainage tubes. Deep-seated abscess on left side opened by cutaneous incision. Condition desperate. Saline infusion. A few days later, on removal of gauze packings, fecal discharge through vagina from cavity on right side, and urinary flow from abdominal wound on left side, evidently from ureter, which, however, could not possibly have been injured by the knife. Gradual closure of both abscess cavities, of fecal and urinary fistulæ. Discharged cured six weeks after second operation. Seen in perfect health one month later.

One case of ovarian tumor with twisted pedicle in a child 13 years of age merits special report, particularly in reference to the differential diagnosis between appendicitis and tubo-ovarian inflammation on the right side.

A girl, 13 years of age, was brought to the Hospital at 3 A.M. with the diagnosis of appendicitis, and was admitted to the general surgical service. On examining her the house surgeon, Dr. W. M. Brickner, found a tense, prominent swelling of the size of a cocoanut in the middle of the subumbilical region, and shrewdly questioned the correctness of the diagnosis. He had her transferred to my service, where I saw her on the same day. The history was that the child had two previous similar attacks of acute abdominal pain during the past few months. I found a tense, boggy swelling in the anterior vaginal vault (the hymen and vagina readily admitted the finger); the uterus was retroverted and two inches and a quarter deep. A fluctuation wave extended from the summit of the abdominal tumor to the vagina. In spite of the age of the girl, I diagnosticated an ovarian cyst, and from the acuteness of the attack, the temperature of 101.5°, and rapid pulse, suspected torsion of the pedicle. The boggy feeling of the vaginal portion of the tumor induced me to hazard the diagnosis of a dermoid cyst, but herein I was mistaken. But my diagnosis of ovarian cyst with twisted pedicle was confirmed at the operation on the following day, when a cyst of the right ovary with a pedicle twisted *three* times was removed, each twist doubtless representing one of the three attacks of pain, etc , given in the history. There was a small amount of free serous fluid in the abdominal cavity. The cyst was almost black, no adhesions, and at its lower portion, just above the twist, the cyst wall was edematous and contained a large, diffuse blood clot, which had given the boggy feel to the vaginal portion of the tumor. The left ovary contained two cystic Graafian follicles, which I obliterated by a single puncture in each with a sharp Paquelin tip at red heat, then dropping the ovary. Convalescence was absolutely uneventful; on the fourth day the child was reading a novel. Neither pulse nor temperature rose above the normal.

Vaginal Section was performed 52 times, chiefly for presumable ovarian abscess (28), for extraperitoneal abscess (6), hematoma (4), and hematocele (2). In 2 cases an ectopic tube was removed per vaginam by Dr. Brettauer. (See special report by him.)

It has been my practice for years in cases of accumulations of serum, blood, or pus in the pelvic cavity which could be easily reached per vaginam, to evacuate such fluids through that passage, formerly by aspiration of small cavities, later by incision and drainage tube; but in recent years by a free, transverse incision in the posterior vaginal pouch, followed by irrigation and gauze packing if the contents were serum or bloody, and by insertion of one or two white rubber drainage tubes if the cavity contained pus. In the former cases the gauze was renewed every two or three days until the cavity contracted; in the latter, irrigation was practised two or three times daily until the purulent discharge ceased, when the tubes were replaced by iodoform gauze. As a rule, no attempt was made to enucleate the sac of the abscess if it was ovarian or tubal. In encysted or extra-peritoneal abscess the most prominent portion of the abscess was usually directly behind the cervix; in ovarian or tubal abscess, if unilateral, the incision was on the diseased side. There is no danger in making a free incision, for only rarely have I wounded an artery.

In small, deep-seated *intraligamentous* ovarian cysts, which are confined more or less to the pelvic cavity, I have a few times thought it safer and equally curative eventually to open the cyst freely through the vaginal vault, instead of attempting the difficult and dangerous feat of enucleating it through an abdominal incision. Care should be taken, in making the effort to peel out the cyst, not to break through the peritoneal envelope and possibly injure the intestine. I have seen even suppurating intraligamentous cysts contract and close in a few weeks when thus freely opened and packed with iodoform gauze.

The number of cases of *Salpingo-oöphoritis* operated on by abdominal (11) and vaginal celiotomy (2), meaning, of course, complete removal of the diseased organs, is small compared to the number of cases thus afflicted (49) which were admitted. The reason for this is the fact that I have always made it a rule, in the probable absence of pus in either tube or ovary, if the inflammation was more or less recent, to give the patient a chance of recovery, that is, of a *restoratio ad integrum* of her appendages, by rest, time, counter-irritation, cold or hot applications, as the case might be, before deciding to remove them. Only in chronic cases, with a history of repeated attacks of inflammation, with firmly adherent, hypertrophied, and very tender appendages which have resisted all previous efforts at improvement, do I think it justifiable to advise their immediate removal. Of course, true pus tubes, whether actual pyosalpinx, or merely suppurating, hypertrophied tubes without an appreciable pus sac, as well as pus ovaries, require operation, if movable, or bilateral and not easily reachable from below, by celiotomy; if adherent and pointing in the vaginal vault, whether single or double, by free vaginal incision, irrigation, and drainage.

Thus many fresh cases of salpingo-oöphoritis have been benefited, and some even cured, at least for the time being. I have seen conception occur in some such cases, where when first examined the extent of inflammation and exudate seemed to utterly preclude the possibility of a restoration of the normal functions of the organs: and, if watched, nothing is lost by reasonable delay.

Without being able to furnish anatomical proof, I do not doubt that all the cases of *pelvic peritonitis* (so designated because the inflammatory exudate was intraperitoneal) originated in a salpingitis from an intrauterine source. The greater frequency of "pelvic peritonitis" in former reports is merely apparent, all the acute cases of salpingitis and resulting exudate being then classed as "peritonitis."

Pelvic Cellulitis was always of puerperal origin, running along the lymph channels between the folds of the broad ligament. Of this character were the 2 cases of ante-uterine abscess, the 14 cases of retro-uterine abscess being both intraperitoneal and extraperitoneal.

Pelvic Hematocele and Hematoma (11) was in 9 cases unquestionably caused by rupture of a pregnant tube, although no fetus was found in most of the cases. In two instances, however, the hematoma followed curetting, which was done for menorrhagia, there being absolutely no sign of a pelvic effusion at the time of the operation. So far as I can remember, these are the only cases in my experience in which an intrapelvic effusion of blood was due to another cause than a ruptured ectopic tube.

When the hemorrhage was intraperitoneal, the amount considerable, and the blood evidently not encysted and confined to the true pelvis by intestinal adhesions, abdominal section was performed, the ruptured tube tied off and removed, and the dark coagula were scooped, sponged, or washed out as thoroughly as possible. In extraperitoneal effusions, or hematoma, or firmly encysted intraperitoneal pelvic hematocele which protruded well into the vagina, the coagula were evacuated through a free vaginal incision, aided by the finger or a vaginal depressor, or large dull curette, and the cavity was irrigated and packed with iodoform gauze, renewed as indicated.

Aneurism of the Uterine Artery cured by Ligation of the Internal Iliac Artery.

This rare and, as I at first thought, unique case deserves a detailed description. In an experience of thirty years not only have I never before met with such an accident, but a careful search through the surgical and gynecological literature at my disposal failed to disclose a mention of its occurrence. I am indebted to Dr. A. Jacobi for a reference to a similar case reported by Prof. Anton Mars, of Cracow, at the meeting of the Physicians and Naturalists of Poland for 1891,[1] which robs my case of its unique character. Prof. Mars describes the aneurism in his case as a "hitherto unknown and undescribed case of aneurism of the uterine artery." in a woman 44 years of age; the aneurism was as large as a hazelnut. Byelicki, of Lemberg, had seen a similar case which rup-

[1] Wiener med. Woch., No. 37, 1891.

tured during labor and the woman died. It is curious that there should have been two cases of aneurism of the uterine artery in Poland and none other reported in any other country. But such seems the case.

None of the surgeons or gynecologists of my acquaintance of whom I have made inquiry has a recollection of seeing any condition in the female pelvis which might be looked upon as an arterial enlargement resembling an aneurism. A supposed case mentioned to me by Dr. E. Pierre Mallett as having been seen by him at the Vanderbilt Clinic during the past year turns out to be the same case as mine Considering the liability of the uterine artery and its branches to frequent prolonged dilatation during the physiological hyperemia of pregnancy and the pathological changes incident to the development of fibroid tumors and ectopic pregnancy, and also the common injuries to which this vessel is subjected at the time of labor and by surgical measures, it is strange that the uterine artery should have remained free from a lesion which occurs so readily in nearly all the more important arteries of the body.

The danger common to all aneurismal enlargements, that of rupture, applies equally to aneurism of the uterine artery, although the course of that vessel in the pelvic cellular tissue lessens the risk in a measure, owing to the comparatively limited space in which the effusion of blood can occur. Still, as is well known to take place, in intraligamentous rupture of an ectopic gestation sac or in a pelvic hematoma due to the bursting of a varicose vein in the pelvic cellular tissue, the escaped blood may be sufficient in amount to dissect up the peritoneum as high as the renal region and produce alarming and dangerous collapse. Hence an aneurism of the uterine artery cannot be considered a trifling lesion, and must be treated and cured as soon as discovered, on the principle applied to all other aneurisms, by shutting off as much as possible the blood supply to the diseased vessel, and thus producing a coagulation and shrinking of the aneurismal contents and sac. And it was on this principle that I treated the present case.

On September 28, 1898, Mrs. N., 32 years old, mother of one child 8 years of age, called on me at my office for an examination, complaining of a "burning, throbbing" sensation in the left inguinal region. She reminded me that I had seen her two years previously at her home, in consultation with Dr. E. C. Savidge, who had operated on her for a lacerated cervix, after which operation an abscess had developed. I remembered the case perfectly: I found pus issuing from the external os when pressure was made with the finger on a boggy, soft swelling in the left vaginal vault, and I judged therefrom that there was a fistulous communication between the cavity of the abscess and the cervical canal. Hence I advised slitting out the cervix from the sinus down to and through the external os and into the abscess, so as to lay the cavity of the latter freely open. This, Dr. Savidge informed me later, was done, and the abscess closed rapidly. A severe *venous* (so Dr. Savidge distinctly told me) hemorrhage took place at the time, which was controlled by tamponade.

The patient stated that she had been perfectly well and under no medical care until three months previously, when, while on a visit in the West, she felt an uncomfortable feeling in the left lower part of the abdomen and consulted a physician in Milwaukee, who examined her and told her that she had a "swelling" in the left side of the pelvis, for which she should consult a specialist on her return home. He gave no opinion, she says, as to the nature of the "swelling."

I expected to find a chronic salpingitis or some chronic inflammatory condition of the appendages or cellular tissue, but was more than surprised to find a softly elastic, strongly pulsating and thrilling tumor of about the size of a hen's egg projecting into the left vaginal vault, close to the cervix and extending slightly down on the left vaginal wall. At one point next to the cervix there was a "purr" so pronounced and distinct as to make me apprehensive that the aneurism, as it clearly was, might burst at any time.

The accompanying illustration, made for me by Dr. W. H. Luckett, former house surgeon to this Hospital, gives an excellent representation of the site of the aneurism as well as of its vascular relations. It was evidently an enlargement of the uterine artery, that being the only arterial vessel in that locality which was sufficiently large to admit of such a dilatation.

The dangerous character of the lesion was evident,

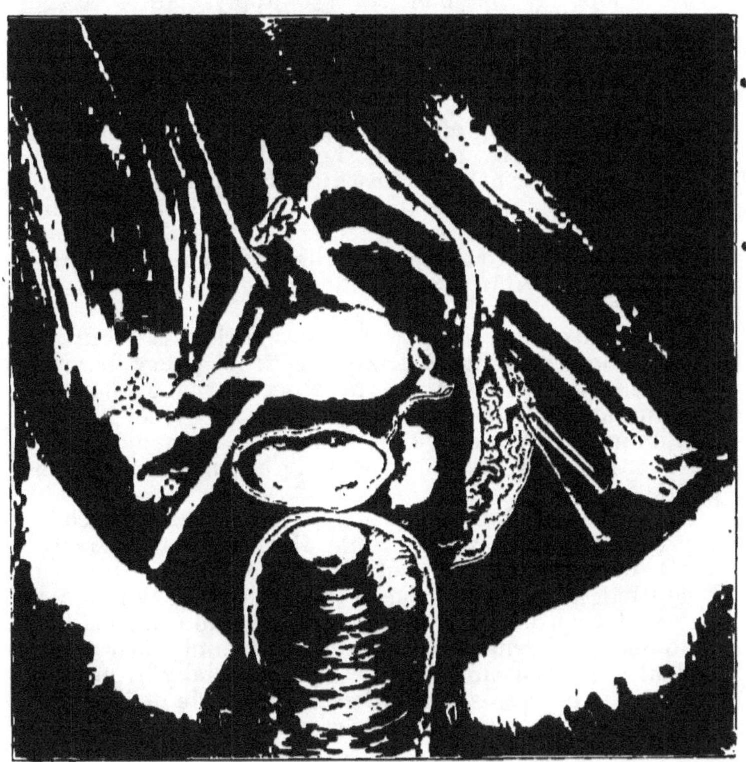

FIG. 6.
(The ligature is seen on the internal iliac artery.)

and the remedy seemed equally clear—namely, the ligation of the arterial trunk from which springs the uterine artery, as well as several other smaller vessels supplying the female pelvic organs. That trunk is the internal iliac artery. It occurred to me that I might be able to reach and ligate the undilated portions of the uterine artery at either end of the aneurism through an incision in the vaginal vault; but the uncertainty as to exact origin and extent of the aneurism, and the danger of wounding a vessel, vein, or artery, the ligation of which through the vagina would prove difficult or impossible, as well as of injuring the ureter, deterred me from adopting this method. To apply clamps to the artery at either side of the dilatation and thus bring about the coagulation of its contents seemed too uncertain and risky.

There remained for me, therefore, only one safe and sure way of cutting off the blood supply to the diseased vessel—namely, by opening the abdomen and ligating the internal iliac artery midway between its separation from the common iliac and its division into the hemorrhoidal and uterine arteries. The direct blood supply of the aneurism would thus be checked, with the exception of the probably trifling amount received by anastomosis with the ovarian artery.

As regards the etiology of the aneurism, it occurred to me that it might be traumatic, the artery having been injured at the time the abscess was opened. I communicated with Dr. Savidge at once by telephone, and he informed me of the violent *venous* hemorrhage at that time, but could throw no light on the causation of the aneurism.

Fearing the risk of delay, I sent the patient at once to a private room in Mount Sinai Hospital and operated on October 1, with the kind assistance of Dr. Howard Lilienthal, adjunct surgeon to the Hospital. Through a four inch incision in the left semilunar line I opened the abdomen in Trendelenburg's position, and after some difficulty in isolating the artery, especially from the ureter which crosses it and lies close to the inside of it at that point, I succeeded in passing a Deschamps pedicle needle under it and ligating it gently but firmly, so as not to injure its coats, with chromicized catgut. Before doing so the finger of an assistant on the aneurism in the vagina informed me when pressure on a certain part of the artery arrested pulsation in the aneurism, and it was at the spot thus indicated that the ligature was applied. When tightened, pulsation in the aneurism ceased entirely. The wound in the peritoneal covering of the vessels was closed by fine uninterrupted catgut suture and the abdominal incision by buried catgut and deep silkworm-gut sutures. Recovery was uninterrupted.

Immediately after the operation there was a faint, apparently transmitted, pulsation in the aneurism, which at the end of a week had increased somewhat, probably owing to the establishment of collateral circulation. The purr and thrill had, however, entirely disappeared, and never returned, and the outer portion of the aneurismal swelling had become hard and solid and had evidently contracted. Wishing to make as perfect a cure as possible before discharging the patient, I decided to try the effects of galvano-puncture of the aneurism, and twice at intervals of three days passed a current of twenty milliampères from a chloride of silver battery through the sac for half an hour, a carefully insulated platinum needle being thrust deeply into the centre of the aneurism and connected with the positive pole, the negative pole being a large wet sponge under the left natis. The effect of these two galvanic sittings in hardening and shrinking the aneurism was very apparent, but I am confident that this method would have proved utterly inadequate, and probably dangerous through the possible detachment of particles from the thrombus and distant embolism, if the chief arterial supply had not been previously shut off by ligation.

When last examined, six weeks after the operation, the aneurism had shrunken to one-half its original size, was hard and painless (at no time, indeed, had it caused any particular pain), and pulsated no more than the normal uterine artery.

I should add that the cervix was normal, the incision at the time of the abscess having healed with scarcely a trace.

While exploring the abdominal cavity during the operation, I could reach the upper border of the aneurism with the tip of my finger, but could not trace out its limits with sufficient clearness to feel justified in attempting to ligate its immediate afferent and efferent vessels; neither did I attempt to ligate the ovarian artery, which I could easily have done at the upper margin of the left broad ligament close to the uterus. I did not estimate its relation to the aneurism by anastomosis with the ascending branch of the uterine artery as of sufficient importance to call for a prolongation of the operation. However, should I meet with another similar case I would take this additional precaution. To endeavor to dissect out the whole aneurismal sac after ligating or clamping its vessels, as has been suggested to me, would, I think, be too hazardous and uncertain, and anatomically too difficult, however tempting and theoretically practicable it might appear.

As regards the ligation of the internal iliac artery, it may be permissible to say that it is by no means an easy operation, even with the vessel exposed as it is in Trendelenburg's position. The difficulty is chiefly the isolation of the artery from the vein and the ureter, and, this accomplished, the passing underneath and around it of the ligature needle. I found the ordinary aneurism needle and a bent silver probe insufficient to force their way through the subjacent areolar tissue, but the slightly sharp tip of the Deschamps ovarian pedicle needle answered admirably, the point being carefully watched by the left index finger.

The operation is a comparatively rare one; Ashhurst (Internat. Encyclop. of Surgery) says that up to 1883 "the whole number of cases is about twenty-seven, with eight recoveries." No doubt, since the perfection of antiseptic surgery and the introduction of Trendelenburg's position, the number of cases of this operation has greatly increased with a corresponding rate of recoveries.

Intravenous Saline Infusion was performed 13 times, before, during, and after operation, or in every case where the exhaustion or shock from loss of blood or some other cause offered a fair indication for the operation. I am confident that several lives (3, at least) were saved by this treatment, and others prolonged. Of course, it is impossible to say in some cases whether the patients might not have recovered without the infusion; but as the latter, properly performed, is devoid of danger, it is well to be on the safe side and to take the chance of performing it unnecessarily rather than to omit it because it seems more or less uncalled for or possibly useless. From two to five pints of decinormal salt solution, at a temperature of 110°, were usually infused from a glass jar into the median basilic vein at the left elbow. Frequently the infusion was repeated once or twice, the median basilic vein of the other arm and the median cephalic veins in each arm being utilized in succession as needed. Any one familiar with the anatomy of the veins of the elbow joint and conversant with the simple technique of the operation can easily find the vein and perform the infusion, even in a fat person and with a collapsed vein. Under intracutaneous eucain anesthesia the operation is practically painless.

Subcutaneous Saline Infusion was little practised, because less rapid and positive in its results, and chiefly because, the instruments being always kept at hand, the intravenous infusion could be performed with equal rapidity and facility. In private practice this would not be the case, and hypodermoclysis might then be preferable.

XIX.

VAGINAL CŒLIOTOMY FOR DISEASE OF THE APPENDAGES.

By J. BRETTAUER, M.D.,

ADJUNCT GYNÆCOLOGIST.

DURING the year 1898 I have operated for disease of the appendages on the following cases:

CASE I.—Mrs. S., aged 28, suffering from a tubal pregnancy of about six weeks' standing. A soft mass the size of the fist could be felt in Douglas' pouch. Operation January 14: After curetting, through an incision in the anterior fornix of the vagina the mass was easily removed. The angles of the incision were closed with catgut sutures and a small strip of gauze left in the pelvic cavity. This was removed in forty-eight hours. Convalescence was undisturbed, and the patient discharged from the Hospital at the end of two weeks.

CASE II.—Mrs. S., aged 30 years, admitted June 30 with a history of acute inflammatory process in the pelvis following abortion. On July 2 an ovarian abscess was removed through the anterior fornix, but not without its rupturing during the manipulations. Adhesions about the intestines caused considerable technical difficulties and parenchymatous hemorrhage. The left appendages appeared normal and were left. The pelvis was packed with iodoform gauze, which was removed on the third day. The patient was discharged on July 20.

CASE III.—Mrs. M., admitted on July 23. After curetting for incomplete abortion, posterior section was made and a dermoid cyst of the right ovary the size of an orange was removed with ease. The incision in the fornix was closed with catgut sutures. Uneventful recovery ensued, delayed only by an anæmia due to profuse hemorrhage before admission.

CASE IV.—Mrs. W., aged 22, admitted July 24. To the left of the enlarged uterus, and somewhat behind it, a fluctuating, immovable mass could be felt. On the right side the appendages were normal. Posterior section was performed on the 26th, and the mass was found to be a pyosalpinx, which was removed with great difficulty owing to adhesions. The patient was discharged cured on August 8.

Case V.—Mrs. G., aged 38 years, admitted August 9 with a diagnosis of tubal pregnancy. A mass the size of an orange could be easily determined in front and somewhat to the right of the enlarged uterus. Through a longitudinal anterior section the pregnant tube was removed *in toto* with great difficulty. The opening in the peritoneum was closed with catgut sutures. The patient made an uneventful recovery and was discharged cured on the 30th.

Case VI.—Mrs. G., aged 27, admitted August 14 and operated upon on the 16th. Posterior section was performed, and a pyosalpinx of the right tube was removed after a tedious operation and the separation of many adhesions. The pelvis was packed with gauze, which was removed after forty-eight hours. On August 26, the vaginal incision had to be reopened to drain an abscess which had formed low down in Douglas' pouch. The patient was discharged cured on September 12.

Case VII.—Mrs. S., 27 years old, admitted August 16. Seven years before she had been operated upon for a left pyosalpinx, which was opened and drained through the posterior fornix. The left appendages were removed one year later by abdominal section. The patient had an attack of pelvic peritonitis on the right side two years ago. She was admitted to the Hospital for diseased appendages of the right side. There could be felt a small cystic tumor on the left which bulged into the posterior fornix. The uterus was somewhat fixed, but not enlarged or tender. On August 17 an incision in Douglas' pouch was made. The cystic mass on the right side, which proved to be of a chronic inflammatory character starting from the old stump, was removed. No ligature was found. The right adnexa were embedded in a dense exudate, and were developed with great difficulty and tied off. The pelvis was packed with gauze, and the wound was partially closed with catgut sutures. The uterus was left *in situ* at the patient's particular wish. On September 1 she was discharged with a freely movable uterus and feeling perfectly well.

Case VIII.—Mrs. B., aged 25 years, was admitted on

August 20 for disease of the left appendages. A posterior section was done on August 23. With great difficulty adhesions of the appendages and omentum were separated and the appendages developed with a rupture of the tube and the escape of foul-smelling pus. The tube was ligated and the oozing controlled by iodoform gauze packing. The right adnexa were not materially changed. Convalescence was disturbed by symptoms of iodoform poisoning, but the patient recovered and was finally discharged on September 22.

During the past few years I have operated upon many patients suffering from pelvic disease by the vaginal method upon whom I was formerly in the habit of operating by the abdominal route. My experience on the whole has been most satisfactory, as I have always tried to select my cases with care. It is, of course, impossible to recognize adhesions to their full extent before operation, and this accounts for some of the difficulty which was encountered in the series reported.

My experience has taught me that in the presence of any freely movable tumor of the appendages situated low in the pelvis, either in the vesico uterine space or in Douglas' fold, the vaginal route is not only applicable, but even possesses advantages over the abdominal method, inasmuch as shock is absent and convalescence is unquestionably shortened. In all cases, and especially in those in which the history informs us of previous inflammatory attacks and in which adhesions seem probable, abdominal cœliotomy is preferable.

XX.

EYE AND EAR SERVICE.

By E. GRUENING, M.D.,
OPHTHALMIC AND AURAL SURGEON.

DISEASES.

Diseases of Mastoid Process and Brain.—6.	Operation. M	Operation. F	Operation. C
Empyema of mastoid, abscess of cerebrum	1	....	....
" " " cerebral meningitis	....	....	1
" " " meningitis, general sepsis	1	....	....
Mastoiditis, general miliary tuberculosis, tubercular meningitis	....	....	1
" thrombosis of lateral sinus and jugular vein, pyæmia	....	1	....
" " " " " " " " general sepsis	....	....	1
Total	2	1	3

Diseases of the Eye—103.	Operation. M	W	C	No operation. M	W	C	Cured. M	W	C	Improved. M	W	C	Unimproved. M	W	C	No treatment. M	W	C	Died. M	W	C	Total.
Burn of conjunctiva and cornea	..	..	..	1	..	..	1	..	..	..	..	..	..	..	..	..	..	..	..	..	..	1
Cataract—14.																						
Cataract, congenital	1	..		..	..	..	1	..	..	..	..	..	..	..	..	..	..	..	..	..	..	1
" mollis	1	..	..	..	..	..	1	..	..	..	..	..	..	..	..	..	..	..	..	..	..	1

Diseases of the Eye—*Continued.*	Operation.			No operation.			Cured.			Improved.			Unimproved.			No treatment.			Died.			Total.
	M	W	C	M	W	C	M	W	C	M	W	C	M	W	C	M	W	C	M	W	C	
Cataract, secondary	1	1					1	1														1
" senile	3	5					3	5														8
" traumatic		2	1																			3
Corneal fistula, secondary iritis		1						1														1
" ulcer				1		1			1	1												2
Conjunctivitis, catarrhal				1			1															1
" purulent				1			1															1
" traumatic				1			1															1
Contusion and emphysema of upper eyelid				1			1															1
Cyclitis dolens	1						1															1
Distichiasis		1						1														1
" entropion		1						1														1
Ectropion		1						1														1
Episcleritis, corneal infiltration					1						1											1
Emphysematous orbit				1			1															1
Glaucoma, acute		6						6														6
" chronic		1																				1
Iris, prolapse of	1						1				1											1
Iritis, plastic		1		2	2		2	2			1											5
" keratitis, corneal ulcer, trachoma	1									1												1
" hypertrophy of inferior turbinated bone	1						1															1
Irido-cyclitis	1	1				1	1	1	1													3
" and perforation of globe		1						1														1
" " trachoma					1						1											1
Keratitis, parenchymatous					1						1											1
" phlyctenular						2						2										2
" " ulcer of cornea					1						1											1
" traumatic					1			1														1
" trachoma		1		1	1	1		1		1	1	1										4

Diseases of the Eye—*Continued.*

Keratitis, fascicular						1			1													1
Kerato-iritis				1						1												1
Lens, subluxation of						1						1										1
Orbit, dermoid cyst of inner		1						1														1
Retina, detachment of					1						1											1
Retrobulbar neuritis				1						1												1
Staphyloma		1						1														1
" ciliary	1						1															1
Scleritis fugans, hypertrophic rhinitis	1						1															1
Strabismus		1						1														1
" divergent	1						1															1
" internal			1						1													1
Symblepharon		1			1																	1
Trachoma, acute	7	2	17				7	2	17													26
" chronic, ulcer of cornea			1	1					1	1												2
" " enucleation	1						1															1
" pannus					1	1				1	1											2
Trichiasis	1	1					1	1														2
Total																						103

Diseases of the Ear—39.

Disease of Mastoid—29.

Mastoiditis, acute	3	2	2	1		1	3	2	2	1											1	9
" chronic, abscess of cerebrum	1																		1			1
" " tubercular			1									1										1
" " extra-dural abscess	1						1															1
" general miliary tuberculosis, tubercular meningitis			1																		1	1
" thrombosis of lateral sinus and jugular vein, pyæmia			1																		1	1
Mastoid, empyema of	5		6				5		6													11

	Operation.			No operation.			Cured.			Improved.			Unimproved.			No treatment.			Died.			Total.
	M	W	C	M	W	C	M	W	C	M	W	C	M	W	C	M	W	C	M	W	C	
Diseases of the Ear—*Continued.*																						
Mastoid, empyema of, meningitis, general sepsis		1																		1		1
" " " cerebral meningitis			1																		1	1
" " " septic thrombus of right lateral sinus, meningitis, general sepsis			1																		1	1
Otitis Media—10																						
Otitis media, acute					1	2			1					1	1							3
" " purulenta		1	1	1	2			1	1	1	2											5
" " " double			1			1						2										2
Total																						39
Diseases of the Nose and Throat—13.																						
Adenoids of pharynx	1		2			1	1		2						1							4
" " " and enlarged tonsils			1						1													1
" " " " blepharitis marginalis			1						1													1
" " " " deviated septum			1						1													1
Ethmoid bone, empyema of	1						1															1
Peritonsillar abscess, double	1						1															1
Perichondritis of nasal septa	1						1															1
Tonsillitis				2			2															2
" hypertrophy of			1						1													1
Total																						13

OPERATIONS.

OPERATIONS ON THE NOSE AND THROAT—23.

	Operations.	Deaths.
Adenoids, post-nasal, removal of	8	
Ethmoidal sinus, curetting of	1	
Nasal septum, enchondrosis on, removal of	1	
" " Asch's operation for d v ation of	1	
" " perichondrosis of, incision and transfixion	1	
Peritonsillar abscess, incision of	1	
Removal of glands, cervical adenitis	1	
Retropharyngeal abscess, incision of	1	
Tonsillotomy	4	
Turbinated bone, middle, exsection of	2	
" " " and inferior, exsection of	1	
" " inferior, exsection of	1	

OPERATIONS ON THE EAR—49.

	Operations.	Deaths.
Furuncle of external auditory canal, incision of	3	
Paracentesis of membrana tympani	10	
Mastoid Operations—35.		
For empyema of mastoid	15	
" " " " cholesteatoma	1	
" " " " meningitis	1	1
For empyema of mastoid, general tuberculosis, tubercular meningitis	1	1
For empyema of mastoid, lateral sinus and jugular vein; thrombosis; ligation of internal jugular	2	2
For empyema of mastoid, extra-dural abscess	1	
For empyema of mastoid, abscess of brain, secondary operation	1	1
For empyema of mastoid, secondary operation, meningitis, sepsis	1	1
For mastoiditis	2	
" " subacute	1	
" " cholesteatoma	2	
Exploratory operation	1	
R visions	5	
Wilde's incision	1	
Infiltration of sterno-mastoid, incision for	1	
Secondary suture after mastoid operation	1	
Intravenous infusion after ma toid op ration	1	

OPERATIONS ON EYE, EAR, NOSE, AND THROAT—185.

Operations on the Eye—113.

	Operations.	Deaths.
A vancement for convergent strabismus	2	
Cataract operations—19.		
complicated, extraction of	1	
secondary, caps lotomy for	4	
senile, extraction of	11	
" " " Critchett's method	1	
traumatic, extraction of	1	

	Operations.	Deaths.
Chalazion, incised	1	
Curetting of cornea for fascicular keratitis	1	
Dacr ocystitis, operation for	1	
Dermoid cyst in inner angle of orbit, extirpation of	1	
Distichiasis, electrolysis for	1	
Ectropion	1	
Enucl ation—7.		
for ciliary staphyloma	1	
" cyclitis dolens	1	
" chronic irido-cyclitis	4	
" traumatic r pture of eyeball	1	
Entropion, Hotz's operation	1	
" Streatfi ld-Snellen operation	1	
Evisceration of eyeball	1	
Exploratory incision through cornea	1	
Iridectomy	6	
" for foreign body	1	
" " glaucoma, acute	1	
" " " subacute	3	
" " occluded pupil	2	
" " wound of cornea with prolapse of iris	1	
Skin grafting (Thiersch) for symblepharon	1	
Sclera, excision and cur tting of	2	
Sclerotomy, posterior	2	
Tenotom of internal rectus for strabismus	2	
Tracho a, expression	40	
" " and scarification with scalpel	10	
Trichiasis, electrolysis for	4	

XXI.

THE MASTOID OPERATION IN ACUTE EMPYEMA AND CARIES.

By E. GRUENING, M.D.,
OPHTHALMIC AND AURAL SURGEON.

THE aural service of the Mount Sinai Hospital was established in 1879. The work of this special department in the twenty years of its existence is best illustrated by the operations performed on the mastoid process, and the books of the institution record 338 such operations. The pathological conditions demanding the operations can be arranged from the material at hand under seven heads.

First: Acute caries and empyema of the mastoid with purulent discharge from the middle ear.

Second: Acute caries and empyema of the mastoid with extra-dural abscess in the posterior cranial fossa.

Third: Cortical or central caries of the mastoid without purulent discharge from the middle ear.

Fourth: Chronic purulent otitis media with cholesteatomatous masses in mastoid antrum.

Fifth: Chronic purulent otitis media with thrombosis of lateral sinus and pyæmia.

Sixth: Chronic purulent otitis media and abscess of the brain.

Seventh: Chronic purulent otitis media and meningitis.

Of the 338 cases of mastoid disease, 248 were acute, and it is my purpose to speak only of these in this communication. The operation was ordinarily performed with the mallet and gouge, and in the first ten years, from 1879 to 1889, according to Schwartze by exposing the mastoid antrum and not venturing much beyond the restricted circular or oval area in the vicinity of the supra-meatal spine. If, in the light of our present knowledge, we consider the manifold pathological changes found in and about the mastoid process, we can readily understand why a gouging operation confined to the mastoid antrum should have proved insufficient in so many instances. The after-treatment was tedious, requiring daily irrigation of the ear, frequently the introduction of a leaden nail to keep the wound open, and often a second or third operation. The tip of the mastoid was forbidden ground, and it was thought hazardous to operate upon a bony region generally consisting of diploic tissue and rarely containing pneumatic cells. It is not just to make Schwartze responsible for this state of things. No one can rob him of his well-earned laurels, yet his operation has been so often described, especially by his pupils, as Schwartze's typical gouging operation to open the mastoid antrum, and so much stress has been laid on this principal feature of the method, that its possibilities of extension and modification have not been sufficiently considered. To do Schwartze full justice it is only necessary to point to page 344 of his book "Die chirurgischen Krankheiten des Ohres," edited in 1885. There he says: "The many pathological conditions found in the course of an operation on the mastoid are really astounding, and it is impossible to determine beforehand the extent of the operation."

The thorough trial given in the Mount Sinai Hospital to the so-called typical Schwartze operation led to its abandonment in 1889, and to the adoption of a modification embodying the chief feature of Schwartze's operation, the opening of the mastoid antrum, but combining with it systematically, even in cases of sound cortex, the laying bare of other pneumatic spaces, especially of those contained at the tip and over the sigmoid groove. The behavior of the mastoid wound after the adoption of the modified operation was an agreeable surprise, and in a paper read before the American Otological Society at the meeting held in Washington in 1891, I was able to report 41 consecutive operations on acute cases with an average healing time of four weeks. Since that time 159 additional operations were performed at the Mount Sinai Hospital in acute cases, and the results obtained were as favorable as those reported in 1891. The operation is begun with an incision extending through the soft part from one-half inch above the temporal ridge to one-half inch below the tip of the mastoid. The periosteum is then lifted from the mastoid process and the tendinous attachments of the sterno-cleido-mastoid muscle are cut close to the bone with scissors, and the tip of the mastoid is fully exposed. If the bone is found diseased and softened, the opening is made with the curette; if apparently healthy and firm, with the mallet and gouge. It is immaterial whether the operation of removing the bone is begun above over the antrum or below over the tip. It is often more convenient to start below, expose the terminal pneumatic spaces, remove granulation tissue and carious bone, determine the course of the sigmoid groove, and finally work the way into the mastoid antrum. The interior of the antrum is then fully explored. Its upper wall being a part of the tympanic roof and its posterior wall usually corresponding to the knee of the sigmoid groove, important indications are derived from such an exploration.

If these bony walls are found diseased, the operation is continued in the direction of the middle or posterior cranial fossa. The operation is completed when the apophysis has been cleared of all diseased material and every fistulous tract has been followed and laid open.

From December 1, 1897, to December 1, 1898, 33 operations were performed on the mastoid process in the aural service of the Hospital.

The cases illustrate various types of mastoid disease, and some of them are of sufficient general interest to be worthy of publication.

CASE I. *Pneumococcus Empyema of Mastoid Cells.* —B. E., schoolboy, aged 8, admitted February 14, 1898. Had measles when quite young. Two weeks ago had a slight attack of diphtheria with dull pain in both ears. Later had acute pain in left ear and chilly feeling. The parts behind the left ear began to ache and swell. Pain was relieved, but swelling increased, by flaxseed poultices. On admission pulse 120, respiration 24, temperature 100.4°. Left ear drum perforated. Canal filled with pus. Behind the ear is a red and œdematous area. Marked tenderness over apex. Right ear normal. Patient looks apathetic. Eyes, lungs, heart, and abdomen negative.

February 14: *Operation.*—Usual incision through the soft parts. Periosteum found much thickened. Cortex of mastoid sound. Bone opened with gouge. Mastoid antrum laid bare; it was filled with pus and granulation tissue. The apical cells were found in the same condition. The ridge of bone intervening between antrum and apex removed with rongeur. All cells were converted into one large cavity. Upper portion of anterior antrum wall removed with mallet and gouge. Sigmoid sinus exposed; it looked healthy. Entire field of operation flushed with alcohol. Upper angle of wound closed with two catgut sutures. Lightly packed with iodoform gauze and dry dressing applied. Gauze in auditory canal. Cultures made by the assistant pathologist of the Hospital, Dr. Libman, showed pneumococcus.

February 15: Pulse 100, respiration 24, temperature 99°. General condition very good.

February 17: Wound dressed; it looks well. Wound sprayed with one per cent carbolic solution; repacked with iodoform gauze; dry dressing applied. Highest temperature 100.4°.

February 20: Wound dressed as before; no discharge.

February 21: Had severe epistaxis. Wound does not look well. Temperature 100.4°. Irrigation through antrum and middle ear. Abundant discharge. Wound sprayed with carbolic acid solution one per cent; packed with iodoform gauze; wet dressing applied.

February 23: Temperature normal all day. Wound dressed in the usual way (dry). From this time the patient made a rapid recovery. Temperature continued to be normal.

March 3: Patient discharged cured.

CASE II. *Streptococcus Empyema with Caries of Mastoid and Secondary Abscess in Substance of Sterno-cleido mastoid Muscle.*—I. S., aged 10, admitted December 21, 1897. For the past week he had purulent discharge from the right ear. Examination of pus showed pure streptococcus of the long variety. In spite of the early incision of the drumhead, marked tenderness remained over the antrum and extended later to the tip and the post-mastoid region. Temperature 101°, pulse 110. Complains of headache.

Operation.—Usual incision through the soft parts. Division of the fibres of the sterno-cleido-mastoid. Full exposure of the tip. The mastoid is very large and has a dull blue color. Mastoid antrum opened with mallet and gouge. Thick pus wells up in large quantity from antrum. There is a large tip cell, which is also filled with pus. The mastoid is one which contains many pneumatic cells with thin partition walls: these were removed with the rongeur, and all cells were found filled with pus. A second incision was carried backward one and one-half inches at right angles with the first to expose the sigmoid sinus. The outer table of bone covering the sinus was removed with the gouge and a great number of pneumatic spaces, all filled with pus, were uncovered. The thin walls forming these cells were removed so that the inner table covering the sigmoid sinus was fully brought into view. The bone appeared healthy. The field of operation was thoroughly cleansed by irrigation and the inner plate covering the sinus removed for exploratory purposes and the sigmoid sinus exposed. It was healthy. The cavity was then disinfected with sublimate solution 1 : 2000. Silk sutures in upper angle of the wound and in the transverse incision. Packed with iodoform gauze and wet dressing applied.

December 22: Temperature 99°, pulse 92. Complains of headache and earache. No discharge from ear. Wound does not look well. Infiltrations and swelling along the sterno cleido-mastoid muscles.

December 23: Temperature 102.2°.

Operation.—Chloroform. Director passed two inches through the inferior angle of the wound into a fistulous tract. Cut down upon the director and found the fistula ended in the substance of the sterno-cleido-mastoid muscle. Skin and muscle opened freely along the director and wound packed.

December 29: Temperature 99°. Condition much improved.

December 25: Temperature 98.5°, pulse 78.

December 26: Wound granulating. Dressing saturated with blue pus. Carbolic spray five per cent. Wound dressed dry.

December 27: Temperature normal.

January 18: Patient up and about all day. Has been dressed every day in the usual manner. Granulations kept down with nitrate of silver. Cavity almost filled. Light packing of iodoform gauze and dry dressing. Discharged cured.

CASE III. *Streptococcus Mastoiditis and Extra-dural Abscess without Purulent Discharge of Middle Ear.*—C. F., expressman, aged 40 years, admitted October 13, 1898. The disease is of four months' standing. Has had very severe pain in left side of head. Was treated with leeches, drops, and various medicines until about ten days ago, when a swelling appeared back of the ear. At the same time all his pain disappeared. The swelling has increased in size up to the present time. There has never been any discharge from the ear. Gives a history of slight fever and chills at varying intervals while he had the severe pains. No brain symptoms.

Physical Examination.—Drumhead is complete, but membrana Shrapnelli and handle much injected. Watch heard in contact. Canal is slightly injected in its supero-posterior portion, corresponding to the injected part of the drum. Mastoid tenderness. Swelling begins on a level with the upper wall of the meatus, extending upward three inches and backward two inches to midway between the auricle and the occipital protuberance. Fluctuation over the central part of the mass.

Eye negative.

Eustachian tube permeable; no improvement after inflation.

On admission pulse, respiration, and temperature normal.

Operation.—Curved incision at the usual site down to the bone; skin found to be lifted from bone so that the finger could be passed its full length beneath it. Another incision was then made about the middle of the first incision and at right angles to it, extending backward to the limit of the swollen area. When the flaps were retracted pus was seen oozing from a small opening in the bone, one and an eighth inches posterior to and a little above the suprameatal spine. A culture was taken of this pus; it proved to be streptococcus longus. The probe passing in about one inch could be turned about in a considerable cavity. The bone was then gouged away in a circle about this opening, when pus and blood came away quite freely. Gouging was then continued downward and anteriorly toward the apex, the previous opening being in the meantime packed with gauze. The sinus was then uncovered. The pus cavity was found to be lined with thick granulations, which were curetted. The cavity was then enlarged above with strong rongeur. The antrum was opened and found to contain pus and granulation tissue. The apex was next attacked; a portion of the tip was taken away; some granulation tissue was found here. The cavity, when completely opened, was located in the posterior fossa of the cranium, triangular in shape; it was bounded above by the dura mater, below by the sinus, internally by untouched mastoid bone, which separated it from the auditory canal. It communicated at its upper anterior angle with the antrum. The edges of the wound were sutured above, behind, and below. Iodoform gauze packing in antrum, and another on the sinus and in the large pus cavity. Dressed dry.

October 14: Temperature 99.4° to 100.2°, pulse and respiration normal. General condition good. Takes nourishment well.

October 15: Temperature 99° to 100°. Soft diet.

October 16: Wound dressed. Packings all removed and renewed. No discharge. Wound very clean. Temperature 99° to 100°.

October 17: Wound dressed. Packings renewed. Lower suture in wound removed. Practically no discharge. Bacteriological report of pus shows it to be streptococcus longus.

October 18: Wound dressed. Some œdema of the scalp over the posterior parietal and anterior occipital region, extending from the upper angle of the wound to the occiput. Temperature normal. General condition good.

October 19: Œdema less marked to-day. Stitches removed.

October 20: Full diet. Wound healing well.

October 25: Out of bed. Wound granulating nicely; all recesses filled up.

November 1: Dressed dry. Wound almost closed. Discharged cured.

CASE IV. *Caries of Mastoid and Subperiosteal Abscess.*—A. M., clerk, aged 17 years. Admitted October 28, 1898.

Was always healthy until two months ago, when, after a swimming bath, pain developed in his left ear. The pain was dull and constant. Patient was treated with injections and drops four weeks, at which time a swelling developed back of the ear. An aurist performed a paracentesis of the drumhead and ordered an ice bag. Since that time he has had a discharge from the ear. Three days ago the discharge stopped. After the ear was cleansed on the following day the swelling back of the ear increased rapidly. Last night the pain was very severe.

Physical Examination.—Auricle stands off from the head, especially the upper portion. There is an elastic swelling occupying the upper part of the mastoid region, extending from the upper wall of the canal to the upper edge of the auricle. At a considerable depth the swelling fluctuates; it is probably subperiosteal. The mastoid process seems thickened along its anterior border, forming a prominent ridge. Severe apical tenderness. Tenderness also above at the posterior border of the fluctuating area, but no post-mastoid tenderness. The drum cannot be seen because of the swelling of the upper wall of the canal, but pus is seen to ooze out from behind. The walls of the external canal are red and swollen.

Nose.—Entire mucous membrane congested. Swelling of both lower turbinated processes.

Eyes.—Normal.

On admission pulse, respiration, and temperature normal. Urine, acid, 1024, negative.

Usual curved incision made behind the ear down to the bone; a short transverse incision was made at the upper third of wound to enlarge the opening. The periosteum was found lifted up from the upper part of the mastoid process, and about one drachm of pus escaped from beneath it. No culture taken. The periosteum was then stripped back and the bone attacked with gouge and mallet. The bone was found roughened over the area where the pus had been confined beneath the periosteum, and much thickened below this point along the anterior border of the mastoid process to the apex. A small cavity filled with granulation tissue and broken-down material was found in the apex. The bone was found to be extensively destroyed. The diseased bone was removed with the rongeur. The supra-sinous cells were found to be filled with granulation tissue, but the lamina of bone (inner table) over the sinus was sound. Sinus not exposed. When the antrum was opened pus welled from it. The opening was enlarged and the cavity curetted. Two stitches were placed above and the cross-cut was closed. Wound left open below, packed lightly, allowing the ear to come back, thus avoiding a gaping wound. Dressed wet.

October 29: Temperature mostly below 100°. Given soft diet. Doing well.

October 30: Temperature normal. Wound dressed. Packings removed and renewed. Wound cleansed with alcohol.

November 1: Temperature remains normal. Wound dressed daily. Painful in lower angle. Given full diet.

November 2: Wound curetted in lower angle, removing white sloughing material. Opening into the antrum closing.

November 4: Wound dressed wet. Opening into antrum closed. Opening into the anterior auditory canal still patent and painful. Temperature normal.

November 10: Patient went on to an uneventful recovery. Wound granulated well. Discharged with a healthy and shallow wound.

CASE V. *Streptococcus Mastoiditis followed by Erysipelas of Head and Neck.*—J. W., tailor, aged 25 years. Admitted March 21, 1888. Patient has had no ear trouble at any time. Two weeks ago had some polypoid growths removed from the left side of the nose. He began to suffer with extreme pain in right ear. Hot applications did not relieve him. Some discharge from the nose. Went to the dispensary and had the drum-head incised. No discharge from the ear at that time. Two days ago he noticed a beginning purulent discharge with pain behind the ear. Felt feverish; had general malaise, nausea. Pain behind the ear is intense. Patient feels depressed.

Physical Examination.—Some slight œdema behind the ear. The whole apex is very tender. Profuse discharge from the ear. Thick purulent coating on left side of nose. Swelling and redness of the cut drumhead. Culture taken from the nose and external auditory meatus.

On admission pulse 80, respiration 22, temperature 99°.

Usual incision carried well down over the apex. Skin very vascular. Bone exposed with periosteal elevator. Antrum exposed with gouge and found to contain granulation tissue. Next, apex exposed, from which pus came. Culture taken. Apex cells well opened and cleaned of pus and débris. Antrum well cleaned out and found to be directly connected with apex cells. In the temporal ridge two cells were exposed and contained purulent matter. About one inch of the sigmoid sinus was laid bare. Sinus soft and sound. Entire operative area cleaned with alcohol and packed. Considerable bleeding from the skin flaps. Over entire packing a wet dressing of Thiersch was applied.

Culture showed both streptococcus longus and brevis from ear, mastoid, and nose.

After operation temperature 99.6°.

April 1, 5 A.M.: Temperature 102°, pulse 70; 10 A.M., temperature 103°, pulse 76. Wound dressed; some bleeding from edges of flap. Bone cavity clean; no discharge. All packings removed, repacked, and wet dressing applied.

April 3: Temperature going up; at 11 A.M. 103.4°, pulse 84. Given phenacetin, caffein, and antipyrin, five grains of each. Given ten cubic centimetres of antistreptococcus serum in the lumbar region. Wound dressed. Sinus found soft and compressible and covered with granulation tissue. Some pus found in upper mastoid cells. These were all cleaned out, sprayed with one per cent carbolic, and wet dressing applied. At 4 P.M. temperature 104°.

April 4: 11 A.M. temperature 104°, pulse 100. Wound dressed; had a gray membrane over the entire surface. Sinus soft and compressible. Thick, grayish discharge on thorough irrigation. On the entire area surrounding the right ear, extending out to the outer canthus of right eye, running on to cheek and temporal part of the head, there is an œdematous rash (erysipelas). Wound lightly packed with iodoform gauze and one per cent carbolic acid dressing applied. Patient was isolated. Erysipelas was treated with a coat of sixty per cent ichthyol painted over the affected area. The erysipelas ran over the bridge of the nose, over the left cheek, and down the back of the neck.

April 6: No further extension. Temperature coming down. General condition good. Stimulated with strychnine and whiskey.

April 9: Temperature 99.5°, pulse 80. Erysipelas almost disappeared. Mastoid wound dressed. Granulations gray and flabby.

April 15: Returned to the wards. Wound dressed. Sinus covered with healthy granulations. Wound has contracted a great deal. Some bare bone exposed. Packed with iodoform gauze and wet dressing applied. Irrigation of mastoid and ear causes fluid to come out of the nose. Dermatitis after the erysipelas improved by applications of vaselin. Patient developed a small abscess in front of right lachrymal sac, which, under applications of heat, opened. Healed in a few days. Mastoid wound slowly granulating, being stimulated at times with balsam of Peru. Patient's general condition improved rapidly under good feeding.

May 24: Discharged cured.

CASE VI. *Caries of Mastoid affecting both Sides; Optic Neuritis; Torticollis.*—W. L., schoolboy, aged 11 years, admitted November 22, 1897. Three weeks ago had bronchitis. Cough lasted but three days, but high fever persisted a week after. During that time patient complained of pain and headache in the right ear; a little later in the left ear also. Poultices were applied. Four or five days later pus began to discharge from both ears, and pain was much relieved. Got out of bed on the tenth day. Temperature then 100°. Discharge from both ears has continued. Frontal headache complained of, but no pain in the ears. Mastoid (apex) tenderness noticed recently on both sides. Temperature yesterday was 98.6° to 100°. Ears irrigated every two hours, Large perforation in right drumhead, small one in left.

November 26: All tenderness has disappeared. Discharge slight.

November 29: Nose filled with discharge ; irrigated with listerine every two hours. Left drum membrane bulging. No mastoid tenderness.

December 1: Discharged (at request) improved.

December 2: Readmitted. Pain in right ear and right mastoid tenderness have returned.

December 4: Swelling has developed behind right ear. Very tender. Temperature has risen from normal to 99° to 100°. Ear and nose irrigated every two hours. Very little discharge from the ear.

December 5: Swelling and tenderness have become more marked. Ear stands out from the head. Temperature 99° to 100.8°.

Operation.—Usual incision one-quarter of an inch behind the auricle. About one-half drachm of pus evacuated. Subperiosteal abscess. On dividing and retracting the periosteum a ragged opening in the bone was exposed. It was found to lead upward and inward into the antrum. The tendinous attachment of the sterno-mastoid was divided. The suprameatal spine was plainly in view, lying on a little higher level than the above-mentioned bone necrosis. The bone was chiselled through behind and above the suprameatal spine; a cavity was exposed. Necrosed bone, pus, and granulation tissue were thus removed. The apex was not involved, and healthy bone was reached all around. The sinus was exposed for a distance of three-eighths of an inch. On syringing the wound the fluid escaped through the auditory canal in small quantity. Wound washed with alcohol and packed. Silk sutures in the upper angle. Usual dressing. Patient's condition after the operation excellent.

December 6: No fever or pain.

December 8: Dressed wet. Wound looks clean. No retention. Discharge moderate.

December 14: Discharge moderate. Feels well. Out of bed. Torticollis on the right side. Much tenderness of the right posterior mastoid region.

December 16: Tenderness of left mastoid very marked.

Operation.—Usual mastoid incision. Periosteum found thickened and adherent. An area of bone caries found behind the suprameatal spine. Bone then gouged through toward the apex and carious bone and granulation tissue removed. Healthy bone overhanging the cavity taken away with forceps. The antrum was curetted and granulation tissue removed. The sigmoid sinus was exposed and found in good condition. The cavity was then irrigated and packed. Silk sutures in the upper angle of the wound. Usual dressing.

December 19: Temperature has been normal. Dressing removed. Wounds clean. On the right side much bone tenderness behind the region of the operation. Neck stiff and motion painful. Much headache. Optic neuritis.

December 26: Wound of left mastoid is in a satisfactory condition on the right side.

December 27: Area of post-mastoid tenderness enlarged. Headache severe. Right torticollis marked. Optic neuritis, vision normal.

December 27: *Operation.*—Wound on right side retracted and increased in size by a transverse incision posteriorly. Bone behind the wound well exposed. Sinus was thus brought into view, and the bone posterior to it removed for a considerable distance, exposing the sinus its entire width and length, a distance of two inches. The bone was soft and succulent, but did not bleed. Removal of bone exposed the dura mater of the posterior fossa over a circular area of two centimetres in diameter. Healthy granulations found around the sinus. Two silk sutures placed in posterior incision. Wound packed. Wet dressing.

December 30: No fever. Dressed. Wound on right side clean. Torticollis disappeared. Optic neuritis less pronounced. No headache.

January 1: Ears irrigated. No discharge. Twitchings of face and body. Put on tincture digitalis 2 minims t. i. d. for rapid pulse rate.

January 3: Right side: wound dressed; granulating nicely; packings removed; sprayed with 1 per cent carbolic; repacked and dressed dry. Left side: granulations curetted, packed, and dressed dry.

January 7: Pulse down to 90. Left side healed. Right side filling rapidly.

January 16: Discharged. Wounds not completely closed. Patient comes to the Hospital twice a week to be dressed.

February 3: Wounds closed. Neuritis and torticollis disappeared. Cured.

CASE VII. *Empyema of Mastoid following Typhoid Fever; Operation with Local Anæsthesia.*—D. O., tailor, aged 17 years. Admitted February 15, 1898. Was admitted to the Hospital on January 2 suffering from typhoid fever. While convalescing he began to complain of pain in the head about February 10. An ice bag was applied without relief. Pain became more localized over the right ear, with a rise of temperature. On February 12 a paracentesis was performed with considerable relief. Ear began to discharge profusely and was irrigated several times daily. Temperature fell to normal and all symptoms abated. On February 13 the patient was well enough to be out of bed. On February 14 the patient had a rise of temperature and mastoid tenderness became marked. Transferred to the Eye and Ear Service.

Physical Examination.—A diffuse œdema situated around the right ear, extending into temporal region. Profuse discharge of pus from the ear. Canal much macerated. Swelling extends around the ear above and posteriorly. Upper wall of external auditory canal swollen.

On admission to the Eye and Ear Ward, pulse 96, respiration 24, temperature 99.6°; ear irrigated every two hours.

February 16: Ice bag stopped. Hot bag applied. Ear irrigated.

February 18: Temperature 99° to 101.2°, pulse 88 to 100, respiration 28. Patient very feeble. It was not thought advisable to use a general anæsthetic.

Operation.—Schleich's local anæsthesia. Usual incision behind the auricle. Wound bled freely. The cortex was opened by gouging, which did not seem to be painful. A large antral abscess was opened on removing the cortex. Apex was also slightly involved. Whole cavity cleaned out; irrigated through; washed with alcohol; packed with iodoform gauze and dry dressing applied. The sigmoid sinus was not exposed. Patient stood the operation well.

After the operation, patient very weak. Stimulating dose of whiskey given. On the following day temperature 100.4°, pulse 100, respiration 26. Soft diet.

February 19: Strychnine, one-hundredth of a grain t. i. d. Bowels moved.

February 20: Superficial dressings changed and wet dressings applied.

February 21: Wound dressed; packings removed; absolutely clean; no discharge of pus; bone not yet covered with granulations; irrigated and wet dressings applied. Temperature still 100°, pulse down to 98.

February 24: Wound dressed daily. Patient out of bed.

February 27: Temperature up to 101.8°, pulse 134. Wound dressed; looked clean; becoming covered with granulation tissue; a small pocket of pus in the lower angle of the wound opened up and drained. Wet dressing applied.

March 2: Temperature normal. Wound dressed daily; rapidly filling up with granulation tissue. From this time on convalescence was uneventful. Temperature normal. Patient on full and extra diet. Free communication between antrum cell and tympanic cavity became occluded. Patient gained rapidly in weight and strength, and the wound soon healed up entirely.

March 14: Discharged cured.

XXII.

RESTORATION OF THE CONJUNCTIVAL CUL-DE-SAC IN A CASE OF TOTAL SYMBLEPHARON BY MEANS OF THIERSCH SKIN GRAFTS.

By CHARLES H. MAY, M.D.,
ADJUNCT OPHTHALMIC AND AURAL SURGEON.

Cases of total symblepharon in which there has been complete obliteration of the conjunctival cul-de-sac are generally regarded as incurable. Even where the adhesions between the ocular and palpebral conjunctiva do not completely obliterate the sac, but yet are extensive, the results of operative interference are frequently unsatisfactory, especially if an examination be made some time after the operation. The connective tissue underlying the new lining has a tendency to shrink, and as a result there are frequently changes which neutralize or minimize the good effects seen immediately after operation. This explains why so many operative procedures have been proposed, especially for cases of posterior symblepharon.

It is for these reasons that the writer has thought the satisfactory cure of a case of total symblepharon by the insertion of Thiersch grafts worth reporting. The eye operated upon presented complete adhesion between both upper and lower lids and the globe as the result of a burn from lime some years before. The symblepharon was so complete that lids and eyeball were kept in one position; the lids could neither be closed nor opened beyond the space represented by the free portion of the globe. As a result of such exposure the surface of the cornea had become tense and tough, resembling skin;

it also presented a well-marked staphyloma due to ulceration following the original injury. The completeness of the symblepharon was not merely apparent. Upon dissecting the lids from the eyeball during the operation no traces of mucous membrane could be found in the fornix nor over any other part of the adherent area.

The report is rendered more satisfactory from the fact that the patient has been under observation for almost two years (more than twenty months) after the first operation, and there has been no shrinking nor modification of the good results originally obtained. The first operation resulted in a perfect cul-de-sac for the upper lid, and this complete restoration still exists. The patient is able to wear an artificial eye and the object of operation has been secured. In the lower lid the first operation restored the central half of the fornix; a second and third operation were needed to obliterate strong bands existing at the outer and inner canthi. Remains of these bands still exist, but do not interfere with the wearing of a prosthesis. The lining of the conjunctival surface of the lids and fornices is smooth, soft, of a modified epidermoid character, but there is now no desquamation and but little discharge.

The operation is not a new one, though the writer is unable to find any mention of a similar case in which the symblepharon was total and in which, after a period of almost two years, the original successful result was maintained. Hotz[1] advocated the use of Thiersch grafts as a substitute for conjunctiva in extensive symblepharon, in trachomatous shrinkage, for enlarging a contracted conjunctival pocket, and in certain cases of pterygium, and gave an account of a number of operations in which such grafts were successfully employed.

In the writer's case much of the success was due to the employment of an effective manner of keeping the grafts in place, immovably applied to the dissected and

[1] Annals of Ophthalmology, April, 1893.

separated surfaces representing the previously obliterated sacs. This was accomplished through the use of a porcelain shell such as forms the basis of artificial eyes. One of these (Messrs. J. T. & A. H. Davis kindly placed a number at the writer's disposal) was selected from a number made to fit this patient. Two large Thiersch grafts, shaved from the thigh, were applied over this shell, completely covering both surfaces, with the epithelial or free surfaces of the grafts toward the surfaces of the shell. Then by placing the covered shell in the dissected sacs the grafts were applied. They were kept in place by stitching together the lids and applying a firm bandage.

The use of such a porcelain shell for the purpose of keeping the grafts in place was suggested by an operation of Dr. Chambers, of Jersey City. The latter presented a patient in whom a partial symblepharon had been operated upon in this manner at a meeting of the Ophthalmological Section of the New York Academy of Medicine some two or three years ago. Subsequently Dr. Marple presented a similar example of operation by this method in partial symblepharon. In August, 1898, Morton, of Minneapolis, recommended the use of a prosthesis after the grafts had been inserted and held in place by a line of sutures,[1] and reported good results in several instances in which he had operated in this manner, with the object of restoring the fornix for the retention of an artificial eye.

Regarding the technique of the operation, a few remarks, in addition to the details given in the history which follows, may be pertinent. The rules which obtain when Thiersch skin grafts are employed in other parts of the body also apply to those upon the eye. The inner part of the arm or thigh answers well for supplying the grafts. The part from which the grafts are taken should be cleansed for a day or two before the operation and then bandaged with sterilized gauze.

[1] The Ophthalmic Record, August, 1898.

Just before operating, after cleansing with soap, washing with sterilized water and then with ether, the selected skin is moistened with warm, sterilized salt solution (six-tenths of one per cent), and the blade of the razor is also kept wet with this solution. Two broad retractors are used to stretch the skin, and then with a very sharp razor held flat, by means of a see saw motion, the very thinnest layer of skin is removed, only the epidermis and the tops of the papillæ being desired.

The grafts should be as large as possible, and the combined grafts (two or three ought to be sufficient to line both upper and lower lids) should be about half again as extensive as the area to be covered, to allow for shrinkage. The grafts must not be handled; they are transferred from the back of the razor to the porcelain shell and spread out as smoothly as possible with the epithelial surface next to the prosthesis. In this way both surfaces of the shell are covered. A defect may, however, be allowed over the centre of the inner surface of the shell corresponding to the cornea. It is important that the margins of the shell be well covered, so that a continuous surface is applied to the deepest part of the fornix. This is insured by applying the grafts so that they cover a part of one surface and then curve over the margin to the other surface of the shell. In one of the operations the writer attempted to stitch the grafts with catgut passed through openings made in the porcelain shell; but this is unnecessary, consumes time, and thus jeopardizes the life of the graft. Limited success in one of the smaller operations is attributed to this circumstance.

The dissection of the lids from the globe having been completed so that the lids are freely movable and all bleeding of the divided surfaces stopped, the graft-covered shell is put in place, the lids stitched together, and a firm bandage applied; both eyes are included in the bandage.

If everything goes well the bandage ought to be left

undisturbed for five days. If there is severe pain or offensive odor the bandage must be removed and the outside of the lids inspected. At the end of five days the stitches are removed and the lids cleansed, but the shell is left undisturbed, if possible, for several days longer. At the end of eight days the shell may be removed. After this the eye requires frequent irrigation with warm solution of boric acid; the shell must be returned after each irrigation and a bandage reapplied.

There is considerable swelling, redness, and some pain. The grafts at first look reddish gray, soft, and somewhat sloughy, but whatever has not been cast off in the discharges will probably take hold and form a satisfactory lining. After a month the artificial eye can be worn.

At the present time the lining of the lids presents a smooth, soft surface, partaking of the characters of both skin and mucous membrane. It is whiter and denser than mucous membrane, but there is no desquamation and no more discharge than is met with in most cases in which an artificial eye is worn after enucleation.

In this case the cornea was staphylomatous and presented a dense, opaque surface; there was barely perception of light. Hence the question of tolerance of the shell was not tested, as it would have been with a transparent and healthy cornea. With a normal cornea frequent examination of the eyeball would be, of course, imperative, and it might be a good plan to have the shell made of transparent glass. The writer has not had, however, any experience with such cases. In the patients already referred to as having been presented at the New York Academy of Medicine, no injury to the cornea resulted from the wearing of the porcelain shell for a period necessary to insure adhesion of the grafts, but these patients had comparatively small symblepharon.

The following is a detailed history of the operations which form the basis for the preceding lines:

Gertrude R., aged 13, was admitted to Mount Sinai Hospital on May 12, 1897. She gave a history of having had lime thrown into the left eye seven years before. She was under treatment for a time after the accident, but despite interference the lids became adherent to the eyeball, there was considerable inflammation, and after the immediate symptoms had subsided the cornea became clouded and sight was lost.

Examination upon admission: Both upper and lower lids are firmly adherent to the ocular conjunctiva, leaving merely the cornea exposed. The latter is staphylomatous, opaque, dense, and its surface dull and epidermoid. The lids cannot be opened or closed, and no movement of the eyeball is possible. The cornea is perfectly dry. There is barely perception of light.

Operation, May 20: Ether anæsthesia. Both upper and lower lids were dissected from the eyeball, going down quite deeply, so that they were freely movable. The cavities thus formed were tightly packed with cotton, so as to arrest hemorrhage. Two Thiersch skin grafts, each about one inch by one inch and a half, were taken from the arm. These were transferred from the razor to a porcelain shell, with the epithelial surface next to the shell. They were smoothed out upon the shell in such a manner as to cover the entire shell. The two grafts met at a line corresponding to midway between the margins, so that when in place the margins of grafts would correspond to the edges of the lids In this way the margins of the shell were covered with a continuous layer. The bleeding having ceased, the graft-covered shell was put in position, the lids were sutured together with three silk sutures, and a firm bandage applied. Next to the eye a heavy layer of cotton soaked in solution of boric acid was placed, so as to keep the grafts moist. Both eyes were included in the bandage.

May 23: The patient complaining of pain, the bandage was removed and the surface of the lids inspected. These were reddened and swollen, and there was a moderate amount of rather offensive discharge upon the dressings. Neither stitches nor shell were disturbed. Bandage was reapplied to the left eye.

May 25: The patient complained of considerable pain. Upon removing the bandage the lids were found red, very much swollen, and tense. There was considerable offensive discharge upon the dressing. The lid sutures were removed. The shell was not disturbed. Appearance rather unfavorable. Rebandaged.

May 27: There is less swelling and redness. Considerable offensive discharge upon dressing. The lids were separated gently and the shell removed. The sac was irrigated and shell reinserted. The grafts have taken hold, but look red, soft, and sloughy. Eye rebandaged.

June 1: The eye is irrigated three times each day, the shell removed and cleansed and reinserted, and bandage reapplied. Solution of boric acid, warmed, is used for irrigation. The grafts look better and the appearances are more favorable.

June 15: The same treatment has been continued since last note. The upper lid is entirely free, except a slight adhesion at inner canthus; this is loosened daily. The lower lid presents a number of firm adhesions, which are also broken up daily.

June 25: The upper lid is now entirely free. The lower lid still presents a number of adhesions, especially at the canthi. The shell is worn constantly. The eye is irrigated three times a day. A light dressing, held on with adhesive plaster, takes the place of a bandage.

July 20: The upper lid is swollen and reddened, and there is some pain. The eye is irrigated frequently and iced pads applied.

July 22: Swelling of upper lid has subsided.

August 22: Condition the same. There is, however, more discharge. For this, solution of bichloride, 1 to 6000, was used for a time, and then solution of peroxide of hydrogen. As a result of these applications the discharge is less in amount.

August 26: Discharged. Examination on this day shows upper lid entirely free and movable; lower lid adherent by means of strong bands at inner and at outer canthus. With the exception of these two spots the grafts have taken hold. There is still a moderate amount of discharge.

September 29: Readmitted to the Hospital. Condition same as at time of last note.

September 30: Operation. Ether anæsthesia. The strong bands at canthi were divided deeply. The shell was covered with Thiersch grafts, corresponding to the separated area. The external canthus was divided so that the graft-covered shell could be applied with greater precision; external canthus stitched after shell had been put in place. Lids stitched together and eye bandaged after a moist compress had been applied. Both eyes included in bandage.

October 3: Patient complains of pain. Bandage removed and outer surface of lids cleansed. Shell not disturbed. Considerable offensive discharge upon dressing. Both eyes rebandaged.

October 5: Bandage removed. Fetid discharge. Sutures removed from lids. Part of grafts upon dressing. Considerable redness and swelling. Shell left in place. Rebandaged left eye.

October 8: Eye rebandaged daily and outer surface of lids cleansed; considerable discharge. To-day shell was removed. The grafts have taken hold, but not over the entire dissected area. Shell reinserted and bandage applied.

October 12: Shell is causing pain; removed and smaller one inserted. The lower lid is now free except at inner portion, where there is a large mass of granulation tissue. The eye is irrigated three times a day, the shell worn constantly, and a bandage kept on. Granulations excised.

October 22: Same as at last note. Discharge is abundant and somewhat offensive. There is still an adhesion at inner canthus.

November 10: Discharged. Examination of the eye at time of discharge from the Hospital shows the following condition: Upper lid free and well lined with epithelial surface. Lower lid free except at inner canthus. Moderate discharge, which is no longer offensive. The shell is kept in place constantly, the eye irrigated several times a day, and a light dressing worn and kept in place with adhesive plaster.

July 5, 1898: Readmitted to Hospital. Upper lid free throughout its entire extent. Lower lid adherent at inner and outer canthus.

July 7: Operation. Ether anæsthesia. The adhesions of lower lid were divided, and grafts placed upon shell and inserted as in former operations, except that catgut sutures were passed through grafts and through holes in shell to keep grafts in place. This consumed considerable time and did not seem to answer any better than in previous operations when this stitching to the shell was omitted.

August 2: The course after this third operation was similar to that after the second. The result was an improvement. There is still a slight adhesion at the inner canthus and a very delicate one at the outer canthus; but these will not interfere with the proper retention of an artificial eye. Patient was discharged.

September 14: Readmitted to the Hospital for removal of the staphyloma and reduction in size of the eyeball to form a better stump. Condition the same as at last note.

September 15: Operation. Ether anæsthesia. Evisceration of left eyeball and abscission of staphyloma.

September 17: Grayish patch on inner surface of upper lid. This was caused by pressure of the retractor at time of the operation.

September 20: Gray patch no longer visible. Shell placed in sac.

October 1: Patient discharged. Examination at this time shows: Upper lid entirely free and covered with grafts, which are soft, smooth, and form an excellent lining surface. Lower lid also lined in same manner. Slight adhesion persists at inner canthus, but does not interfere with retention of prosthesis. There is but little discharge.

March 17, 1899: Patient is now wearing an artificial eye, and the cosmetic effect is good. The lining to lids has remained effective. There is the same freedom as existed at last note. There is but little discharge. The eyeball, reduced in size by the last operation, forms a good stump.

XXIII.

REPORT OF DR. CARL KOLLER,

ADJUNCT OPHTHALMIC AND AURAL SURGEON.

From August 1, 1898, to September 6, 1898, 17 patients were admitted in my care to the Eye and Ear Department. The diagnosis in these cases was as follows:

Diagnosis.	No. of cases	
Distichiasis	1	Cured.
Trachoma	4	"
Convergent squint	1	"
Traumatic keratitis	1	"
Corneal fistula	1	"
Senile cataract	2	1 cured, 1 improved (preparatory iridectomy).
Optic neuro-retinitis	1	Improved.
Detachment of retina	1	"
	12	
Purulent otitis media	1	Cured.
Chronic mastoiditis with caries and necrosis	1	"
Chronic mastoiditis with sclerosis	1	"
Tubercular meningitis (of aural origin)	1	Died.
Thrombosis and phlebitis of the sigmoid sinus (of aural origin)	1	"
	5	

OPERATIONS PERFORMED.

On the Eye:

Bowman's operation for obstruction of the tear duct	1
Electrolysis for distichiasis	1
Expression for trachoma	4
Tenotomy and advancement for convergent squint	1
Iridectomy (preparatory)	1
" for corneal fistula	1
Extraction of senile cataract	1
	10

On the Throat:

Removal of adenoids.......... 1

On the Ear:

Opening of the mastoid antrum (Schwartze)........ 2
Radical operation (Stacke)..................................... 2
Exposing and opening of the sigmoid sinus and ligature of the jugular vein... 1

5

XXIV.

A CASE OF THROMBO-PHLEBITIS OF THE SIGMOID SINUS AND THE JUGULAR VEIN.

By CARL KOLLER, M.D.,

ADJUNCT OPHTHALMIC AND AURAL SURGEON.

Among the cases treated there are several which present features of sufficient interest to justify publication. From their number I have chosen as contribution to this report the case of thrombo phlebitis of the sigmoid sinus and the jugular vein, as this condition and its surgical treatment engage at the present time the attention of aural surgeons and surgeons in general. Hardly ten years have passed (1888) since the operation of opening the thrombosed sinus was performed (by Lane) for the first time, although recommendations to that effect had preceded it several years before that time, and the surgical treatment of sinus-thrombosis has already an uncontested place among surgical operations, and quite an extensive literature has accumulated on the subject. Perusal of the latter makes one point very clear, that is, that the sooner the diagnosis of sinus thrombosis is made, and the sooner the operation is performed, the greater are the chances for a favorable result. The cases in which the pyæmic condition has been allowed to last for a week or longer, or where pulmonic metastases are present, have hardly any chance of recovery; whereas with early diagnosis and operation the chances are in favor of the patient.

In order to contribute my share to the establishment of this fact, and because each case presents some individual and interesting features, I will record the following case:

Sarah Magrowitz, 13 years of age, was admitted to Mount Sinai Hospital on Tuesday, August 15, 1898. Patient was conscious, looked septic, and was very hard of hearing. Soon after admission she had a chill of five minutes' duration; temperature 104°. Two hours later she had another chill; temperature 106°. After that she was very apathetic, in fact hardly conscious; later, entirely unconscious, perspired profusely, and looked intensely septic.

According to the statement of her family physician, she had scarlet fever when 3 years old; from that time she suffered with her ears. The left ear was repeatedly operated on. The ear discharged; sometimes the discharge stopped and she had fever with chills and vomiting. With the reappearance of the discharge she felt better. The present spell is said to date back two weeks, since which time she has had two chills daily. For the last two days the right ear also discharged, with pain behind the ear and down the neck.

Present Condition.—Well-developed girl of medium build. General appearance septic: skin sallow and mottled. Herpes-like eruptions on the upper lip and over the right nostril, also on several fingers of the right hand; on the fingers more recent vesicles grouped together, of slightly hemorrhagic discoloration. Sclera of yellowish tinge. Pupils small, equal, react to light. Tongue moist and coated brown. A few soft crepitant râles can be heard in both axillæ. Liver normal; spleen enlarged to percussion; abdomen slightly distended and tympanitic; reflexes normal. Ophthalmoscopic examination of the fundus negative, except some venous hyperæmia.

Examination of Ears.—Over the left processus mastoides extended scars, partly adherent to the bone. Tympanic membrane missing; medial wall granulating; whitish cholesteatomatous masses toward the attic. On the right side the membrane also missing, the medial wall granulating, partly denuded; from the attic a purulent discharge comes. No visible signs of inflammation on the mastoid: strong pressure upon the apex or the fossa mastoides causes pain. A hard cord can be felt in the anterior triangle of the neck along the course of the jugular vein; intense pain on slight pressure. This sensitiveness also exists, to a lesser degree, on the left side. The right occipital region is very painful to percussion.

Diagnosis.—Thrombo-phlebitis of the right sigmoid sinus and the jugular vein. On account of the ambiguous aspect of the case and history of persistent trouble on the left side, Dr. Fred. Whiting was called in consultation, corroborated the diagnosis, and advised operation on the right side.

Previous to the operation the patient was unconscious. Physician in charge of anæsthesia observed pleural scraping on the left lower lobe.

Operation.—Incision as usual for opening the antrum. Bone of healthy appearance. The antrum was opened with gouge and chisel. The antrum and posterior mastoid cells were filled with broken-down granulations and inspissated pus, which led toward a loose, shell shaped sequestrum of the interior plate of the sigmoid groove three-eighths of an inch in diameter. Beneath some more inspissated pus the sinus was found presenting a greenish, glistening surface, pulpy to touch. The incision was extended backward at right angles to the original incision; by removing the bone with the rongeur forceps the sigmoid was exposed almost its entire length up and down from the point where it was first struck. The bone contained broken-down granulations and pus. I inserted an aspirating needle into the sinus and aspirated thin, greenish, ill-smelling pus. Then I asked Dr. Lilienthal to ligate the jugular vein. He made an incision on the anterior border of the sterno cleido-mastoid muscle in the lower part of the triangle, dissected down into the depth, ligated some branches, and found the jugular vein as a thin, flaccid cord. He ligated deep downward, incised the thrombosed vein, passed a probe up toward the bulb, and continued the original incision through the deep muscles of the neck, until almost the whole length of the vein was exposed, with the exception of a small piece near the base of the skull. The exposed part was slit open and a sharp spoon passed up toward the bulb. The thrombus was half solid. After that I made an incision into the sinus at the point of aspiration and evacuated several drachms of ill-smelling pus. Then I curetted down toward the bulb, afterward up toward the lateral sinus, from which locality crumbling, inspissated matter and gelatinous pus issued; finally came a gush of blood. This was stopped in the usual way by placing iodoform gauze under the edge of the bone; then I allowed it to bleed once more, and afterward washed the sinus and jugular vein thoroughly with sterile saline solution, packed with iodoform gauze, and applied a bandage. Toward the end of the operation about two pints of saline solution were infused into the cubital vein.

After the operation the pulse was 140, respiration 36, temperature 102.2°; later the temperature went down to 101.4°. Immediately after the operation the patient looked cyanotic. An hour and a half later she recovered from the anæsthetic, was fully conscious, and asked for a drink.

The next morning the pulse rose to 156, respiration 40, temperature 104.2°. The patient looked sallow and septic. At 2 P.M. the pulse was 168, respiration 48, temperature 105°. The patient became very noisy and had to be given morphine. Severe pains in the chest developed, very hard breathing, and cyanosis, with drawing-in of the jugulum. Over the lower lobe of the left lung crepitant râles could be heard; breathing diminished; the pulse became imperceptible, respiration shallow, and at 2.45 the patient stopped breathing.

The patient had no more chills after the operation, and this, together with the returning consciousness, were the only favorable symptoms. Considering the two weeks' duration of the pyæmic condition and the involvement of the left lung at the time of the operation, the latter had little chance of saving life and was performed as a forlorn hope.

No autopsy was allowed.

The diagnosis of phlebitis and thrombosis of the sigmoid sinus in a case of chronic ear suppuration must be based on pyæmic symptoms supervening on the symptoms of chronic ear suppuration: high temperature with great fluctuations, chills, vomiting, persistent cephalalgia. These are the most constant symptoms. The local symptoms, due to disturbed venous circulation (Griesinger's, Gerhardt's, and others), may be absent, as they were in this case. The ophthalmoscopic examination may show optic neuro-retinitis, or simple venous hyperæmia, or normal conditions. The diagnosis of thrombosis of the sigmoid sinus is made certain if thrombosis of the interior jugular vein is present, which shows itself by a cord-like hardness in the upper part of the lateral triangle, very sensitive to touch. Pain and sensitiveness to pressure on the occiput and down the posterior part of the neck is indicative of the continuation of the thrombosis into the condylar veins and those of the deep muscles of the neck. In our case both these symptoms were present; not only this, but the tenderness along the jugular vein existed also on the other side, which, according to Macewen, is not infrequently the case, and which he attributes to the venous communications with the other side.

As in our case chronic suppuration had existed in both ears since earliest childhood, and a number of bone operations had been performed on one side (not the one which we rightly assumed to be the seat of the present trouble), the presence of hardness and sensitiveness along the upper part of the jugular vein on both sides was very embarrassing. The tenderness over the right occipital region and along the deep muscles of the neck decided the question in favor of the right side.

As to the method of operation, it is worth mentioning that, according to Körner's statistics, the results are better if the jugular vein be ligated before the sinus is opened and emptied. This mode of operating recommends itself; by first ligating the jugular vein the possibility of disseminating infectious material while manipulating the thrombosed sinus is excluded.

Still, the most important factor of prognostic value is the time when a case of thrombosis of the sinus comes into a surgeon's hands. So long as the vital powers are not yet exhausted by a pyæmic condition of long duration, and so long as no metastases in the most important organs exist, the prospects are fair. With the view of encouraging our colleagues in general practice to keep the possibility of a sinus-thrombosis in mind in cases of chronic ear suppuration with acute symptoms, I thought it of interest to record the above case, although it ended fatally and no autopsy was made.

XXV.

FROM THE PATHOLOGICAL LABORATORY.

A REPORT OF A SERIES OF UNUSUAL PATHOLOGIC CONDITIONS.

By F. S. MANDLEBAUM, M.D.,
PATHOLOGIST,

AND

E. LIBMAN, M.D.,
ASSISTANT PATHOLOGIST.

THE material that comes to the Pathological Laboratory for examination in the course of the year is so extensive and varied that it is impossible to attempt a report of all the interesting observations noted. We have, therefore, selected simply a number of unusual or especially instructive cases from the autopsy records of the past year. To these we have added a few of the rare cases observed in the past few years, this being the first opportunity we have had of incorporating them in a report of the hospital. Aside from these cases several other reports of postmortem examinations will be found in the articles by members of the attending staff.

Only such clinical data as are essential have been included, and no attempt has been made to enter into a discussion of the literature of the various subjects. The details of the histologic examinations which were made in every case have been purposely omitted on account of lack of space, and main attention has been paid to the gross pathologic lesions.

CASE I.—*Addison's Disease; Tuberculous Bronchial Glands; Cardiac Hypertrophy; Chronic Splenitis; Fatty Degeneration of Liver; Tuberculosis of Adrenals.*

I. F., male, aged 24 years, presented all of the usual manifestations of Addison's disease. The patient died four days after admission, in coma which followed a general epileptic attack accompanied by transient left hemiplegia. The autopsy, made six hours after death, showed the usual pigmentation of the skin, distributed over hands, feet, face, sternum, penis, and scrotum, and along the inner surface of both lips. Enlarged bronchial glands, some of which were pigmented, were also found. At the root of the right lung were several cheesy glands, and one gland was found to be calcified. The spleen was much enlarged, weighing 400 grammes, and on section showed a marked increase in interstitial connective-tissue fibres. The right adrenal was found to be adherent to the lower border of the liver, was much enlarged, and on section presented cheesy degeneration and necrosis with the formation of several small cavities. The left adrenal was somewhat smaller than the right, but otherwise presented similar conditions. At the inner side of each adrenal were several enlarged, pigmented, tuberculous glands.

This case was one of primary tuberculosis of the bronchial glands, the adrenals becoming involved secondarily.

As a marked contrast to this case the following is of great interest, as in it the Addison's disease was caused, not by direct involvement of the adrenals, but by the pressure of tuberculous glands on the adrenals and on the abdominal sympathetic nerves.

CASE II.—*Addison's Disease; Chronic Miliary Tuberculosis of Lungs; Pleurisy with Effusion; Pericarditis; Tuberculous Bronchial and Mediastinal Glands; Tuberculosis of Spleen; Amyloid Degeneration of Liver; Tuberculous Retroperitoneal Glands.*

J. S., male, aged 16 years, was under observation for ten weeks, during which time the diagnosis of Addison's disease was unquestionably established. The autopsy was made fifteen hours after death. The body was markedly emaciated and the skin presented a brownish discoloration, most marked on the face and chest, with decided pigmentation, however, on the penis, in both axillæ, and upon the mucous membrane of each cheek just within the angle of the mouth. In each pleural sac was about 500 cubic centimetres of clear serous fluid. Both lungs contained miliary tubercles scattered throughout all of the lobes, and at the apex of the right lung was a healed nodule undergoing calcareous changes. Large masses of cheesy glands were found at the root of each lung, filling the entire mediastinum and being firmly attached to the sternum on its posterior surface. Some of these glands were soft and cheesy, while others were pigmented and showed recent small hemorrhages. The pericardial sac contained 250 cubic centimetres of clear serum. On the visceral pericardium were a few brownish spots resembling those found in the mouth and distributed over most of the heart's surface. The heart muscle and the valves appeared normal. The spleen was slightly enlarged and soft, and the surface was covered on its inner aspect with a thick layer of fibrinous exudate which could be stripped off easily. One large anæmic infarct was found. On cut section about one dozen miliary tubercles were seen, varying in size from a pin's head to a split pea. The liver was the seat of amyloid degeneration. The kidneys were somewhat enlarged, but on their cut surfaces did not present any abnormal appearance. The adrenal bodies were not enlarged, and on section were absolutely normal, but surrounding the left adrenal were many enlarged glands, reddish in color and of the size of hazelnuts. The stomach and intestines were quite normal. The pancreas was somewhat enlarged and was entirely surrounded by enlarged glands, some of these being the size of a hen's egg. After the thoracic and abdominal organs were removed, an enormous chain of glands was seen extending from the upper part of the thorax down along both sides of the vertebral column to the pelvis.

The case next to be described belongs to that class of interesting cases where marked disease of an adrenal may occur without either the skin pigmentation or the constitutional manifestations of Addison's disease.

Case III.—*General Tuberculosis; Tuberculous Enterocolitis; Tuberculosis of Right Adrenal; Fatty Degeneration of the Liver.*

S. B., male, aged 38 years, was under observation for

three weeks. His illness was of six weeks' standing, during which time he complained of constipation, abdominal cramps, and general weakness. The diagnosis rested between typhoid fever and acute miliary tuberculosis, but nothing was demonstrated to establish the diagnosis conclusively. The autopsy revealed extensive tuberculous ulceration in the lower ileum and the ascending colon, and miliary tuberculosis of both lungs. The heart muscle was somewhat pale, and a few atheromatous areas were seen at the beginning of the aorta. The spleen was slightly enlarged and on section showed a few miliary tubercles. The kidneys also were involved with miliary tubercles, but otherwise were quite normal. The mesenteric glands were enlarged. Under the right lobe of the liver and attached to its inferior surface was a hard tumor the size of a hen's egg. On dissecting downward it was found that this tumor was firmly attached to the capsule of the right kidney at its upper pole. Upon making sections of this tumor it was found that it consisted mainly of broken-down, cheesy matter with giant cells about the periphery of these areas. Here and there were remnants of the adrenal. The left adrenal was normal.

It has been shown that extensive involvement and destruction of both adrenals may occur without any of the manifestations of Addison's disease. The following case is a good example of this kind:

CASE IV.—*Lympho-sarcoma of both Adrenals; Infiltrating Lympho sarcoma of Lungs; Lympho-sarcoma of Bronchial and Retroperitoneal Glands; Cardiac Hypertrophy and Dilatation; Interstitial Myocarditis; Interstitial Nephritis; Fatty Degeneration and Congestion of Liver; General Arterio-sclerosis.*

J. H., male, aged 61, was a patient in the hospital for three weeks. He gave a history of three months' standing, and complained of pain in the chest, cough, and bloody expectoration. No tubercle bacilli were found in the sputum. Bloody serous fluid was aspirated repeatedly from the right chest, and a diagnosis of malignant tumor of the lung was made. The autopsy was performed eleven hours after death and disclosed the following: the right lung was compressed by a large amount of blood-stained pleural exudation, and on section showed dense whitish masses of newly-formed tissue extending along the bronchi and infiltrating the lung parenchyma. The left lung was the seat of similar changes, but to a less degree. Large bronchial and mediastinal glands pressed upon the pulmonary vessels and trachea, and infiltrated the walls of the latter. A purulent bronchitis also existed. The pericardium contained a slight increase of fluid somewhat tinged with blood. The left ventricle was hypertrophied, the right auricle and ventricle dilated. The heart muscle showed brown atrophy and interstitial myocarditis. The heart valves appeared normal, but above the aortic valves there was marked atheroma, extending into the coronary arteries. The spleen was enlarged and congested, and its pulp was somewhat soft. The kidneys showed chronic interstitial nephritis. The liver was pushed downward to the level of the umbilicus, and upon section was found to be congested and fatty. Above each kidney, and firmly attached to the same, was a large tumor mass the size of an orange. That on the right side was soft, and on section was much degenerated and necrotic. Here and there small remnants of adrenal tissue could be seen. The tumor on the left side was firm and nodular, and sharply defined from the kidney substance proper. A large glandular mass was found near the head of the pancreas. On section this was mottled and of a yellowish color, otherwise it resembled the other tumors in general appearance. The stomach, intestines, and mesenteric glands were normal. The retroperitoneal glands were enlarged and infiltrated. Microscopic sections of the various tumors and of the newly-formed tissue in the lungs showed same to be lymphosarcoma. A careful examination points to the right adrenal as the primary seat of involvement.

CASE V.—*Empyema; Septicemia; Hemorrhagic Inflammation of both Adrenals*

F. L., female, aged 18 months, was operated upon for an empyema of the left pleura and died ten days later with the usual signs of sepsis. Beyond this the patient had no evidence of any other pathologic condition. At the autopsy it was found that both adrenals were the seat of large hemorrhagic inflammation, that on the left side being the more extensive. This interesting condition was first described by Virchow in 1864 as occurring at times in the acute infectious diseases, but its presence in a case of empyema, as far as we have been able to ascertain, has not been reported hitherto. Microscopic examination of the adrenals showed an extensive hemorrhagic infiltration throughout the entire glandular substance. The liver was the seat of a fatty infiltration, and the kidneys presented the appearance of an acute parenchymatous nephritis. An unresolved bronchopneumonia was also found, being most marked in the lower lobe of the right lung.

CASE VI.—*Perithelioma of the Ilium.*

A. L , male, aged 65 years, was treated in the hospital for one week. His family and previous history, with the exception of an attack of rheumatism thirty years before, was entirely negative. His present illness dated back nine months and began with pain in the right tuber ischii, the sacrum, and along the course of the sciatic nerve. Examination over the right sacro sciatic notch revealed a tumor, pulsating synchronously with the heart, and having a distinct bruit. A diagnosis of pulsating sarcoma was made, but upon aspiration, as a syringeful of bright arterial blood was obtained, the diagnosis was changed to aneurism of the superior gluteal artery. The patient was operated upon and the right internal iliac ligated. After this the pulsation and bruit entirely disappeared. The patient survived the operation but a few days.

As permission to perform an autopsy was not granted, a simple exploration of the parts through the operative wound was made. Under the muscles in the right gluteal region a whitish, nodular tumor was found, the size of a large orange. The centre of the tumor was filled with a soft, purulent mass containing long spiculæ of bone. A similar condition was found at the periphery of the tumor. The muscles were not infiltrated. A few large blood vessels were seen running through the tumor mass. In the ilium, near the right sacro-iliac synchondrosis, was a defect, extending completely through the bone and measuring 7 by 9 centimetres in extent. The edges of the bone were roughened, but the muscles on the inner aspect were not involved. It was most unfortunate that none of the internal organs could be examined, as the microscopic examination showed the tumor to be a metastasis from a primary tumor of an adrenal or an adrenal rest. The stained sections presented the typical picture of a perithelioma or perithelial sarcoma, consisting of many small capillaries along whose margins were rows of densely packed polygonal cells, the cell bodies taking up the stain with difficulty and appearing fatty. This case is of great interest, as it is well known that when tumors of this kind are deeply situated they may frequently simulate aneurism, their richness in blood vessels accounting for the distinct pulsation.

CASE VII.—*Multiple Mixed-celled Sarcoma; Thrombosis of Left Innominate, Subclavian, and Internal Jugular Veins; Occlusion of Thoracic Duct; Chylous Ascites and Chylo thorax.*

R. K., male, aged 19 years, was operated upon fifteen months before his admission to the hospital, and a small tumor, which had been present for four months, was removed from the left side of his neck. At this time he first noticed a swelling in both axillary regions. Three months later his abdomen became distended, and in the scar left from the operation a small tumor became noticeable. He now entered the hospital. Several hard, nodular masses were felt in both axillæ and on both sides of the neck, most prominent, however, on the left side. As signs of a pleural exudation existed in the right chest, he was aspirated and a white, milky fluid was obtained. Chemical and microscopic examination showed this fluid to be an admixture of serum with chyle, without the presence of distinct fat globules. His abdomen was also aspirated and contained similar fluid. It became necessary to aspirate both the chest and abdomen every second day, and at each sitting an average amount of 1,500 cubic centimetres was withdrawn from the chest and 4,000 cubic centimetres from the abdominal cavity. In five weeks' time over 37 quarts of fluid were removed from the abdomen and nearly as much again oozed through a canula which was left *in situ*. His urine was clear and normal at all times, and no parasites were to be found in the blood. The patient steadily lost in weight, and died in an asthenic condition five weeks after entering the hospital.

The autopsy was made eighteen hours after death. Both pleural sacs and the abdominal cavity were distended with chylous fluid. The mediastinum was entirely filled with a tumor mass made up by a fusion of many gland-like tumors. The lungs presented signs of compression, and upon section several small glandular tumors were found in the right lung. The thyreoid gland was somewhat enlarged and was the seat of hyaline degeneration. The heart was small, the valves and muscles being normal. Remains of thymus gland were seen, but did not present any important changes. The spleen was slightly enlarged; upon section it was negative. The liver was the seat of chronic congestion. The pancreas, kidneys, and adrenals were normal. The intestine did not show any involvement of its lymphatic elements. The mesentery was fused by a large tumor mass similar in character to that found in the mediastinum. The retroperitoneal glands were also involved in a similar manner. Upon cut section all of the tumor masses gave the homogeneous appearance of lymphosarcoma, but stained sections showed the picture of a mixed-celled sarcoma containing many large irregularly shaped cells and a few giant cells.

All of the veins in the left side of the neck were embedded in a tumor mass that compressed them to a marked extent. These were all carefully dissected and the following interesting condition noted: The left innominate vein contained a well-organized thrombus, firmly adherent, and measuring 3½ centimetres in length. The thrombus extended into the subclavian vein for 2½ centimetres and into the internal jugular for 2 centimetres up to its valve. The thoracic duct opened into the subclavian at the posterior and upper aspect at the junction of the innominate, but its opening was entirely obliterated by the thrombus. Below this point the duct was dilated in a circumscribed manner, measuring 2 centimetres in length. The thoracic duct was dissected out into the abdomen, but, excepting a few beaded and slightly dilated portions, nothing abnormal was found. The thrombus in this case was undoubtedly the result of pressure made by the large tumor mass, and the occlusion of the thoracic duct was simply a result of its presence at this situation.

CASE VIII.—*Chronic Otitis Media; Empyema of Mastoid; Abscess of Brain (Temporo-sphenoidal Lobe), with Fistula.*

A. S., male, 17 years. The history of the otitis media in this case dated back almost sixteen years, having then followed an attack of scarlet fever. For an account of the symptoms on admission, the subsequent course, details of operations, etc., we refer to Dr. Gruening's report. The case is so interesting, both from the pathologic and bacteriologic aspects, that we have considered it advisable to give a detailed account of the results of the autopsy. We had permission to examine the brain only. The autopsy was made three and a half hours after death.

The vessels were much distended, especially the veins. There was an accumulation of fluid under the pia, and numerous gas bubbles were present. Along the vessels and at the base was a cloudy exudate. In the centre of the right temporo-sphenoidal lobe was an abscess, into which the finger could be inserted to a depth of 5 centimetres. The outer opening was laterally placed and measured 5 by 6 centimetres. Its edges were irregular and ragged. At the base of the lobe was an opening leading from the abscess cavity, measuring ½ by 1 centimetre, and presenting a well-defined margin. The margin was adherent to the tentorium cerebelli. The descending horn of the lateral ventricle was converted into an abscess cavity; its walls were thickened and necrotic. There was a communication between it and the abscess in the temporo-sphenoidal lobe. The pus in both cavities had a very disagreeable odor. The right optic thalamus was greenish in color and very soft.

The left lateral ventricle was distended. Its walls were very soft. There was a slit adjacent to the right lateral sinus, just above it, which led to the posterior fossa. In the sinus was a firm thrombus, adherent to the wall and partially decolorized. At the place where the lower small opening of the abscess was adherent to the tentorium cerebelli there was a small perforation of the tentorium, allowing the discharge of pus into the posterior fossa. This pus had been drained by the operator by means of an incision just above the lateral sinus. This corresponds to the slit mentioned above.

On May 12, when the first operation was performed, the mastoid being opened and the pus in the posterior fossa drained, cultures were made from the pus in the mastoid and the pus coming from the posterior fossa. Both showed the bacillus proteus vulgaris in pure growth. On May 21, when the brain abscess was opened, cultures from the pus in it gave the same result. At the autopsy on May 31, cultures were made from the pus in the right lateral ventricle. They showed the same bacillus. On May 24 a blister was raised on the patient's thigh, and the serum used for testing for an agglutination reaction, when added to the various cultures mentioned above. Dilutions of 1 : 10, 1 : 20, and 1 : 50 showed good agglutination reactions when viewed in the hanging drop after twenty-four hours. The serum gave no reaction when tested with typhoid bacilli, several cultures of coli, and a proteus culture from another case of extra dural abscess. Sera from other cases did not agglutinate the proteus bacilli except in one instance, when the serum from the case of extra-dural abscess just referred to was used.

Note.—The tests were examined after twenty-four hours, as the reactions are not present after short intervals. This is a point that has been brought out by Pfaundler.[1] He claimed that if fever were present the reaction, after twenty-four hours, would consist in a peculiar thread-formation; if no fever were present, in an agglutination reaction at a time when fairly high fever (102° F.) was present.

CASE IX.—*Cerebral Endarteritis (Specific); Thrombosis of Left Sylvian Artery; Atheroma of Aorta and Aortic Valves; Aortic Insufficiency; Calcareous Nodules in Right Lung and Spleen.*

Of special interest in this case, which presented an extreme grade of atheroma of the aorta with ulcerations and thrombotic deposits, was the occurrence of large calcareous deposits In the base of the right lung were several, measuring about one-half to one centimetre in diameter. The spleen contained numerous globular nodules, varying from the size of a pea up to that of a lima bean, easily isolated from the surrounding tissue, but attached at one point where a vessel seemed to enter. The microscopic examination of these "spleen stones" after their decalcification revealed no definite structure. In one there were found, in the centre, the remnants of a vessel with scarcely any lumen. They were evidently areas of calcific impregnation, secondary to the changes in the vessels. They are of interest mainly because of their large size.

CASE X—*Gonorrhœal Arthritis; Acute Dilatation of the Stomach.*

P. B., male, 16 years. This patient, after suffering from a gonorrhœal arthritis of the left elbow joint for three weeks, developed symptoms that resembled in every way those of an acute peritonitis, and died five

[1] Centralblatt für Bacteriologie, vol. xxiii., No. 1.

days later. At the autopsy the following interesting and unusual condition was found: the stomach was very markedly dilated, extending down to the pelvis, and placed so that the pylorus was in the right iliac fossa, the greater curvature resting against the bladder. The organ was nearly vertical in position. The measurement from the cardiac orifice to the pylorus in a straight line was 28 centimetres; the transverse measurement was 18 centimetres. The duodenum showed a sacculated dilatation for nearly its entire length. At the horizontal part it was constricted, probably from stretching due to the malposition. The entire remainder of the small intestine was greatly collapsed, being no larger in diameter than an ordinary lead pencil.

The condition here found is so rare that it will be of value to take a glance at the literature of the subject. Hilton Fagge,[1] in 1873, reported the first two cases of acute dilatation of the stomach, in both of which the etiology was obscure. Later cases were reported by Kelynack,[2] Schulz,[3] Boas,[4] Fraenkel,[5] and Albu.[6] In some of the cases the condition was attributed to some gross error in diet, in others the causative agent was undetermined. Fraenkel's case is of interest, as the picture presented postmortem is exactly the same as in the case here reported. He also found a sharp bend at the horizontal duodenum, due to the malposition of the stomach. The case of Albu's occurred in a man of 26 during the desquamative period of an attack of scarlet fever.

CASE XI.—*Calculus in Cystic Duct; Empyema of Gall-Bladder; Obstruction of Duodenum by Adhesions; Acute Dilatation of Stomach and Duodenum.*

M. W., male, aged 20 years. Two years ago the

[1] Guy's Hospital Reports, 1873.

[2] Kelynack: Medical Chronicle, 1892.

[3] Jahrbücher der Hamburger Staats-Krankenanstalten, 1890; Leipzig, 1892, page 145.

[4] Deutsche med Wochenschrift, 1894, No. 8.

[5] Ibidem.

[6] Deutsche med. Wochenschrift, 1896, No. 7.

patient had an attack of abdominal pain and vomiting lasting one day. On admission to the hospital he gave a history of having been sick four days, having had severe abdominal pain, especially on the right side, vomiting, and fever. He always vomited much bile. The clinical picture was that of an empyema of the gall-bladder. After three days he was operated on, a cholecystostomy being performed. Six days later he died, in the meantime suffering from symptoms referable to an obstruction of the intestine.

At the postmortem examination the stomach was found markedly dilated. The stomach extended to three inches below the umbilicus, and was full of a dark fluid material, the walls being congested. The upper part of the duodenum was also markedly dilated. About four inches from the pylorus there was an area of marked congestion of the walls of the duodenum, extending for a distance of three inches. There were also some submucous hemorrhages. This part of the duodenum was adherent to the liver and gall bladder, and was constricted. Below this part the duodenum was narrower than normal. The gall-bladder was surrounded by adhesions. The omentum was much congested and adherent to the gall bladder. The gall-bladder was dilated, its walls thick and trabeculated. The cystic duct was obstructed by a stone that presented irregular surfaces.

CASE XII.—*Carcinoma of the Stomach; Tuberculosis of the Liver.*

L. W., female, aged 43 years. In this case, which was that of a very large adeno-carcinoma of the fundus of the stomach, there were seen on the surface of the right lobe of the liver two nodules. These were of the size of small peas, grayish in color, granular, and quite dry. They did not look like metastases from the gastric tumor. A search through the body revealed no epithelial carcinoma to which they might be secondary. Microscopically they proved to be large tuberculous nodules. As some tubercles, with cheesy degeneration, were found in the bronchial glands, they were considered the point of entry of the infection.

Apart from the interest attached to the coincidence of these two diseases in one patient, a coincidence not nearly as rare as has been supposed, the localization of the tuberculosis is worthy of special comment.

CASE XIII.—*Carcinoma of the Stomach; Stenosis of the Pylorus; Pulmonary Tuberculosis; Chronic Nephritis; Myocarditis; Coronary Thrombosis; Chronic Aneurism of the Heart.*

W. F., male, aged 70 years. This case *intra vitam* gave the clinical picture of a carcinoma of the stomach. Postmortem the heart and lungs showed changes of which there had been no signs during life. The heart showed brown atrophy and interstitial myocarditis. There was some old thickening of the mitral. The aorta was markedly atheromatous, as were also the coronaries. In the anterior coronary artery, about two centimetres from its opening, there was an organized thrombus adherent to the wall of the vessel, the latter being entirely plugged. Near the apex of the heart, in the anterior wall of the left ventricle, there was an area of softening and thinning of the heart muscle. This area bulged outward somewhat. Its inner surface was filled out with a partially organized thrombotic mass. There were infarcts in the spleen and liver.

Of further interest was the presence of large, firm, cheesy nodules in both apices, especially in the right. There was also a small cavity in the right apex. The cheesy nodules were nearly all encapsulated. The patient had been seen thirty-five years before by Traube, who had made a diagnosis of pulmonary tuberculosis, but had made a good prognosis.

CASE XIV.—*Ulcer of Stomach; Perforation; General Peritonitis; Status Lymphaticus.*

A. G., female, 34 years of age. This patient was admitted to the hospital moribund. She had never been ill until four days before admission. She then complained of abdominal cramps, specially marked in the right iliac region, nausea, vomiting, and constipation. She was sent in for intestinal obstruction.

The autopsy revealed a clean-cut perforation of the stomach, about half a centimetre in diameter, located in the lesser curvature near the pylorus. Its edges were thickened and infiltrated. There were free gas and a large amount of brownish fluid in the peritoneal cavity. The spleen lay in a sac, made by adhesions, filled with fluid. Microscopic examination of the edge of the perforation showed that the infiltration was entirely inflammatory. The usual lesions found in cases of status lymphaticus were also present.

CASE XV.—*Perforated Gastric Ulcer; Thrombosis of Upper Branch of Splenic Vein; Infarction and Gangrene of Spleen; Necrosis of Lung; Abscess of Liver.*

S. F., female, aged 33 years, was admitted to the hospital with a history of having been treated for ulcer of the stomach for some time. Seven weeks before admission to the hospital she was suddenly seized with abdominal pain in the umbilical region. Since then she had been in bed with fever, at first with, later without, profuse sweats. After the first week the pain had disappeared. Two days before her arrival at the hospital pus was found, on aspirating on the left side, in the subphrenic area.

The patient was operated upon on the day following her admission. At the operation there was found a large cavity near the spleen, filled with a mass of gangrenous, pultaceous, gray-black material weighing 120 grammes, which was considered to be part of the spleen. This was surrounded by a collection of fetid black fluid apparently encapsulated. There was also seen a large perforation of the stomach wall. The patient's temperature continued high, and she died six days later.

The gangrenous mass removed was examined microscopically and showed nowhere any tissue elements. Cultures from it showed the bacillus proteus vulgaris in pure culture. The blood showed a moderate polynuclear leucocytosis.

The postmortem examination, which was restricted to the parts in the neighborhood of the wound, showed a very unique state of affairs. In the fundus of the stomach there was a fairly circular opening about 6 centimetres in diameter. The mucous membrane was everted and had firmly grown to the serous coat of the stomach. From the edge of the perforation ran a vein filled by a partially organized thrombus, which anastomosed with the splenic vein. The thrombus was continued into the upper branch of the splenic vein. The spleen was necrotic at its upper end and was ragged. A large piece of its upper pole was missing. About the middle of the spleen was a raised margin, above which the spleen was swollen and congested. This area, together with the piece missing, was taken to represent the area normally drained by the upper branch of the splenic vein. The diaphragm was perforated at the base of the left lung and there was a defect in the lung.

The edges of the perforation of the diaphragm were adherent to the lung. The lung itself looked clean and smooth, and the lower half of the lower lobe was in a state of chronic interstitial inflammation. There had evidently been gangrene of part of the lower lobe, and the gangrenous area had completely separated.

In the left lobe of the liver, posteriorly, was a large cavity containing pus and having a ragged, necrotic wall infiltrated with pus. The vessels supplying the part could not be examined.

CASE XVI.—*Dilatation of the Colon; Brown Atrophy of the Heart; Pulmonary Edema.*

F. S., male, 60 years of age. This patient entered the hospital with a history of intestinal obstruction of five days' standing. He had previously had attacks of obstinate constipation, sometimes with vomiting, the attacks usually lasting five or six days. Soon after admission he was operated upon. No obstruction could be found. To relieve the patient a colostomy was performed and the ascending colon was opened. The patient died the next day with the symptoms of pulmonary edema.

The autopsy failed to reveal an obstruction anywhere. The colon was markedly distended and contained fluid feces. Above the colostomy wound the intestine was less distended. The sigmoid flexure was very long and the rectum was ballooned out. Nowhere was there a sign of any inflammatory process. The mesenteric glands were large.

We believe the case belongs to that class of cases called "acute idiopathic dilatation of the colon," of which there are but twelve cases on record.

CASE XVII.—*Lymphosarcoma of the Duodenum, with Extensive Metastases.*

H. G., male, aged 12 years. This case is not only of interest because of its rarity, but also because of the short history. The boy on admission had appeared sick for only nine days. He complained of abdominal pain, and inability to walk because of weakness. Three days after the onset the parents noticed that his abdomen was growing larger. For three days before admission his bowels had to be moved by cathartics and enemata. He appeared to be rapidly growing worse. The pain in the abdomen increased and was located below the umbilicus. He had dyspnea, attributed to the abdominal distension. The whole illness appeared so acute that the physician who sent the case in suspected the presence of an acute peritonitis, possibly due to some appendical trouble.

On admission his temperature was 100.6° F. Physical examination revealed a nodular mass lying across the hypogastrium and extending into the pelvis, which was concave above. There were other masses felt in the abdomen, which appeared to be enlarged glands. Rectally a large, bulging mass could be felt anteriorly. There was some ascites present. The case was considered to be one of malignant disease of the peritoneum.

An exploratory incision evacuated a large amount of seropurulent fluid, and there were seen large masses lining the peritoneum and involving the omentum. These masses were white, smooth, and hard. They extended up to and over the liver. In both iliac regions large nodules could be felt which seemed to be retroperitoneal. A piece of the tumor was removed and microscopic examination showed it to be lymphosarcoma.

The boy died twenty-eight days after the operation. Previously he had developed signs of consolidation at the left base, and the abdomen had become so enlarged that it was tapped and two quarts of purulent fluid withdrawn.

Postmortem examination: The external glands are not enlarged. The mesentery and omentum are much thickened, due to an infiltration by white tumor masses, which consist partly of uniform thickenings and partly of nodular growths. All the glands are large, and on section whitish and homogeneous. In places the intestinal coils are bound together by the new growth, in some parts there are collections of green pus between the coils. The parietal peritoneum is not involved. The intestinal coils are attached to the bladder by some of the tumor masses. In the free abdominal cavity is much pus and grumous material. The walls of the large intestines and part of the ileum are thickened by diffuse infiltration with a whitish growth. The mucous membrane is intact.

The primary growth appears to be in the lower part of the duodenum. Here is a large white mass, the size of a fist, encircling the intestine and projecting into its lumen. The mucous membrane seems to be complete.

The duodenum is stenosed and just admits the index finger. The stomach is moderately dilated. The liver is covered by numerous flat growths, white in color, some of which are attached to, and involve, the parietal peritoneum. The entire wall of the gall-bladder is very thick, due to a uniform infiltration with new growth. The spleen shows the same flat surface growths. The kidneys present streaks of uric acid in the medulla, resembling much the uric-acid infarcts found in new-born infants. The anterior surfaces of the kidneys are covered by flat growths. The pancreas shows the same growths on the surface and upon section. The left lung is compressed by a large purulent exudate. The diaphragm is infiltrated by the growth, and there is an extension into the base of the left lung.

Microscopic examination of the primary tumor and the metastases in the mesentery, glands, and organs showed them all to be of the same character, viz., lymphosarcoma.

Lymphosarcoma of the intestine is a very unusual disease. Nothnagel states that of 2,125 carcinomata recorded in Vienna from 1882 to 1893, 243 involved the intestine; of 274 sarcomata, but 3 involved the intestine; of 61 lymphosarcomata, 9 involved the intestine. So that, although lymphosarcoma of the intestine is rare, it occurs more often than other forms of sarcoma. Lymphosarcoma attacks by preference the small intestine, arising from the lymphatic apparatus in the submucosa. Instead of stenosing the gut, like the carcinomata, it usually dilates it. The case we here report is an exception to this general rule.

CASE XVIII.—*Perforating Typhlitis with Secondary Abscesses in Abdomen, Liver, and Spleen; Adhesive Pleuritis.*

D. V., male, aged 38 years, entered the hospital with a history of two months' duration, and complained of general abdominal pain, some diarrhea for four days prior to his admission, and cough. He was much emaciated, had a distended abdomen, tympanitic in the centre and dull at the sides, with prominent superficial veins. His liver extended five centimetres below the free border of the ribs, but the spleen appeared normal in size. The patient was in an extremely feeble condition and had a slightly elevated temperature for two days after his admission. Subsequently the temperature became subnormal, the patient passed into a condition of stupor, and died a week after admission. The diagnosis rested between appendicitis and tuberculous peritonitis.

At the autopsy, made nine hours after death, firm adhesions were found at the base of each lung. A lobular pneumonia with some edema was also present. The heart muscle was soft and friable and the aortic valves somewhat thickened. The spleen was moderately enlarged and was extremely soft, and upon section an abscess filled with thick, greenish pus was found. The kidneys were of the large white variety. Between the right lobe of the liver and the diaphragm was a large abscess which compressed the liver. The liver itself contained many small abscesses, most of which were found in the right lobe. The anterior abdominal walls were adherent to the intestines in various situations. In the hypogastric region thick, greenish pus welled upward from the pelvis, but the abscess was shut off from the general abdominal cavity by dense adhesions. The intestines were pushed over to the left, and between the various coils small abscesses were found, the intestinal walls at these situations being firmly adherent to each other. To the right of the ascending colon was a collection of thin, brownish pus which extended upward to the liver. Under the left lobe of the liver, and limited by the spleen, stomach, and posterior abdominal wall, was another abscess cavity. In the right iliac fossa the cecum, appendix, and a few coils of the ileum were adherent. *The appendix was perfectly normal.* Upon opening the cecum several small perforations were found, having ragged edges, but not infiltrated and not presenting any signs of tuberculosis. Nor could any stenosis or dilatation be demonstrated in this situation.

In the majority of cases of perforation of the cecum the underlying cause is to be found outside of the gut, and usually it is an abscess following a perforating appendicitis. In this case, however, the appendix was normal, and consequently the case must be considered one of perforating stercoral ulcers, notwithstanding the fact that in the very few cases hitherto reported there has been but one ulcer that has perforated.

CASE XIX.—*Thrombosis of Superior Mesenteric Vein.* H. B. male, aged 50 years, was admitted with a history of four weeks' illness, during which time he suffered from pain in the right iliac fossa, radiating to other parts of the abdomen, and diarrhœa. He had nausea, but no vomiting. Physical examination revealed nothing of any importance. On the following day he went into collapse and then passed a bloody stool. An exploratory incision was made, and some coils of intestines, dark colored and hemorrhagic in character, were found. Owing to the patient's wretched condition the operation had to be discontinued.

At the autopsy, made on the next day, there was found a thrombus in the superior mesenteric vein, extending about two centimetres into its main branches. The thrombus was firm and closely adherent to the wall of the vein. The large intestine was practically normal. The entire small intestine was filled with dark fluid blood, and there were numerous small hemorrhages in the mucosa. The spleen was somewhat enlarged and deeply congested: there were numerous small, pin-point hemorrhages on its surface. The other organs were practically negative.

As in nearly all the other recorded cases of this condition, the etiology in this case is unknown.

CASE XX.—*Intestinal Anthrax.* W. S., male, negro, aged 21 years, was a patient in the hospital for one day. A satisfactory history could not be obtained, but it was learned that he had been ill for several days with pain in the right iliac region, accompanied by chills, high fever, and great prostration. A tentative diagnosis of typhoid fever was made, but the patient died before any satisfactory diagnosis could be established.

At the autopsy a localized peritoneal exudate was seen, about two centimetres in thickness, firmly uniting the cecum to the anterior abdominal wall. The lower ileum and cecum were intensely congested. Just above the valve an ulcerating mass was seen, four centimetres in diameter, extending deeply into the mucosa and submucosa, of a brownish-black color and having at its central part a necrotic area. At this situation a small perforation had probably occurred, which accounted for the peritoneal exudation mentioned above. The intestine surrounding this ulcerating mass was edematous and intensely congested. The remainder of the alimentary tract was negative, with the exception of an area in the colon which was deeply congested, the peritoneal coat in this situation being somewhat thickened. The spleen was much swollen and congested, and upon section was of a semi-diffluent character. In size it measured 23 by 10 centimetres. Unfortunately no cultures were made from the blood or spleen, but stained sections of the spleen showed large numbers of long bacilli with square ends scattered throughout the spleen tissue and giving a positive reaction with Gram's stain. From this find, together with the acute and severe sepsis and the single large ulcer, a diagnosis of anthrax seems positive. The patient had worked as a porter in a large clothing store, but had never handled raw wool as far as could be ascertained.

CASE XXI.—*Congenital Cardiac Disease; Open Foramen Ovale; Open Septum; Stenosis of Pulmonary Conus; Transposition of Vessels.*

B. J., male, aged 14 months, was admitted with a history of four days' standing for broncho-pneumonia An examination of the heart led to the diagnosis of a congenital lesion, most likely a pulmonary stenosis, with a defect in the septum. The physical signs were as follows: the right border of the heart extended to the mid-sternum, the left to one-half inch outside the nipple line. The apex-beat was felt in the sixth space outside the nipple line, being forcible and diffuse. There was a loud, rough systolic murmur heard at the apex and over the mitral and pulmonic areas. It could also be heard distinctly behind. The toes showed fairly marked clubbing. Cyanosis was hardly noticeable when the child was admitted, but became very marked several days before death.

Postmortem examination: There is marked dilatation of the left auricle and auricular appendix. The right auricle is moderately dilated. The left ventricle is markedly hypertrophied. The right ventricle is moderately hypertrophied. The aorta springs from the right ventricle, and the auriculo-ventricular valve is composed of two flaps with thickened edges (mitral valve). The pulmonary artery springs from the left ventricle, and the auriculo-ventricular valve consists of three flaps, two of which show a partial subdivision. The origin of the pulmonary artery lies behind and slightly to the left of the aorta and is very small in diameter. There is a marked narrowing of the entire pulmonary conus, there being a strong fibrous ring present. The pulmonary valves are three in number, thick and rudimentary, but competent. There is an opening between the two auricles, protected by a well-marked valvular fold, lying on the side of the left auricle. There is also an opening about 1.5 centimetres in diameter at the upper part of the septum ventriculorum, partly covered by one flap of the mitral valve. The ductus arteriosus barely admits a probe.

CASE XXII.—*Ulcerative Endocarditis of Aortic Valve; Inflammatory Tumor of Septum stenosing Orifice of Pulmonary Artery.*

H. A., male, 21 years of age. This patient suffered from an acute endocarditis of the aortic valve, which presented nothing atypical until two days before he died, when there appeared a loud, rough systolic murmur over the pulmonary area, which was referred to a probable lesion of the pulmonary valve.

The postmortem examination showed an ulcerative endocarditis of the aortic valve with enormous vegetations in the sinuses of Valsalva. In the septum, directly continuous with the process in and behind the aortic valve, was a large, globular, hemorrhagic mass, which bulged into the right ventricle and made the entrance to the pulmonary artery almost impassable. The centre of the swelling was quite soft. Microscopic examination showed it to be an acute inflammatory process with beginning abscess.

A blood culture made four days antemortem (10 cubic centimetres of blood from a vein being used) showed the staphylococcus albus. A culture from the heart blood made directly postmortem gave the same result. Smears made from the centre of the swelling of the septum, at the autopsy (nine hours postmortem), showed enormous numbers of staphylococci.

CASE XXIII.—*Dermoid Cyst of the Mediastinum.*

F. G., female, 30 years of age. This case was of ten months' duration when admitted to the hospital. The first manifestation was a small nodule on the right side of the chest. On admission it was of the size of an orange and was adherent to the deeper tissues, but not to the skin. There were no other symptoms. On aspiration a thick, yellow fluid was obtained. The operation (see surgical report) revealed a large dermoid cyst. The patient died two months later with the symptoms of a gradual exhaustion due to a slow sepsis

At the autopsy the following condition was found: In the right second interspace there is an oblique incision about five centimetres long, leading to a cyst about the size of a large egg. The cyst lies between the pleura covering the mediastinal surface of the right lung and the pericardium, and is attached to both of these parts. The cyst is thick-walled: on its walls are a number of polypoid excrescences jutting in and outward. In the cavity is some sebaceous material mixed with hair. The liver is slightly fatty. The spleen is large, soft, and congested; microscopically it shows acute inflammation, with small hemorrhages.

This case is notable mainly because of its rarity. There are but fourteen cases of dermoid cyst of the mediastinum on record. They form, however, a fair percentage of the total number of tumor formations in the mediastinum. They are supposed to originate from the ectoderm over the thymus. According to Hoffmann, they can be divided into three classes:

1. Real dermoids;
2. Those containing cartilage and lined with cylindrical cells, which probably originate in the bronchi:
3. Dermoid cysts combined with lymphoid tumor.

The case which we record is of interest in connection with the third class of cases, because there were such large tumor-like masses in the walls. The suspicion was aroused that it was a dermoid cyst plus lymphoma or lymphosarcoma. The microscopic examination, however, proved that the case belongs in the first class mentioned above, for the large masses were seen to consist of skin elements (mainly sebaceous glands) only.

CASE XXIV.—*Gonorrhœal Pyelonephritis: Prostatic*

Abscess; Gonorrhœal Cystitis with Hemorrhage; Gonorrhœal Urethritis in a Boy Ten Years of Age.

J. J., male, aged 10 years, contracted gonorrhœa while coming to this country as a steerage passenger. The exact mode of infection was not ascertained. He entered the hospital one month later, complaining of pain over the region of the right kidney and a discharge from the urethra of about two weeks' standing. Just before his admission he also noticed that he had some pain over the left kidney. The urine was diminished in amount and contained much pus and some blood. He had vomited two days before, also had a slight chill and high fever. Upon entering the hospital the entire surface of his body was covered with an urticarial erythema such as is occasionally seen in septic cases terminating fatally. Gonococci were present in large numbers in the urethral discharge, and a diagnosis of gonorrhœal pyelitis was made, as a distinct tumor could be felt occupying the position of the right kidney. The patient was operated upon and the right kidney drained, but he survived the operation but a day.

The autopsy was made ten hours after death, but only an examination of the genito-urinary apparatus was allowed. Both kidneys were much enlarged, the right being fully twice its normal size. Its substance was filled with abscesses, from the very minutest size to that of a hazelnut. The cortex appeared somewhat widened, the capsule was adherent, and beneath it were numerous small abscesses. The pelvis was thickened and congested and contained a large blood clot. The vermiform appendix was found adherent at its lower pole. The left kidney appeared congested and contained but one abscess, holding about four cubic centimetres of pus. Both ureters were congested at their openings into the bladder. The bladder wall was thickened and the mucous membrane studded with small hemorrhages. The prostate was enlarged and congested, and in its substance was an abscess containing two cubic centimetres of pus. The urethra appeared congested.

Cover-glass preparations from the pus found in the kidneys showed the presence of gonococci and staphylococci, while those made from the prostate showed simply staphylococci. Cultures were made upon blood serum and serum agar, and the staphylococcus albus and gonococcus were isolated from the kidney and the staphylococcus albus from the prostate. In stained sections of the kidney staphyloccoci and gonococci were also demonstrated.

CASE XXV.—*Carcinoma of Duodenum, Pancreas, and Liver; Obstructive Jaundice; Anomaly of Lung; Horseshoe Kidney.*

C. L., male, 52 years of age. This case is notable because of an unusual pulmonary anomaly and its occurrence with a horseshoe kidney. The lower lobe of the right lung was entirely separate from the upper and middle lobes, and was supplied by its own separate vessels and bronchus. The line between the upper and middle lobe was poorly marked The hilus of the kidney was located anteriorly. There were two ureters, which joined just below the hilus and then again divided. The arterial supply consisted of two branches, arising from the aorta.

CASE XXVI.—*Tabes Dorsalis; Bilateral Suppurative Pyelonephritis; Subphrenic and Psoas Abscess; Purulent Pericystitis: Pulmonary Tuberculosis.*

L. A., male, 35 years of age. This case is reported to show how extensive can be the results of a pus kidney. The case was diagnosed as locomotor ataxia with cystitis and double pyelonephritis, and pulmonary tuberculosis. At the postmortem the characteristic changes in the cord were found, and there was advanced tuberculosis of the right apex, with cavity formation, and miliary tuberculosis of the left lung. The right kidney was very large and was surrounded by adhesions. The pelvis was dilated, and there was marked purulent pyelonephritis. The left kidney was still larger and showed extensive suppuration, with streaks of pus in the medulla and abscesses of various sizes in the cortex. One abscess had perforated and the pus had infiltrated the psoas muscle as far down as the groin, where there was a distinct swelling to be seen externally. There was also a large collection of pus around the kidney and in the subphrenic space. The bladder was small, its wall being much thickened and showing prominent trabeculæ. There were numerous small abscesses in its wall. To the left of the bladder, in the connective tissue, was a large pus sac.

XXVI.

A REVIEW OF THE WIDAL TESTS MADE DURING 1898, WITH A DESCRIPTION OF THE METHOD USED.

By E. LIBMAN, M.D.,
ASSISTANT PATHOLOGIST.

Nearly all of the tests which form the basis of this report were made with dried blood. The method ordinarily used for making the reactions was found to be unsatisfactory, as it did not allow of even moderately accurate dilutions being made. We therefore used the following method, by means of which quite certain dilutions can be made. After the finger-tip has been cleansed and pricked, several platinum loopfuls of the exuding blood are deposited side by side on a slide. After these have dried, there is added to one of the drops fourteen loopfuls of sterile water measured with the same loop. Each loopful of this mixture represents a dilution of 1 to 14 or 1 to 14 +, as the dried blood has a certain small volume. One loopful is intimately mixed with a loopful of a bouillon culture of typhoid bacilli, the dilution thus being 1 to 14 +. As the dried blood, according to the most recent analyses, consists of about two-thirds serum, we have a dilution of 1 to 21 +, or, roughly, 1 to 21 reckoned on a serum basis. In the same way dilutions of 1 to 30, 1 to 51, etc., can be made.

To make the method shorter, one can make a dilution of 1 to 21 by adding seven loopfuls of water to one loopful of the dried blood, and then adding two loopfuls of the culture to one of the mixture. The platinum loop can be of any size, provided the same loop is used for making the dilutions as that used in taking the blood. If the blood-taking is carefully performed, the drops of blood on the slide are of almost exactly uniform size. A slight inaccuracy is avoidable, but the same inaccuracy is present even when the platinum loop is made for making dilutions with serum. We believe this method is as nearly accurate as any can be when dried blood is used, with one exception. The latter is the method used by some observers, and consists in diluting the blood in the melangeur of the Thomas-Zeiss hæmocytometer (Pfaundler), but it is not practicable to do this when 15 or 20 Widals must be made. We have made all our dilutions 1 to 20 (1 to 21, as described above).

The stock culture is one on agar, obtained from the laboratory of the Health Board through the kindness of Dr. Park. This culture is reinoculated on agar every two weeks. From the agar culture daily inoculations are made into bouillon, and these are used after standing in the thermostat at 30–35° C. (at which temperature we obtained better growths than at 37°) for a period varying from 16 to 22 hours. During the summer months we obtained cultures showing very active motility of the bacilli by allowing them to stand in the laboratory, outside of the thermostat. Albolene was used instead of vaseline for preventing desiccation (Mandlebaum).

The reactions were viewed directly after being made. If not immediately positive, they were placed in the thermostat, for a period not exceeding twenty minutes, and again examined. In our report we do not note whether the reaction was immediate or not. When no reaction was obtained in cases which appeared to be typhoid fever, the reaction was usually repeated, using serum obtained by raising a blister. The result always remained the same. When a positive reaction was obtained, the test was generally repeated on the following day. When a reaction was obtained in cases only suspected of being typhoid fever, but not being clearly so, the test was repeated, using dilutions of 1–50. In all such cases the latter dilution also gave a positive result.

From February 20 to January 1, 960 examinations were made in 223 cases. Of these, 98 were clinically cases of typhoid fever. Five of these cases never showed a positive reaction, making a percentage of five and one-tenth. The blood of these five cases was examined nearly every day during their stay in the hospital. The earliest age at which a positive reaction was obtained was thirteen months. The remaining 125 cases covered the greatest variety of febrile diseases, such as pulmonary tuberculosis, acute miliary tuberculosis, pneumonia, suppurative processes, bacteremia, meningitis, malaria, malignant endocarditis, Weil's disease, etc. In no instance was a positive reaction present, the blood of some of the cases being tested from ten to twenty-five times.

In trying to fix upon the day of the disease on which a Widal reaction is first positive, there are two sources of error to overcome. Firstly, we can rarely state definitely when the disease began; and, secondly, if the first test we make proves positive, we cannot be sure that the patient may not have had typhoid fever at some previous time, as the histories given by the patients cannot be relied upon. In 71 cases of our series we have attempted to fix upon the date of onset of the disease. In these 71 cases a positive reaction was found:

On the 3d day in 1 case.
" " 5th " " 6 cases.
" " 6th " " 2 "
" " 7th " " 6 "
" " 8th " " 1 case
" " 9th " " 2 cases.
" " 10th " " " "
From the 11th to the 14th day (inclusive) in 19 cases.
" " 15th " " 19th " " " 10 "
" " 20th " " 25th " " " 15 "
On the 30th day in 2 cases.
" " 32d " " 1 case.
" " 42d " " 2 cases.
" " 67th " " 1 case.

The case in which the reaction was positive on the third day was that of a boy aged 9 years.

In some of the cases the blood showed a positive reaction the first time it was examined, and of course one cannot say that the day on which we found the reaction was the first day upon which a positive reaction existed. If we exclude these cases we find that the reaction occurred for the first time:

On the 5th day in 1 case.
" " 7th " 1 "
" " 9th " 2 cases.
" " 10th " 1 case.
From the 11th to the 14th day (inclusive) in 11 cases.
" " 15th " 19th " " " 10 "
" " 20th " 25th " " " 12 "
On the 30th day in 2 cases.
" " 32d " 1 case.
" " 42d " 2 cases.
" " 67th " 1 case.

In some of the cases the reaction first appeared after complete defervescence or during a relapse. Summed up they are as follows:

1.	Widal	positive	on 23d	day,	being	the 5th	day	of	normal	temperature.
2.	"	"	" 16th	"	"	" 2d	"	"	"	"
3.	"	"	" 21st	"	"	" 4th	"	"	a relapse.	
4.	"	"	" 54th	"	"	" 4th	"	"	"	
5.	"	"	" (?)	"	"	" 9th	"	"	"	

No extended observations were made as to the persistence of the reaction. In some instances, however, it was noted that it lasted but three days. This refers to cases in which the reaction had been found positive only after a number of examinations. From this fact it is evident that some of the cases which showed no reaction may have had one before admission.

In a very large number of the cases the Widal test was only of corroborative value, as the cases were clearly typhoid long before a positive reaction was obtained. In a fair number of cases, however, it was of the greatest service in establishing a diagnosis. We shall not attempt to review all these cases, as it would make the article inordinately long. We wish to refer to two groups of cases only, in which the test was very useful. These are the cases of typhoid fever resembling meningitis and those resembling pneumonia. We do not refer particularly to the cases of typhoid fever, late in the course of which marked pulmonary or cerebral symptoms develop, but to those in which the clinical picture from the outset is that of meningitis or pneumonia, cases in which the primary or main localization of the bacilli seems to be in the lungs or pia mater. In two such meningeal cases and three pulmonary cases the Widal reaction established the diagnosis, which was confirmed by the subsequent course of the disease or the autopsy. So valuable has the reaction been in these cases that it seems advisable during the summer and autumn months to test the blood of all the pneumonia and meningitis cases.

In the course of our remarks it will be noticed that we mention only positive reactions and draw no attention at all to partial reactions. We designate a reaction as partial when all motion of the bacilli has stopped but the clumping is imperfect, there being a fairly large number of bacilli lying singly between the clumps. This form of reaction, to us, is of no significance, and does not lead us to suspect that a positive reaction will occur later, as we have found it nearly as often in cases not clinically typhoid fever as in those of typhoid fever. We have found it most often in cases of acute miliary tuberculosis and tubercular meningitis. We therefore believe it inadvisable to report "fair reactions" or "incomplete reactions." Only a thorough agglutination with very few or no loose bacilli is of any significance whatsoever.

As the Widal reaction in the large number of cases appears after the end of the first week, it may be thought useless to examine the blood before that time. This is, however, erroneous. The examination early in the disease is really of the greatest advantage, as, if it be negative, the later occurrence of a positive reaction stamps the case as one of typhoid fever; whereas if we wait until the second week and the Widal is then positive at the first examination, we must frequently remain in doubt as to whether the reaction is due to a former attack of typhoid fever or not. This is a point to which Leube has recently drawn attention.

Summary.—First, in a series of 98 cases the reaction was absent in 5. Second, in 206 examinations of the blood in 125 febrile cases that were not typhoid fever, the reaction was never positive. The earliest date of the appearance of the reaction was the third day. If we consider only those cases in which the reaction was not positive at the first examination, the earliest was the fifth day and the latest the sixty-seventh day. Fourth, in two cases the Widal first appeared during convalescence and in three cases during the relapse. Fifth, the occurrence of an "almost complete" reaction is of as little value for diagnosing the presence of typhoid fever as a negative reaction is for excluding it. Sixth, during the summer and autumn it is advisable to repeatedly test the blood of cases which clinically appear to be instances of pneumonia or meningitis. This is especially necessary in the case of children. Seventh, to make the diagnosis sure, a test should always be made early in the disease, even before we hope to find a positive reaction.

Our thanks are due to Dr. Hauswirth, the house physician, for keeping the laboratory in touch with the cases and supplying many necessary data.

1898.

NUMBER OF PATIENTS TREATED DURING THE YEAR.

	Males.	Females.	Adults.	Children.	Total.
Remaining from last report .	125	80	169	36	205
Admitted during the year...	1,606	1,476	2,557	525	3,082
Discharged during the year .	1,427	1,330	2,318	439	2,757
Died during the year..... ..	205	120	222	103	325
Remaining in Hospital......	99	106	181	24	205

Whole number treated during the year 3,287
Discharge cured 1,930
" improved 632
" unimproved 192
Transferred to other institutions 3
Deaths 325
In Hospital November 30, 1898 205
Percentage of deaths 9.88%

Died each Month.

Month.	Year.	Males.	Females.	Adults.	Children.	Total.
December..........	1897	15	12	21	6	27
January...........	1898	15	10	20	5	25
February	1898	17	12	24	5	29
March............	1898	14	8	16	6	22
April......	1898	16	8	18	6	24
May	1898	19	12	23	8	31
June...	1898	18	11	18	11	29
July	1898	17	10	12	15	27
August............	1898	24	14	22	16	38
September	1898	14	7	16	5	21
October............	1898	20	8	15	13	28
November.........	1898	16	8	17	7	24
		205	120	222	103	325

XXVIII.

GENERAL SYNOPSIS FOR 1898.

Total number of patients admitted		3,287
Medical patients	1,020	
Pediatric "	385	
Surgical "	1,916	
Genito-Urinary patients	189	
Gynecological "	480	
Ophthalmic, Aural, and Laryngological patients.	103	
Accident War		426
Total number of operations		1,986
Surgical	1,052	
Genito-Urinary	107	
Gynecological	572	
Pediatric	70	
Ophthalmic, Aural, and Laryngological	185	
Total number of patients discharged CURED		2,019
Total number of patients discharged IMPROVED		678
Total number of patients discharged UNIMPROVED OR NOT TREATED		186
Total number of deaths		325

www.ingramcontent.com/pod-product-compliance
Lightning Source LLC
Chambersburg PA
CBHW030319240426
43673CB00040B/1214
* 9 7 8 3 3 3 7 1 7 3 5 6 2 *